FIVE LOVE AFFAIRS AND A FRIENDSHIP

BY ANNE DE COURCY

The English in Love
A Guide to Modern Manners
1939: The Last Season
Society's Queen
The Viceroy's Daughters
Diana Mosley
Debs at War
Snowdon: The Biography
The Fishing Fleet: Husband-Hunting in the Raj
Margot at War: Love and Betrayal in Downing Street
The Husband Hunters: Social Climbing in London
and New York
Chanel's Riviera

FIVE LOVE AFFAIRS AND A FRIENDSHIP

THE PARIS LIFE OF NANCY CUNARD, ICON OF THE JAZZ AGE

Anne de Courcy

WEIDENFELD & NICOLSON

First published in Great Britain in 2022
by Weidenfeld & Nicolson
an imprint of The Orion Publishing Group Ltd
Carmelite House, 50 Victoria Embankment
London EC4Y 0DZ

An Hachette UK Company

1 3 5 7 9 10 8 6 4 2

A CIP catalogue record for this book is
available from the British Library.

ISBN (hardback) 978 1 4746 0741 3
ISBN (trade paperback) 978 1 4746 0742 0
ISBN (ebook) 978 1 4746 0744 4
ISBN (audio) 978 1 4746 1745 1

Typeset by Input Data Services Ltd, Somerset

Printed and Bound in Great Britain by Clays Ltd, Elcograf S.p.A.

MIX
Paper from
responsible sources
FSC® C104740

www.orionbooks.co.uk

CONTENTS

><+>+O+<+><

INTRODUCTION

Whatever one thought of Nancy Cunard, it was impossible to ignore her – her beauty alone would have seen to that. Although in photographs she is usually seen with unflatteringly pursed lips, her looks were something commented on by everyone who met her, with her huge blue-green eyes, emphasised by their circles of kohl, invariably remarked upon.

Her personality was equally extraordinary. Around her shimmered a force field of energy that drew people in, often influencing them in ways they could hardly have credited before they had met her. Osbert Sitwell talked of her 'ineffable charm and distinction of mind'; Alannah Harper thought that 'whatever she did – however violent – Nancy always looked more distinguished than other people'. Harold Acton believed that she had inspired half the poets and novelists of the Twenties.

What was not always obvious was that much of her extraordinary energy drew its power from an underlying anger – sometimes explosive on behalf of a cause, or a righting of what she saw as an injustice, sometimes a slow-burning resentment that simmered below the surface, as in her relationship with her mother. Later, it would power her campaigning against injustices, especially those perpetrated against black people, fights which she pursued with immense courage and complete scorn for what anyone else thought.

This hostility to her mother, to her mother's attitudes, friends and social life – Emerald Cunard was perhaps the greatest hostess of the inter-war years – gradually built up during Nancy's adolescence. Born into a life of wealth and privilege, yet one in which she hardly saw her parents, her childhood was lonely and constrained by a stern and unpleasant governess. Highly intelligent and a poet from early on, she rebelled against what was expected of her and her contemporaries – a debut, followed by a London Season or two, marriage to some suitable young man, children and the running of a large house, probably in the country. What she wanted instead was a life in the arts, with the constant company of artists, writers, poets and painters, found in the great Soho cafés rather than the ballrooms of Mayfair.

Escaping from her mother's influence through an early marriage, quickly followed by its disintegration, she soon made what was arguably the most formative decision of her life – she would live not in England, but in Paris.

She arrived there at the beginning of 1920, to stay for approximately fourteen years, the period I cover in this book. Here was everything she wanted: the richest and most stimulating artistic life in the Western world, untrammelled sex and plenty of alcohol (the last two quickly became addictions). In addition, it was close enough for her to keep in touch with her English friends, including, and especially, George Moore, her mother's lover and the man Nancy herself had loved since early childhood; and the 'Friendship' of my title. (They would remain close until Moore's death just before she left Paris.) Moore, then a major literary figure, had taken a great interest in the lonely little girl, talked to her as an equal, encouraged her writing, reviewed her poetry and kept in constant and loving touch, often coming to Paris to visit her.

It was in Paris that Nancy became a cultural icon, a muse to Wyndham Lewis, Aldous Huxley, Tristan Tzara, Ezra Pound and Louis Aragon. Mina Loy wrote poems to her; Constantin Brâncuşi sculpted her; Man Ray photographed her; she played tennis with Ernest Hemingway, and after meeting her the poet William Carlos Williams kept her photograph on his desk at all times.

A poet herself, she set up a publishing house called the Hours Press, and published the poems of others (Nancy was the first person to publish work by Samuel Beckett). It was during these Paris years, too, that what to my mind were Nancy's five most important love affairs took place – affairs that are just as much a portrait of Paris as it was then as of romances, sweeping her into circles and ideas that she might otherwise not have met.

Everyone has their own definition of 'important', but in these pages I am taking it to mean the loves that had either the most impact on Nancy or on the literature and life of the time. The first of these, which throughout most of her first year in Paris did much to sear the city's romance and glamour into her mind, was with the Armenian writer Michael Arlen. Vividly accurate descriptions of Nancy are threaded throughout his stories; and it was the picture of Nancy as heroine of *The Green Hat* that shot him to global best-sellerdom and for which she is often remembered.

After they had parted – somewhat acrimoniously – came Ezra Pound. Nancy had met him when she was sixteen, by which time he had already made a name in English literary circles, but they did not become close until her Paris years. She admired Pound enormously, not only for his somewhat theatrical good looks and deep classical learning but for the way in which he tirelessly promoted the work of writers in whom he believed, and also for his ability to discover new talent – to one friend who ran a small magazine he sent off the early work of three future Nobel Prize in Literature winners, Yeats, Rabindranath Tagore and T.S. Eliot.

The married Pound, a tireless pursuer of women, was perhaps the only man whose feeling for Nancy was less powerful than hers for him, so much so that she remained in his thrall for several years, only finally giving up after she heard his wife had become pregnant – wives were, to Nancy, if not exactly an irrelevance, certainly no barrier to a liaison.

The third of the five affairs that to me seems noteworthy was with Aldous Huxley, author of *Brave New World* and nominated nine times for the Nobel Prize in Literature, who became so obsessed with her that he was unable to work and was forced to flee the country in order to continue writing – there are vivid echoes of Nancy and his hopeless passion for her in several of his books.

When she met Louis Aragon, the handsome, brilliant poet and writer who was co-founder of the Surrealist movement before becoming the leading intellectual of the Communist Party, the two fell passionately in love. His influence on her was strong: through this (fourth) affair she became ever more left-leaning. Yet although she could never have been described as a champagne socialist, she saw no contradiction in fervently advocating communist principles while leading a life only possible because of a large income that came from inherited money.

For two years the couple were blissfully happy, until Nancy's self-destructive streak asserted itself. Not for the first time, while attached to one man she began an affair with another. Much of Aragon's best poetry about her was written after their break-up.

This was caused by Henry Crowder, a black jazz pianist whom she had met while in Venice with Aragon and who was the unwitting catalyst for her eventual irrevocable breach with her mother. For Nancy, this was the most formative – as well as the longest – of her many relationships. It was Crowder, himself a peaceable man, who inspired her in her battle with the many injustices suffered by his race, culminating in her major work, *Negro*, an anthology of writings by and about black people. As she said later, 'Henry made me.' With their eventual parting came the end of her Paris life.

CHAPTER I

>⊷•⊶O⊷•⊷<

The Friendship

No two people could have been less suited to each other than Nancy Cunard's parents. Sir Bache Cunard (the grandson of the founder of the Cunard shipping line) was a fox-hunting squire interested only in outdoor sports and, unusually, silversmithing and wrought ironwork; Maud Alice Burke, Nancy's mother, a blonde and pretty San Francisco heiress almost twenty years younger than her husband, was intelligent, witty and cultured and seldom set foot out of doors (the story goes that when he built her a rose garden to tempt her out she only entered it once). Maud had, in her usual headstrong fashion, married her much older husband partly because his English title made him seem a highly suitable *parti*, but largely to avoid the appearance of being jilted – the Polish prince at whom she had set her cap had publicly stated that they were not engaged, and indeed had gone on to marry another rich American girl.

Nevill Holt, the large country house in Leicestershire to which Sir Bache brought his bride, is situated on a slight rise that gives it a view clear across the Welland valley. Built of grey and yellow stone with a turreted façade, at its centre is a high, timbered late-fourteenth-century hall. At one end is a small thirteenth-century church, with a modest graveyard behind it, the headstones aslant with age, to which Nancy often retreated as a child. The large Victorian dining room overlooks lawns and the red-brick walls of the kitchen garden. Inside, the Cunards had introduced dark Jacobean wood panelling. Outside, some of Sir Bache's wrought

5

ironwork still remains – waves and anchors symbolising the origins of the Cunard fortune, in Sir Bache's case sadly depleted.

When the couple married (in 1895), Maud's money enabled her to begin work on the large, isolated house in which she found herself – house decoration was always one of her passions – repainting walls and woodwork, adding oriental rugs and silk curtains and assembling various suitably medieval effects, from suits of armour to tapestries. While Maud rearranged the drawing-room furniture, Sir Bache worked in his room in the house's sixteenth-century tower, where he made silver leaves to decorate the dining-room table and turned half-coconuts into silver-mounted cups.

Although often depicted merely as a featherbrained socialite thanks to her later career as a leading hostess, Maud was anything but. She had a deep love of music and literature; Osbert Sitwell, who knew her well, claimed that she had read many Latin and Greek writers as well as the whole of Shakespeare and Balzac. In the evenings she would play Chopin and Beethoven and read the classics and French literature late into the night, tastes which must have influenced her daughter.

Their only child, Nancy Clara Cunard, was born on 10 March 1896, to a childhood that was then typical for the upper class – numerous servants, fresh flowers in her room every morning and absentee parents. Often she did not see either of them for months at a time, a loneliness-inducing practice that affected girls more than boys, as the latter almost always went off to school at around thirteen. More stultifying still must have been the lack of physical contact – the cuddles, kisses and hand-holding that are so necessary for small children and part of normal child-parent relationships. Brothers and sisters would have helped mitigate this but Nancy was an only child, Maud having felt that with her daughter's birth she had done her duty and could carry on with her own life.

Although Nancy was too young to recognise such feelings, she was desperately lonely and craved affection. She longed for her mother's presence and was happy to be dressed up and shown off by her, sometimes in black velvet that set off her golden hair, sometimes in simple cotton. All her life Nancy was to have a love of beautiful clothes with an original twist to them – her later diaries invariably mention new outfits and how pleased she is with them. This showing-off would happen during Maud's house parties, unusual and stimulating groups of people that, instead of merely the usual run of aristocratic couples, included anyone from the Prime Minister, H.H. Asquith, and his wife Margot to musicians, poets, artists and writers.

One of these was the man who became Nancy's lifelong friend, the Irish novelist George Moore, who was her mother's lover and who some thought might have been Nancy's genetic father. It was a rumour fairly widespread at the time, probably fuelled by the obvious interest he took in this engaging child; but there is no evidence to support it and today it is largely discounted. Nor, except for the fact that both were fair rather than dark, did she resemble him at all physically, as she herself noted later on. Moore (the Friendship of my title) was always known by Nancy as GM.

Moore and Maud Burke (as Lady Cunard then was) had first met at a banquet at the Savoy. Maud, who admired Moore greatly for his defence of Emile Zola,* was so determined to meet him that she had slipped in earlier and changed the place cards so that she could sit next him. Looking extremely pretty in a grey and pink shot-silk dress, she sat beside him drinking in every word. When he paused for breath, she placed her small hand on his arm, turned her ardent blue gaze on him and said passionately, 'George Moore, you have a soul of fire!'

For Moore it was a *coup de foudre* and she remained the love of his life. Twelve years after that first meeting he wrote to her, 'I am the most fortunate of men; surely the most fortunate man in the world is he who meets a woman who enchants him as a work of art enchants . . . if I have failed to write what I dreamed I might write, one thing I have not failed in – you. You are at once

---

* The English translation of one of Zola's books, published by Moore's publisher, Vizetelly, had fallen foul of the National Vigilance Association, for 'obscene libel'.

the vase and the wine in the vase . . . A sky full of stars does not astonish me more than your face, your marmoreal eyes . . . you can never form an idea of the wonder it is to me to see you – to think you and dream you.' Much later he evoked her 'brightly coloured cheeks and fair hair, fair as the hair in an eighteenth-century pastel . . . very few men have seen their ideal as close to them and as clearly as I have seen mine.'

George Moore was born in February 1852, the eldest son of George Henry Moore, of Moore Park, a nationalist Irish politician who was also a Westminster MP and who died in 1870, leaving the eighteen-year-old GM a rich man. Once independent at twenty-one, Moore handed the management of the estate to his brother Maurice and left for Paris to study art, which he had always wanted to do, in large part because of the opportunities it offered of legitimately gazing at naked women (by his own admission he spent hours daydreaming of undressing women), since most Parisian models happily posed nude. In Paris he lived, like many art students, in the Latin Quarter – although, unlike them, he stayed in a smart hotel and kept his own valet – until, having published a book of poems at his own expense, he decided instead to become a writer.

When he published *Esther Waters* (his seventeenth book) in 1894 it became an instant best-seller, receiving rave reviews everywhere (earlier books had been banned from the powerful circulating libraries because their themes had been considered too immoral). Set in England from the early 1870s onwards, the novel is about a young, pious woman from a poor family who, while working as a kitchen maid, is seduced by another employee, becomes pregnant, is deserted by her lover, and against all odds decides to raise her child as a single mother – then, she would have been thought of as a 'fallen woman'. Even the former Prime Minister Gladstone, whose favourite hobby – along with chopping down trees – was saving such females, praised the book in a letter to the influential Liberal newspaper the *Westminster Gazette*. It brought Moore both kudos and financial security.

Nancy described GM as her 'first friend'. As her mother's long-time lover and adorer, he came often to Nevill Holt. Here he took a close interest in Nancy, spent time with her, never talked down to her and indeed became the central figure of her childhood. She first remembered him when she was four and he was forty-eight and famous.

The first thing Nancy noticed about GM was that he spoke differently from the rest of her parents' friends: his rich voice was tinged with an Irish brogue, and while he talked he gesticulated constantly with his plump white hands with their tapering fingers. He had champagne-bottle shoulders, the red hair of his youth had faded to a golden-white, his face was pink and white and his eyes pale blue; he moved so softly that Nancy often thought there was something cat-like about him.

He was known as a good conversationalist, if rather too uninhibited for the era. Harold Acton, the son of an Anglo–Italian baronet who as a youthful aesthete* had become a member of Maud's circle, described how, when the rest of the party went off to play bridge, he would join Moore, who was invariably outspoken about the other guests, even when they were within earshot: 'his directness and the round steadiness of his gaze fell like an icy shower on prevailing conventions. Nothing appeared to embarrass him . . . he would tell of his troubles with an enlarged prostate, describing them with clinical detail. Egoism in him had become a shining virtue.' He once left a grand house party† without warning, leaving only a note for his hostess that said, 'I am sorry to leave without seeing you, but I can no longer stand the love-making of the doves by my window.'

GM was witty, he was amusing and he loved gossip. At Nevill Holt he had a licence to be the *enfant terrible*. When he was offered salt, Nancy heard him say, 'I thank you, no I do not wish for any of that salt. Oh, of course, if you insist, go ahead. *But you will be eating the bones of your ancestors.*' To him, salt should

---

* At Oxford, he declaimed passages of T.S. Eliot's *The Waste Land* from the balcony of his rooms through a megaphone, an incident later fictionalised as performed by Anthony Blanche in Evelyn Waugh's *Brideshead Revisited*. Acton soon became regarded as a leading figure of his day.
† Given by Grace Duggan at Trent Park.

be sea salt, not the sort 'refined with detestable chemicals and powdered bones for whiteness'.

If people found some of his conversation too near the bone, Maud would tell her guests that not only was GM the life and soul of the party but he should not be taken too seriously – many of his remarks were exaggerations, to provoke a reaction. Some of Maud's country neighbours did not know what to make of his frequent frankness about things that – then – were thought better left unsaid. While watching a field of lively young bullocks, some of which were attempting to mount each other, GM, instead of politely ignoring them, remarked, 'Poor bullock, poor bullock – he would like to but he can't.' He would also rail against prudery: fig leaves, it seemed, were coming in again, and in Rome the finest statues of antiquity . . . oh, it didn't bear thinking about.

One of the guests who enjoyed these occasions was the young writer Osbert Sitwell. 'Very often, [George Moore] was out to shock; and when he had said something that he hoped would appal everyone in the house or even in the garden, a seraphic smile would come over his face, and remain on it, imparting to it a kind of illumination of virtue, like that of a saint, for several minutes; the bland unselfconscious smile of a small boy.'

But Maud did not hesitate to berate GM if she thought he had gone too far. Coming from Ireland, where Catholicism was so entrenched it sometimes verged on superstition, GM talked frequently about what he called 'papistry' – mocking not sincere religious faith but dogma, the inordinate ascendency of the priests in Ireland, the threat of hellfire. Suddenly he would interject a flippancy – what would they do about Holy Communion if Prohibition came in?

'Really GM,' said Maud crossly one day, '*Can't* you be more tactful? Miss X is the daughter of one of the great Catholic families of England, and you know it. And yet you go walking with her and upset her thoroughly with your nonsense . . . she went straight to her room when you came in from walking and hasn't been seen since.' For several days GM was uncharacteristically silent and in disgrace.

Maud was also angry if he was late for meals: in a house with a large staff of servants, punctuality was essential if everything was to run like clockwork.

'Go and tell Mr Moore we can't wait any longer,' Maud would say to a footman about to serve lunch. 'Where is he?'

'Mr Moore is still writing in the Long Room, your Ladyship.'

'Go and tell him to come down *at once!*'

After some time, the footman would return, red-faced and out of breath, to face an angry Maud, a temperamental butler and hungry guests.

'What have you been doing for so long, William?'

In confusion the poor footman would answer, 'Mr Moore wanted to ask me everything I thought about cricket, your Ladyship.'

Well after lunch had been started GM would appear, realise he really was late, excuse himself volubly and explain how he had become interested in the footman's views on cricket.

Sometimes GM would walk around the garden with Nancy, looking at the rooks and jackdaws or starlings; sometimes they would go further afield. She remembered one walk in particular, to Holt Wood, on a July day when most of the wildflowers were gone.

'Flowers, like us, Nancy, have their season,' said GM. 'But that is the yaffle's cry! I am not mistaken. *He* is with us the whole year round.' 'Yaffle' he told the ten-year-old Nancy, was a much nicer word than 'woodpecker'.

As a small child, Nancy longed to read. She could manage small words like 'cat' and 'dog' but longer ones, and phrases, were too much for her. The lonely, precocious little girl would question GM vigorously about anything that interested her and he would do his best to answer. Once, when she was five, she took GM to the little churchyard behind the Holt chapel, where they sat on one of the beautiful old gravestones. 'I often come here alone,' she said. 'And I often wonder where we go after we are dead.'

When Nancy was nine, her life was taken over by an appall-ingly strict governess, whose reign instilled her with a powerful, lifelong dislike of authority. Miss Scarth, who had arrived with excellent references, was indeed a good teacher – albeit one who reinforced her methods with a steel ruler. Nancy's daily regime now began with a cold bath, in winter and summer, followed by porridge and a heavy English breakfast that she found hard to swallow – one of Miss Scarth's diktats was that Nancy had to finish every scrap of food on her plate, and the small child would often sit for hours before she could bring herself to swallow the slowly congealing mess that remained, a treatment that left her with a lasting distaste for food, which she would always associate with punishment.

It was, of course, the custom for the children of upper-class families to be handed over to nurses and governesses almost from birth, but even by the standards of the day Maud's neglect of her daughter was virtually total – her social life and its demands took up all her time. Once Miss Scarth had been engaged, Maud felt she had done everything necessary for her child. Nancy's complaints about her treatment by her governess were disregarded while Maud continued her own life unhindered, an abandonment that must have gone much of the way to fuelling Nancy's later resentment of her mother. Her father, a vague, distant but affectionate presence, left the upbringing of his daughter to his wife, as was then customary. It was during these years that Nancy's affection for GM, the only person who took a real interest in her, became so firmly grounded.

When Nancy was ten and Moore was in Dublin he wrote to Maud, 'Do speak to her sometimes of me, for I don't want her to forget me,' and soon afterwards, 'Kiss Nancy for me and tell her I look forward to hearing from her and going for a walk with her.' Sometimes Nancy pressed wildflowers and sent them to him to remind him of these walks. Wild forget-me-nots were the ones he particularly liked – something she remembered years later when he visited her in Paris.

Nancy had a precocious taste in literature and read widely in English and French. The education of this clever child fascinated GM, and when one day he discovered that she was learning the answers to questions like 'What is Leeds famous for?' and 'What is Bradford famous for?' he was so indignant that all the adults were told – and also told how useless this was. 'When she grows up and goes down to dinner on the arm of a young man,' he said crossly, 'is she going to turn to him and say, "What is made in Sheffield?"'

He would often open the schoolroom door in the middle of lessons, saying, 'Well, here is Nancy at it, just as I expected. She is at what *I* have come to be informed about, French irregular verbs.' In fact, thanks to his seven years in Paris, his own French was excellent and spoken fluently with what seemed a real French accent; and he had even written poems in French.

Everyone came to Holt, with its vivacious, glittering, restless, dominant chatelaine who managed her guests and their conversations rather as a conductor draws the best from his orchestra (perhaps it was no coincidence that she herself later fell in love with a conductor). There were always house parties, with women of fashion, diplomats, wits and politicians. To Holt came the Duchess of Rutland, her lover Harry Cust, today the acknowledged father of Nancy's later friend Lady Diana Manners, statesman and former 'Soul' George Wyndham, the wasp-waisted Mrs Hope Vere, the polymath Edward Marsh, the polar explorer Fridtjof Nansen, the young poet Francis Meynell, F.E. Smith (later Lord Birkenhead) and Somerset Maugham – then known as a playwright – and A.J. Balfour, Prime Minister from 1902 to 1905.

As the summers drew on and the host was away for long periods shooting and fishing in Scotland, from August onwards the men became intellectual rather than good riders to hounds and worldly. In summer there were elaborate long teas on the lawn under the ancient cedar tree while tennis and croquet were played, on colder days was bridge for hours on end in the hall or morning room, where great log fires blazed.

In winter women arrived in smart tailor-mades, swathed in furs with a bunch of Parma violets pinned to the shoulder; in summer they wore striped taffeta or muslin as they strolled the lawns. In the early evenings some wore floating tea gowns of beige lace or lilac chiffon. The spotted veils, the long feather boas and the ruffled dresses fascinated the small Nancy and made her long to be old enough to wear such things.

For a long time, Nancy's only playmate was her cousin Victor, two years younger than her, who lived a few miles away at Lubenham, meetings that would form a lifetime bond. Like Nancy, Victor had golden hair and blue eyes. Occasionally there were other gaieties: when she was twelve she was involved in teenage amateur dramatics. 'More rehearsing. Harewood is <u>so</u> tiresome, keeps on saying "I ham he" and does not know his speeches,' records her diary for 4 January 1909. 'Little Eileen is very annoying as well, she speaks as if her mouth were full of plums. Today we acted the play. The Grand Duke Michael and his family were present. The play went well. Lady Sarah Wilson managed it all!!'

But it came to an end all too soon: '7 Jan. Mother has gone to Belvoir today by train. Things here begin their usual course again and lessons recommence. Therefore during this period while Mother is in America and after K.P. have left, things will not be very bright and nothing much happens . . . I am not going to write a diary while Mother is in America as nothing amusing or interesting happens.'

When GM was at Holt when there was no house party, Maud would make use of him for her favourite pastime, rearranging the furniture or enhancing what was there with one of her purchases of cushions, brocades or Chinese bowls of potpourri. Moore was knowledgeable about antique furniture and loved it, so that any new arrival was thoroughly discussed as to provenance and placing. As for Nancy, she enjoyed going around the bedrooms with a housemaid to see that everything was in order for the expected guests; she would check that there was ink, pens, writing paper on the writing table. She would also concoct a small vase of wildflowers to put beside the bed.

Often GM would go walking with Nancy and her governess, Nancy running on ahead while Moore and Miss Scarth, a woman highly educated and extremely well read, discussed some aspect of French literature, walks that would usually put Miss Scarth temporarily in a better temper. Equally often, Moore would walk with Nancy on her own, talking of everything from the landscape that lay in the valley ahead of them ('there, to the left, is Castle Rockingham, a sturdy place, at which the cannons of Cromwell were once fired from Holt') to how to write a story.

Only one disagreement between the two friends is recorded. One teatime, when GM was demonstrating a waltz step as someone played the piano, Nancy's dog Buster, a Scottish terrier with a withered leg, got in the way, to be kicked hard by GM. Immediately Nancy flew at him and gave him a furious slap on the face. Everyone – except GM himself – was angry with her and she was confined to the schoolroom in disgrace for two days.

An even worse explosion occurred when it was realised that she had read *Three Weeks*, the red-haired, green-eyed novelist Elinor Glyn's tale of a passionate affair between a beautiful woman, first seen lying seductively on a tiger skin, and a younger man. Bound in purple (Elinor's favourite colour), the novel, published in 1907, was considered so scandalous that it created a furore. To the eleven-year-old Nancy, who read it clandestinely in bed, it was fascinating. 'So that was an adventuress – beautiful, perfidious, dashing, and exactly what I wanted to know about! She blazed across the repressions of my childhood,' she wrote. But there was no one she could talk to about it – until the arrival of GM on a visit.

When he called her into his workroom one day for a chat she told him, and they discussed the book for about twenty minutes. Unfortunately her governess, walking past the door, overheard the subject of the conversation, reported it, and that afternoon there was a furious outburst as this 'sin' was related. To everyone's surprised indignation, GM firmly stood up for the crimson-faced Nancy, with the result that both of them were in disgrace for days – and Nancy became fonder of her 'first friend' than ever. She called him her 'constant and endearing companion'.

Nancy's feeling for lovely clothes started early. Her parents took the thirteen-year-old Nancy to Paris in April 1909, where she was immediately struck pleasurably by the Louvre ('What a store of glorious work it contains!') and by the French habit of taking a cup of chocolate at teatime, something she found delicious. Then came her first steps in fashion; it was a time when most smart women who could afford it went to Paris for their clothes: 'We tried on dresses and bought some new hats this morning and such lovely things too.' Next day, 'we tried on all morning at the Galeries Lafayette . . . Father and I visited the furniture in the Louvre and then joined mother and tried on at Lanvin.' This was followed by a visit to Rome and Florence ('the most divine city'), then back home via Paris, where 'I had to try on all morning at the galleries Lafayette where they had made me a sweet little blue dress.' After this, much of her diary was written in impressively good French.

At the end of March the Cunards travelled to Germany. Nancy talked of the wonderful pictures she had seen, of walking in the Tiergarten, of pine woods and lakes, but concluded by saying, 'I hate Germany.' As it was the last time Nancy and her parents would be together as a family, this might have been the reason – Sir Bache was spending more and more time away on visits, her mother was as social as ever and Nancy herself had embarked on a long course of reading, from Shakespeare and Dickens to Corneille, Goldsmith, Daudet and Borrow.

In 1911 Maud, then thirty-eight, left her husband and moved to London, taking Nancy with her, largely because she [Maud] had fallen in love with the conductor Thomas Beecham, the rising star of British music and a witty and entertaining conversationalist. Beecham, six years younger than Maud, was tall and handsome with dark hair, a small moustache and beard. He was also married, although soon after Maud arrived in London he separated from his wife (who refused to divorce him).

As her London home, Maud rented 20 Cavendish Square, the house belonging to Margot Asquith and her husband H.H. Asquith (the Asquith family were ensconced in No. 10 Downing Street). Here she began the frenetic social life for which she became known, while assisting and promoting Beecham in any way she could, attending all his concerts, wheedling money out of her wealthy friends to support English opera and giving glittering first-night parties for him. The story goes that she pressured her friend the Prime Minister into creating his father Joseph a baronet (in 1914)* so that her beloved Tom would have a title to inherit.

As a hostess Maud was supreme at a time when to fulfil this role was a full-time occupation, almost a profession – the endless writing of invitation or thank-you notes, the juggling of guests, often so that there could be two, three or four tables of bridge after dinner, the notes taken of preferences, rivalries or enmities, the concoction of menus, the buying of flowers, clothes and small gifts, the knowing whom one could ring up without affront if someone fell out at the last minute. Trivial it may have been, but it demanded an ability to organise, an excellent memory, the personality to command success and enormous stamina – entertaining at Maud's level was a ceaseless, almost daily round.

On most days there were luncheons and dinners in the dining room, newly decorated by Maud with shot green lamé curtains and black lacquer screens embossed with bristling silvery porcupines. Opposite was a tapestry in which giraffes pushed their heads through a forest of birch trees; the Diaghilev Ballet, with its vividly coloured and exotic designs by Bakst, had just come to London, so Maud's décor was cutting-edge. Much more than most, she also invited poets, novelists, painters, musicians and sculptors to her table, where they would have met many potential patrons.

Maud's parties became famous; she herself was cultured and knowledgeable, and she had a genius not only for mixing people but for throwing some unexpected remark into the conversation that drew out the best and wittiest from her guests. 'Lady Cunard ... had a greater capacity for keeping a dinner table alight than anyone I have known,' said the politician Bob Boothby a few

---

* Lady Diana Manners, later Nancy's great friend, asserted that Joseph had to pay £10,000 for his baronetcy, of which £4,000 went to Maud and £500 to herself. (See Philip Ziegler, *Diana Cooper*, p.94, 1981.) Beecham was knighted in 1916, a few months before his father Joseph died and he inherited the baronetcy.

years later, and most of London society would have agreed with him. Or as the diarist Chips Channon put it of one luncheon party, 'the usual potpourri and brilliant chat'.

Nancy, now fifteen, was well aware that Beecham was the real reason they had left her beloved Nevill Holt and the father to whom she was deeply attached (the Cunards were now formally separated, by mutual agreement). Just as she was going through adolescence – a turbulent time in itself – her whole life was turned upside down. The double break, from the home she loved and from her father and his protective aura, must have been traumatic and one of the strands that underlay her growing distance from her mother. (It was a considerate aunt who explained some of the facts of life to her.)

At the same time, GM moved from Dublin to London, settling in 121 Ebury Street, where he was cared for and cosseted by two devoted maids. Most of his time – sitting, eating, writing – was spent in what he called the Morning Room, a ground-floor front room with a bow window through which he could see the street but was invisible to those outside. Its stone floor was covered with an Aubusson carpet splashed with great pink roses on which stood a large, long table, usually strewn with books, proofs and typescripts, which were pushed aside or removed when it was time to lay for a meal. Around him hung some of his wonderful collection of pictures – two Manets, two Berthe Morisots, a David and a small Constable.

His beloved Maud's affair with Beecham upset the faithful GM. 'I did not remain till the end of the concert because I wished to fly from your world, which is not my world,' he wrote on 21 January 1913; and again, 'I thought you might be coming to dine with me,' he wrote in January 1914. 'You didn't because you feared you mightn't be amused all the while, and of course life is intolerable if it be not always at concert pitch.' Yet more than ever, GM had become a fixed point in Nancy's life; for his part, as he wrote to Maud that summer, 'You and Nancy are my realities – all the others are shadows.'

In London, there was no hated Miss Scarth ('my odious governess', as Nancy referred to her later). Instead she attended a private school in South Audley Street, run by another excellent teacher, Miss Wolff, where girls sat at round tables in the drawing room rather than at desks. In these civilised surroundings she met the girl who would become her greatest friend for the next few years, Iris Tree, the daughter of the celebrated actor–manager Sir Beerbohm Tree and his actress wife, Helen Tree.

Iris, whose mother used to dress her and her sister Viola in black velvet frocks with apricot silk sashes to play up their red-gold hair, was exactly the kind of free spirit to appeal to the adolescent Nancy. Although a year younger than Nancy, at fourteen she was in embryo the complete bohemian, impervious to convention, determined on a life in the arts lived according to the rules of romance or, as she would put it in a later poem, 'And like a firefly through the twilit trees/Romance, the golden play-boy of my days.'* Already the two of them wrote poetry, which they would read to each other, Nancy in her small, clipped, high-pitched voice, Iris in a resonant, sonorous tone. Nancy was encouraged by GM, who wrote to her in May 1912 from Paris, 'I suppose you are too young to write "pure poetry", poetry about things, but remember that that is the only poetry that lasts … one truth I have gathered; and it is, that the artist should avoid sentiment as he would the plague – as sentiment passes away like the clouds. There is not a tear in Shakespeare …'

Through Iris, Nancy met the dazzling Lady Diana Manners, and through her the circle that included Osbert Sitwell and Augustus John. The lovely, witty Lady Tree, Iris's mother, was the closest friend of the Duchess of Rutland, Diana's mother, who was fascinated by all things theatrical, and their respective daughters had become equally close.

Every summer the Trees would rent lodgings near the Manners' cottage near Bognor; every Christmas they would stay at Belvoir, arriving on Christmas Eve when Sir Herbert, who hated the country, would 'unexpectedly' receive a telegram telling him of a crisis in his theatre that necessitated his immediate return. Off he would go, to spend Christmas with his mistress in

---

* From 'Far Away the Lost Adventures Gleam', 1917.

Putney Hill. No one was deceived, but convention was observed.

At fifteen Iris, already determined to become a painter, left Miss Wolff's for Venice, as her parents were allowing her to study art there under the aegis of her older sister Viola (a true sign of parental liberality, when one considers the girls' ages and the proclivities of most Italian men). Sixteen-year-old Nancy, to complete the 'finishing' process thought necessary for upper-class young girls, was sent to Munich, to continue her German and her musical education.

Much to her surprise, she enjoyed it; by comparison, the *pension de jeunes filles* she was sent on to in Paris was three months of boredom – her French was already so good that the language lessons fell flat, and the girls were heavily chaperoned. However, one great benefit, largely manifested later, was her friendship with Marie, the youngest of the three Ozanne sisters who ran the school. With Marie, when she was able to detach her from the others, there were plenty of enjoyable concerts and the opera.

Nancy got to know Paris by walking everywhere, once passing the Closerie des Lilas. Ironically, in view of her later life, she said to herself, 'Dearly would I have liked to be taken there to meet some of the poets – but by whom?'

Soon afterwards, in the summer of 1913, Maud Cunard took a palazzo in Venice and invited several friends to stay, including the Asquiths, the Duchess of Rutland and, to Nancy's delight, the Duchess's daughter Diana. In another palazzo nearby were Diana's group of special friends, mainly the children of the 'Souls', that loose grouping of those among the aristocratic elite of the late nineteenth century who preferred intelligence, wit, an interest in art, music, philosophy and fine writing to the more philistine values of the Marlborough House Set, as the circle around the then Prince of Wales (later Edward VII) was known. Both Margot Asquith and the beautiful and artistic Violet Rutland were Souls.

The Souls' children called themselves the 'Corrupt Coterie'; at their heart were Diana and their leader, Raymond Asquith, the eldest of the Asquith family. Although most of the Coterie were, like Diana, a few years older than Nancy, to mix with people so close to her own age for the first time, and to know that this glittering band enjoyed her company, was a huge boost to her social confidence – something she would need when she was 'out'. Already prepared to be rebellious, she also admired their reputation for the flouting of convention and disregard of scandal, something unusual in those pre-war days when the shadow of Edwardianism still hung heavy: young girls were supposed to be chaste, modest, and certainly completely shielded from anything sexual – a few were not even allowed to walk down St James's Street in case they encountered lascivious glances from the windows of the gentlemen's clubs that lined it. But although Diana declared of the Corrupt Coterie, 'Our pride was to be unafraid of words, unshocked by drink and unashamed of "decadence" and gambling,' their so-called wickedness was fairly mild: swimming by moonlight, escapades that involved visits to men's flats without chaperonage (though Diana herself remained virginal until her marriage), group parties without their parents' knowledge.

When the radiant Diana referred to the Duchess as Her Grace, instead of 'my mother', Nancy began her habit of always talking of her own mother as Her Ladyship. But where Diana always spoke of the Duchess in affectionate tones, Nancy's had a distancing sharp edge; the resentment of her mother that would eventually occupy much of her life was already there.

The social ritual that led up to Nancy's debut in the adult world through presentation at Court, to be followed by a Coming-out Season, was to take place the following spring. First, Maud, determined to do the right thing by her beautiful daughter and launch her in style, took her to Paris to buy clothes for this all-important year – ballgowns by Poiret, the designer of the moment, morning and afternoon dresses, Ascot outfits, hats and a leopard-skin coat. But, much as Nancy loved clothes, this generosity had little effect on her: Maud's attention had come too late.

More and more she began to despise and resent her mother – forgetting, of course, that it was from Maud that she had inherited her gold-blonde looks, intelligence, literary leanings and love of music. Nor did Maud's entertaining of some of a younger generation help, although often the teenage Nancy enjoyed meeting them. One of these young men was the American poet Ezra Pound, already known for trying to help and promote other writers he admired. He would visit Maud for tea, stressing to her how necessary it was to give financial aid to the Irish writer James Joyce (when a sum of money was eventually raised it was known as the 'King's Bounty'), so that Joyce could fulfil what Pound believed was his immense potential. Maud, who realised that Pound too was in need of money, would also, as she put it, 'help him out occasionally'.

Nancy liked Pound from the start. She was deeply struck by his appearance; she noted that he was tall and had 'green, lynx-like eyes, a head of thick, waving red hair and a pointed red beard'. He emphasised this dramatic colouring with clothes theatrical for that day – a swirling black cape over a black velvet jacket and black and white check trousers, the whole topped with a wide-brimmed black felt hat, so that he looked, she thought, 'like Rodolpho in *La Bohème*'. She recognised at once that beneath the flamboyance lay a deeply cultured man who could draw on anything from the classics to China and Japan for his subjects. Although they did not become close for some years, the door to the world of ideas had opened another inch or two.

Nancy was presented at Court in March 1914, wearing a pink dress with a tulle train scattered with rose petals – a month earlier, Maud had given a dance for her at Cavendish Square (which had a large ballroom), at which Maud was reported as wearing blue silk shot with mauve and ropes of pearls, while Nancy 'looked charming' in pale primrose-yellow with clusters of orange roses. She danced with the Prince of Wales, who gave her a gold cigarette case engraved with his crest, which must have raised Maud's hopes. But Nancy hated the Season; it would be, she swore to herself, 'my first and last, as one ball succeeded another and the faces of the revolving guardsmen seemed as silly as their vapid conversation among the hydrangeas at supper'.

It was one of the last times that convention held her in its sway. From now on, grown up at last, she was determined to live life on her own terms.

CHATER 2

※—⊱—◦—⊰—※

Grown Up

Nancy at eighteen was a spectacular beauty – tall, slender, elegant and gleamingly blonde. The writer David Garnett remembered her coming into the Café Royal in a party with Viola Tree: 'She was very slim with a skin as white as blanched almonds, the bluest eyes one has ever seen and very fair hair. She was marvellous. The world she inhabited was that of the rich and smart and the gulf between us then seemed unbridgeable.' Allied to her extraordinary beauty was a personality mesmeric in its depth, intelligence and passion. The writer Sybille Bedford called her 'incarnately alluring', saying that 'never for a second was it possible not to be aware of Nancy'.

Her closest friend when she came out was her schoolmate Iris Tree, at seventeen a year younger than herself but already leading a remarkably free, and busy, social life – in part through her links to the Coterie and her involvement in the art world, in part through her parents, who gave lavish first-night supper parties in the dome of the theatre built and owned by Sir Herbert, Her Majesty's, in London's Haymarket, to which came the cream of haut bohemia.

While Nancy was in Munich and Paris, Iris had been attending the Slade School of Fine Art. Here she became a close friend of Dora Carrington, both girls appearing with the Slade haircut – a bell of golden hair (as an act of rebellion, Iris had cut off her long red-gold plait and left it in a train). Also in Iris's circle were the three Sitwells – Osbert, his older sister Edith and his younger brother Sacheverell – the poets Robert Nichols and Tommy Earp, painters like Álvaro 'Chile' Guevara and Nina Hamnett, ex-debutante turned publisher Allanah Harper and, of course, Diana Manners.

Everything about Iris was generous, warm and abundant, including her contempt for conventional behaviour. She had, said Osbert Sitwell, 'a honey-coloured beauty of hair and skin that I have never observed in anyone else'. She was sought after as a model, being painted by Augustus John, Duncan Grant, Vanessa Bell, Roger Fry and (in the nude) by Modigliani and sculpted by Jacob Epstein* (it was through Epstein that Nancy first took an interest in African art and artefacts, later to become synonymous with her public persona). These were exactly the sort of people Nancy wanted to meet.

Sometimes Nancy would take Iris with her to visit her father, now living at Haycock House, once a sizeable coaching inn, at Stibbington in Cambridgeshire (the parting with Maud and her money and his own growing debts had forced his departure from Nevill Holt). Or they would go down to the Trees at the seaside, always spending as much time out of doors as possible and often walking for miles – both enduring loves for Nancy. In the evenings they would read each other the poetry they had written, Nancy being the more introspective and self-critical.

Iris lived a life of seemingly complete freedom. Even more telling, she cared nothing for what others thought. To Nancy, already embarked on the battle against everything her mother thought 'suitable', this attitude was irresistible. When the two of them secretly rented a studio in Fitzroy Street, they were able to put these attitudes into practice. 'The Fitz', as it became known, had a red and white checked floor on which Nancy and Iris installed a large black-velvet sofa and a mirror-topped table with red edges. Black-velvet blinds hung on the windows.

Nancy and Iris also did what was then done largely only by actresses and prostitutes – they used cosmetics freely, though always, of course, out of sight of their respective parents. Meeting

---

* This sculpture is currently displayed in Tate Britain.

at the Fitz before an evening out, they would delve into their stash of theatrical make-up acquired by Iris from her father's theatres: sticks of greasepaint, rouge – applied with a hare's foot – and Reckitt's Blue powder for their eyelids. For the fancy-dress parties then so popular, they also kept a collection of costumes. One early morning, so dressed, the two of them were returning in such high spirits from a Royal Albert Hall Ball that they jumped into the Serpentine, emerging with bedraggled feathers and dripping chiffon to find themselves confronted by a policeman, who took down their names and addresses and brought a charge against them. This of course got to their parents, who confiscated their latch keys and imposed a curfew; but as the existence of the studio was still secret and they managed to get new keys forged, life went on much as before.

It was Iris, too, who introduced Nancy to the Eiffel Tower, the restaurant that would play so large a part in her life, so much so that she called it 'our carnal-spiritual home'. It was at 1 Percy Street, an address just north of present-day Soho, but then very much part of what was known as Fitzrovia, an amorphous area renowned for its literary and artistic associations and louche bohemian atmosphere.

The Eiffel Tower was kept by the Austrian-born Rudolph Stulik, the illegitimate son of a Viennese opera dancer and once a chef, first in a big hotel in Monte Carlo, then to Lord Kitchener. Stulik looked and sounded the part of genial, prosperous restaurateur: a stout man with black mustachios waxed at the ends and a thick Austrian accent. He was endlessly indulgent to his patrons, often keeping the restaurant open so late for them that his waiters missed the last bus and had to walk the six miles home; and many years later having to close it because so many of those to whom he had been so generous did not pay their bills.

In his wine cellar were amazing bins of Imperial Tokay from famous Hapsburg vineyards – Stulik had bought, for more than he could afford, the yacht of the last Crown Prince; this included its wine cellar, worth several times as much as the boat.

The Tower, as it was known to habitués, had been discovered by Augustus John in the 1890s, and through him soon became an artists' rendezvous – later, it managed to combine this with being a high-priced, fashionable eating place, usually full of those who wished to enjoy a bohemian atmosphere in comfort. The restaurant walls were covered with paintings, some left in time-honoured fashion by those who could not pay their bills, there were red lamps on the white tablecloths of the ten-odd tables and the ceiling was hung with brass pots full of trailing plants. Its menu design was by Wyndham Lewis,* whose paintings hung in the Vorticist Room upstairs and who was the founder of the Vorticist Movement – painting that combined early Cubism with imagery derived from the angularity of machines and the urban environment, supposedly to express the dynamism of the modern world.

Lewis himself was a dramatic personality. He was tall, with pale skin and dark hair and eyes – he often wore black – and he fizzed with energy and ideas. His looks were the sort that either greatly appealed or repelled equally strongly: he was handsome in a dark and arrogant way that women – whom he pursued vigorously – and most men found irresistible. Nor did he have any hesitation about promulgating his ideas. To castigate what he saw as the effeteness of contemporary British art, he founded the short-lived (two issues only) *Blast* magazine; its first edition, published on 2 July 1914, had a lurid pink cover, with the word 'Blast' written diagonally across it in thick black capitals. It was referred to by Ezra Pound as the 'great MAGENTA cover'd opusculus'.

At the same time, Lewis was proclaiming almost nightly that war was a necessary evil. Until he left in 1915, posted to the Western Front as a second lieutenant (in 1917 he was made an official war artist for both the Canadian† and British governments), Nancy and her friends would listen enthralled to his expositions and to the discussions of art and literature in the Vorticist room, dedicated to their use. This they treated like a club, often

---

* His name was Percy Wyndham Lewis but he quickly dropped 'Percy', a name he disliked.
† Born in Canada to an American father and a British mother, Lewis had both Canadian and British citizenship.

turning up if at a loose end or simply to see who else was there.

In one of her poems ('Sublunary') Nancy described the Tower's atmosphere of 'wits and glamour, strong wines, new foods, fine looks, strange-sounding languages of diverse men'. The night before Augustus John left for America for the first time, he dined on peacocks (which came from Germany), served with their feathers on. Another time, the menu was based around Minnie, a sucking pig that had been a pet of the restaurant. Iris wept bitterly when she heard of Minnie's death but managed to eat a slice of her.

Another attraction of the bohemian society found at the Tower was its attitude to sex. In girls of Nancy's class, leading the sort of life prescribed for them, virginity until marriage was a cardinal principle, but even before the war had produced a generation determined to rebel against the old certainties, the habitués of the Café Royal, the Tower and other such haunts had thrown off most moral taboos.

Bohemia believed that love should be expressed to its fullest and it was mere prudery to deny this. Augustus John, one of its leading figures, seduced every woman who allowed him to; one girl who went to stay with John and his wife in Dorset was advised by his sister-in-law to put a heavy chest of drawers against her bedroom door when she went to bed. Enid Bagnold, the daughter of a colonel, escaped the conventional life of her parents by going to work as a staff writer on the magazine *Modern Society*, founded by the notoriously priapic Frank Harris in 1913. 'Sex', he told Enid, 'is the gateway to life.' As she recorded, 'So I went through the gateway in an upper room in the Café Royal . . .'

Nancy and Iris would sneak fresh-faced out of their respective houses, smother their faces in chalk-white face powder emphasised by scarlet lipstick and set off to smoke and drink among their friends, in the Fitz, the Tower or the pulsing heart of bohemia, the Café Royal, with its marble-topped tables, red plush seats and gilded mirrors. Under its ornate turquoise ceiling, usually half hidden by tobacco smoke, artists like Jacob Epstein or Augustus John, piratical in his swirling black cape and brass earrings, would sip pale, cloudy absinthe or suck green crème de menthe frappé through a straw. Or perhaps it would be the Cavendish Hotel, run by the great Rosa Lewis, who, knowing that Iris was a favourite of her adored Lord Ribblesdale,* served them champagne that went on to the bills of others.

They would visit pubs in Limehouse or call in at cabmen's shelters for a cup of sweet tea or sometimes an early breakfast of bacon and eggs (but never at the shelter at Hyde Park Corner, known as the Junior Turf Club, because there Iris's father Sir Beerbohm Tree would often play dominoes with the cabbies until six in the morning).

With Diana Manners, they made a glamorous threesome for the gossip columns. Diana and Nancy were the two most usually featured, Nancy because it was her debutante Season ('Miss Nancy Cunard wearing white charmeuse' at a ball at the Ritz), Diana because, as the *Tatler* pointed out when it snapped them walking in step together at Melton Mowbray on 15 April for the Melton Hunt Steeplechases, she was 'invariably in the foreground of the innumerable house parties, bazaars, amateur theatricals and other cheerful functions that Society, with a big S, includes in its daily round and common task'.

The two of them were reported as maids of honour in different-coloured mirror-velvet† dresses at a wedding, Diana's rose-pink, Nancy's lime-green, both with hats of silk beaver trimmed with roses. With her mother chaperoning her, Nancy went through most of the big events of the Season, attending the opera, Ascot and balls, such as those given by Mrs Leggett, where the panelled walls of the dining room were hung with Rose du Barry brocade and the three dining tables piled with pink roses and tulips.

Despite their attendance at these compulsory rituals, both Nancy and Diana wished to show that they were not bound by the way of life to which they had been born. The difference was that while Nancy was rebelling on principle against everything her mother stood for, Diana flouted convention largely to draw attention to herself. At one ball, for instance, which stated on the

---

* Before the Licencing Act of October 1915, pubs were allowed to stay open roughly nineteen hours a day. After it, they had to close at 9.30 p.m.
† Velvet with the pile pressed flat to give a satiny sheen.

invitation that medals might be worn, she appeared wearing two that she had won for swimming and a Coronation medal. At a 'theme' ball at the Royal Albert Hall, when she and eleven other girls had been told to dress in white, with swansdown trimming, she appeared in a black dress. Nancy's gestures, on the other hand, such as turning up late for Maud's dinner parties or the opera or appearing at a dinner party before a ball wearing a man's black waistcoat, were designed to irritate Maud and be as openly hostile as she dared. But they did nothing to free Nancy from a life that she was finding more and more constraining.

She was constant in one major part of her life, however, lunching regularly once a week with her 'first friend' George Moore. By now, the rumour that he might be her father had inevitably reached Nancy, and with her usual straightforwardness she decided to tackle it head on. At one of these lunches she asked him unexpectedly, 'GM, people around London are saying that I am really your daughter. Is that true?' GM, as was his habit when bewildered, puffed out his cheeks and 'popped' (in Nancy's words) his eyes before replying noncommittally, 'My dear, I fear I cannot say,' before adding in a panic, 'Nancy, you haven't mentioned this to your mother, have you?' She reassured him that she had not, but much later wondered how different her life might have been had the rumour been true.

Before the end of the summer, everything changed. When the Archduke Franz Ferdinand of Austria, heir to the Austro-Hungarian Empire, was assassinated on 28 June 1914, to most people it was an event of little import. No one thought it would be the spark that lit the fire; indeed, most of the British government was more concerned at the prospect of civil war in Ireland, as Ulster fiercely resisted the demands of the South for complete Home Rule. So when war with Germany was declared less than six weeks later, on 4 August, after the Germans had overrun Belgium and ignored the British ultimatum to withdraw, it came like a thunderclap to many (with no television or radios and few telephones, newspapers were the main source of news, often unavailable to those in the depths of the countryside).

There was an immediate rush to the colours and, among high-spirited young men like Nancy's friends, a feeling that this was, if not exactly a lark, at least a good adventure. In London, the declaration of war brought cheering crowds to fill Trafalgar Square; there was constant singing of the national anthem and in country towns people fought over the batches of newspapers as they arrived. The general belief was that it would soon be over, perhaps by Christmas.

Even during the long and bloody conflict that followed, civilians were little affected – without aerial bombardment, there was no blackout and daily life was mostly no more hazardous than usual.* To the outward eye, the main differences were the disappearances of young and youngish men, the arrival of paper money instead of gold coinage and, soon, the growing casualty lists that began to appear in *The Times*.

Social life went on as normal, although already drink was playing a larger part than usual in the lives of young women like Nancy (until the war, most of them drank little if at all). 'Dined at Cavendish Square with Nancy Cunard,' wrote Duff Cooper in December 1915. 'Everybody got rather drunk but I got very drunk and unfortunately Lady Cunard came back after dinner.' Next morning he felt 'a complete wreck' and was 'horrified to hear that Lady Cunard had noticed my drunkenness last night and spoken about it to Nancy ... I wrote an abject letter of apology and remorse to Lady Cunard.'

Soon the first casualty lists began to appear, often with a friend's name in them. 'Gradually every man with the (rough) average number of limbs & faculties is being sucked out to the war,' wrote Violet Asquith to Rupert Brooke in March 1915. 'I feel as if I were sitting on a beach at low tide amongst old boots & wreckage. Those who have remained have acquired an artificially inflated value – Montague & Duff Cooper the only two men left in London – from whom in peace women with aesthetic sensibilities shuddered & shrank – now swoon on divans surrounded

---

* The first Zeppelin raid did not take place until January 1915, the last in August 1918 with total fatalities of 557.

by troops of odalisques – Ruby [Peto] – Diana [Manners] – Viola [Tree] – Katharine – Nancy [Cunard] – Ly Essex – Ava Astor etc, etc etc.'

Nancy and Iris did more than hover around non-combatants. For them, the habit of casual sex began early. At the Fitz they gave parties to which their friends – now officers fighting in the trenches – would come when home on leave. These parties, fuelled by endless champagne, became ever more abandoned: a young man, knowing that he might never return, did not want to die without knowing the embrace of a woman; the girls felt equally that they should do all they could for someone they might never see again. Yet while Iris, a true romantic, seemed untouched, these encounters left Nancy with a feeling of rueful despair, often to be drowned only by more alcohol.

Sometime in 1915–16 – probably in the autumn of 1915 – she wrote a poem entitled 'Remorse':

I have been wasteful, wanton, foolish, bold
And loved with grasping hands and lustful eyes
All through the hectic days and summer skies

which concluded:

I sit ashamed and silent in this room
While the wet streets go gathering in their gloom.

And once, whether to excuse or explain herself, she said to Diana Manners 'My mother's having an affair with Thomas Beecham; I can do what I like.'

As word of the doings at the Fitz got about, Iris and Nancy began to acquire what was called 'a reputation'. 'Iris quenches a dozen blue-flies' thirst, and God knows her face betrays her,' wrote Diana to a friend that May. 'Nancy too is in the same boat of iniquity, with better show yet a smuttier name, God help them both! They have more courage than me – and can seize an opportunity and hug and crush it against their palates irrespective of the taste and they are very happy while I go starved, and hesitating and checking my every impulse for fear of losing my pedestal of ice.'

Nancy and Iris would often urge Diana to join them for their parties at the Fitz but, less abandoned in her rebellion, she always refused – a refusal that became adamant after she once helped clear up after one such party. Here she saw champagne bottles broken at the neck to save the bother of uncorking them, pools of blood and vomit, sordid-looking unmade beds and the black-velvet sofa thick with dust. It was a life of 'drink, cynicism and unlimited promiscuity', as one friend described it. Or, as Iris herself put it in a poem of 1916:

> You have not felt the abandon
> Of light love . . .

Inevitably there was gossip, with Nancy's reputation in particular suffering. In part, perhaps, to hide from herself the sordidness of some of the goings-on and her own role in them she was beginning to rely on the champagne that was the favourite drink of everyone in their circle, so that she was often, in the slang of the time, 'buffy' – i.e. tipsy – to a lesser or usually a greater extent. When Diana and Duff Cooper, the man Diana would later marry, called on Nancy one morning at eleven, 'We found Nancy not yet dressed, looking squalid, having been very drunk the night before,' wrote Duff in his diary. 'Diana was disgusted. Nancy's *dégringolade** is so complete I find it rather romantic.'

By contrast, daytime activities were entirely proper. Like other society girls, Nancy would pose in tableaux or sell at bazaars to raise money for comforts for the troops. In November 1915 she was a bridesmaid at Iris's sister Felicity's wedding; at the end of the month she was selling at her mother's stall at the Grand Bazaar in aid of war victims held in Claridge's.

In 1915, Iris departed for a long tour of the United States with her father, leaving a great gap in Nancy's life, a lack of intimate

---

* Plunge, fall.

companionship that left her more under her mother's sway and probably encouraged the events that followed.

Hostesses, hampered by the huge shortage of men, leapt at the chance of entertaining gallant young officers, wounded or home on leave. One weekend in 1916 Maud and Nancy went to stay at Trent Park, the grand country house and estate in the London borough of Enfield that the wealthy and newly widowed Grace Duggan* had rented from Sir Philip Sassoon. There, too, in the house party was Sydney Fairbairn, a young officer home on leave because he had been wounded at Gallipoli; Nancy's scrapbook has a photograph of him lying asleep on a hospital bed, blood showing on a bandaged leg. Sydney Fairbairn was from a prominent and rich Australian family, with a father who was one of the most famous athletes of his day. Sydney had been brought up in a country house in Buckinghamshire and educated at Eton before going to university in Germany. He was tall, dark, good-looking, husky-voiced, cheerful, friendly and himself a superb cricketer, having played for the MCC against Barbados during their tour of the West Indies in early 1913. He had joined the Royal Buckinghamshire Hussars before the start of the war.

In the luxurious surroundings of Trent Park – 'four footmen in the hall and dinner beginning with caviar', reported one visitor – Nancy and Sydney became engaged.

'Maud did not approve of the engagement,' wrote Grace. 'Unhappily we – the house party and the children – were unwilling listeners to a rather acrimonious dispute one afternoon at tea. Maud, who had little self-control when annoyed, started to find fault with the newly engaged couple, who were there too.' The dispute became so heated that Grace had to send away her sons, having tea at a nearby table with their tutor.

Maud had realised, though Nancy refused to, that the couple had little in common; and, although Sydney was perfectly 'suitable', she might also have wished for a grander match for her dazzling daughter. But Nancy was determined, seeing marriage as the fastest route – as it was – to the independence she craved.

---

* Later Lady Curzon.

No longer would she have to live at home, she could see those she wished quite openly – in short, she would no longer be under Maud's eye or control. She countered her mother's objections by saying, 'I have given my word and I cannot break it.' In her diary she wrote that she 'did it. Went through with it all, so as to get away from Her Ladyship and have a home of my own.'

'Nancy Cunard is one of the best-known girls in town, and as far as publicity is concerned, runs her bosom friend, Lady Diana Manners, very close indeed,' accurately summed up one of the many reports when the engagement was announced (if ever such a report was wide of the mark, it was the one that stated confidently of Nancy that after the marriage 'her hobby will probably be dogs'). Sydney, now in the Grenadier Guards, and Nancy were married on 15 November 1916, in a wedding as unconventional as Nancy could make it. She spurned the customary bridal white ('she looked beautiful in a gold dress', thought Duff Cooper); there were no bridesmaids, no gloves, no bouquet, and instead of a tiara a toque of orange blossom (at the reception, in a fury at something said, she ripped this off and threw it on the floor). After a honeymoon in Devon and Cornwall, the couple moved into a house in Montague Street, Maud's wedding present to them.

That same month Nancy received an even better 'present'. Hers was the opening poem in the first issue of *Wheels*, an annual poetry anthology edited by Edith Sitwell along with her brothers Osbert and Sacheverell. One hot evening in 1915, Sacheverell had met Nancy and Iris at the Eiffel Tower, although he had been too shy to talk to these two slightly older, very beautiful girls who already wrote poetry; but there and then he made up his mind that he too would devote his life to becoming a poet. When Nancy had the idea for *Wheels* it was immediately seized on by Edith, who saw it as the launching pad for an avant-garde literary movement spearheaded by the Sitwell trio. *Wheels* was characterised by its contributors and editors as being 'in open revolt not only against conventional techniques and subjects but also against the war, its ethos one of destruction rather than innovation' – indeed, the *Times Literary Supplement* called it 'on the whole dour and morose'.

Nancy's half-dozen poems were stigmatised by one critic as being 'conceived in morbid eccentricity and executed in fierce fictitious gloom', but praised by George Moore – praise that was partly inspired by his affection for her. It served its purpose: to encourage her. To her mother he was more enthusiastic, writing, 'Nancy's poems seem to me on second reading much better than they did on a first reading. She has got an exquisite ear for rhythm, and the poems published in *Wheels* vindicate my prophecies pronounced years ago at Holt.'

But, as Nancy would recall much later, she found it impossible to write poetry while living with Sydney, whose friends bored her with their talk of sport and bridge, and with her own consciousness that the marriage had been a mistake. One of the problems was that she had no real template for a marriage: that of her own parents had been at best almost one of two strangers living in the same house and, since her early adolescence, non-existent. After her years of loneliness as a child, what she did know was something that remained with her all her life: she did not like to be alone. So when Sydney returned to the Front, Nancy and Sybil Hart-Davis, Duff Cooper's sister, to whom she had become close when Iris had left, arranged to rent a house together for the summer.

The one they settled on was largish, just outside Kingston Bagpuize in Oxfordshire, set in flat fields – '*un peu lugubre*', commented Nancy's French maid – and surrounded by gardens, lawns and orchards at the end of a long drive. To it came all Nancy and Sybil's friends, from the Sitwell brothers and 'Chile' Guevara to Augustus John (now in the uniform of a war artist), as well as countless officers home on leave, to enjoy long, rather drunken parties. In the intervals, Nancy was constantly writing poetry in the drawing room.

Once, they planned to entertain GM for a weekend, but when Nancy's husband unexpectedly arrived home on leave she put GM off at the last minute – in fact, just as he was climbing into a taxi to go to the station. It would have been intolerable, she thought, for GM to witness the rows between herself and Sydney.

GM told her later that she had been right to put him off. 'Rows between others,' he said, 'are unendurable. I would have left the house.'

She was, at least, away from her mother. Maud, no whit checked by the war, was continuing her social career at full flood. Cynthia Asquith, staying at Glynde in the same house party as her that September, noted in her diary, 'Maud was looking more like an inebriated canary than ever. I love her slight concessions to country clothes! She was in amazing, startling, soprano soliloquy form and has come on immensely since I first saw her. She's a priceless woman – like most of the great laughter-raisers, she often doesn't know when she's being most amusing and sometimes blinks with astonishment when one laughs at her sweeping absurdities. She fell upon a volume of Donne – new to her – and read 'The Flea' out loud and thought him some poet: "Do you know Donne? He's a most lecherous poet."'

It was the same a few months later when Maud lunched with the Asquiths, who had returned to Cavendish Square in March 1917 (after Asquith's replacement as Prime Minister by Lloyd George in December 1916). 'We lunched at Cavendish Square,' wrote Cynthia Asquith in January 1918, 'Margot, in another gorgeous new dress, was going off to a *thé dansant* at Lord Curzon's . . . Maud Cunard was in marvellous form, holding the whole table – even Margot listening quite silently. She browns the covey, shoots away the whole time and occasionally really hits the target.'

Nancy's marriage was given its death blow when, in the summer of 1918, she invited one of her husband's brother officers, Peter Broughton Adderley, to stay for the weekend. They fell in love almost at once. 'My love and I sitting in a tree, and under a tree, read aloud to each other several days running,' she wrote. When Peter's leave was up he went back to the fighting. Just under a month before the war ended he was killed; Nancy was told he had been so badly shot that he had died of his wounds.

She was completely devastated. Although they had only known each other for three weeks, Peter, she believed, then and always, had been the love of her life, the only man she could have lived happily with, a love with which nothing could compare because it had been so brief and so perfect. Like her, Peter had been sensitive and a lover of literature, with a sweet nature and linked to many of her friends. But he was dead and her husband alive – one reason, perhaps, why she would later describe the twenty months of her marriage as among the most miserable of her life.

One of Nancy's biographers believes that the reason for her antipathy to her husband may have been sexual incompatibility; certainly, Sydney's talk of war and sport bored and alienated her whereas to her the life of the mind was all-important, and she was correspondingly unpleasant about him for the rest of her days. Another factor in her castigation of him as a 'foul man' could have been a smothered sense of guilt at having deliberately used someone she did not love merely as an avenue of escape – Nancy's instinct was always to attack, rather than question her own behaviour; it was she, after all, who had forced the marriage through against the wishes of both her parents. Even Sydney's return to the appalling dangers of the Front did nothing to rekindle their relationship.

The war ended with the signing of the Armistice on 11 November 1918. London began to revert to its peacetime self. Wounded soldiers, in their blue suits and red ties, were everywhere, ballrooms that had been hospital wards became ballrooms again and the dancing craze that was to last through the Twenties took hold. At *thés dansants*, girls with pulled-down hats and fringed dresses foxtrotted with their escorts before going home to change into evening dress for a ball – which was always brightly lit, with chaperones sitting on gilt chairs ranged around the room. Nancy, who had left the Season and its entertainments well behind her, preferred dancing in restaurants like Claridge's, the Criterion or the Café Royal.

Soon after New Year's Day 1919 Nancy caught Spanish flu,*

---

* Overall, the epidemic would kill around 250,000 in the UK and somewhere between 20,000,000 and 100,000,000 worldwide. Unusually, it particularly attacked young adults in seemingly good health rather than the very young or the old.

her resistance probably lowered by the depression into which her failed marriage and Peter's death had sunk her. For most of January, February and March she lay in bed, weak and furious, in her mother's house. Despite feeling that it was like a prison, it was from this fortress that she and Sydney finally separated: she had told him on his return from France in January that she felt unable to go on with their marriage. Nor, when Sydney was awarded the Military Cross that same month 'for conspicuous gallantry and devotion to duty at Preux au Sart on 4th November 1918', did this make any difference, although he still hoped. 'Dined with Sydney Fairbairn at the Junior Carlton,' wrote Duff Cooper on 19 January. 'We drank two bottles of champagne and he told me all his sorrows. Nancy won't live with him – he still loves her and believes her faithful. Husbands are incredible. I expect I shall be as gullible as the best.'

In April, when Nancy was fit enough to travel, she left for the South of France to convalesce with Marie Ozanne, the friend from her French finishing school. 'Unaccustomed yet to the heat and God! The flies,' she wrote in her diary on 12 April. Nor did the citizens of the south get a warmer reception: 'There is an unending procession of cars hermetically sealed with awful bourgeois in them, not a touch of local colour, not even a cocotte.' For Nancy, to be 'bourgeois', or as her friend Diana Manners would characterise it, 'common', was the cardinal sin.

Her muscles had become so weak from lying in bed that she acquired a physiotherapist, known to her as 'the Doctor', who soon began to fall in love with her ('those erotic persistent eyes always cast up to heaven'). Used to a whirl of activity in her London life, she was now thrust – as she saw it – into two months of enforced seclusion and loneliness, with too much time to brood over her unsuccessful marriage: 'I have too long leisure to worry about nerves and being letterless.'

Fortunately, an admirer – more correctly, a sporadic lover – was not long in turning up: 'A querulous note from Hutchinson. So he has appeared on these coasts and typically enough is unable to trace one.' St John Hutchinson was a successful barrister, fourteen years older than Nancy, whose wife Mary was having a prolonged and open affair with the art critic Clive Bell and who, whenever given the chance, made a play for Nancy. When she had dinner with 'Hutchy' on 17 April, there was 'a serious talk of personalities, H. exclaiming that he has the best influence on me of anyone I know . . . later I nearly die with laughter at his so well known sudden change to sugared sentimentality and the struggle in a dark street . . . I return to find the doctor has been talking to Marie about me for an hour.'

With a move from La Réserve to Cap Ferrat came excruciating boredom, one of the factors that often drove her behaviour: 'The Doctor therefore now becomes the only link with the past (a short one as yet but lurid in regard to one night).'

Even in a nightclub, where the amorous Doctor 'was pulling faces at one and talking of people who dance too wildly dropping dead', she acquired an admirer: 'The Tenor goes to Marie and offers her 500,000 francs to let him take me away.' But the dancing and the admiration did little to cure her underlying unhappiness. On 28 April she was talking of 'lying here in a litter of old letters from Hutchinson and cigarette ash at 5 in the afternoon, with racing pulses, in an attitude of waiting (oh that <u>waiting</u> is always with one) and who has ever explained away the sudden onset of despair'. Two days later she felt a deep need for her oldest friend: 'All day I have a longing for George Moore and somehow see him hurrying after one in deed and speech, catching one up, and standing squarely on some cliff and declaiming against Europe.'

To judge by the misery, hopelessness and boredom that fills page after page of her diary, she felt her life was purposeless, lonely and leading nowhere. Even her sexual adventures had lost the thrill of defying outdated morality and had become a semi-automatic habit.

But neither boredom nor unhappiness seem to have dimmed Nancy's powers of fascination. In May she was writing, of the man known as the Tenor, 'Lord, how quickly they fall in love here, how utterly, with all the hot-headed impulse of a southern opera, if one would believe such phrases . . . *je souffre, je suit malade, je ne dors pas depuis deux nuits* – erotic, frantic and funny . . . This unknown man so suddenly destroyed with love and consumed with a violent intense desire for one – <u>if one is to believe words?</u>'

The diary talks of the long, arid stretches of the day with no occupation. Pages and pages of it are written in French ('I find I write French as easily as English now'), with a fluency built up first by the hated Miss Scarth and later by the Ozanne sisters. Letters from Hutchinson pour in, but 'I think George Moore understands me now better than anyone else . . . Oh God, I miss those long sessions of expounded thought, rare fruit that one craves for.'

Slowly, the long convalescence drew to an end. In the train back to Paris she was offered a seat and given champagne by an officer: 'Marie again rattled and shocked, but champagne is champagne, in a train more than anywhere, and I shall certainly always drink with anyone as indeed will I talk with any stranger.' In Paris there were friends and more champagne: 'got quite buffy – an excellent buffiness'. On the last night there was dinner at the Ritz with Diana and Duff Cooper and the Aga Khan, 'a large excellent meal with a good deal of wine and rare excellent conversation – but <u>why</u> must everything be shut at 11.30 . . . no, one won't get into Montmartre tonight – boring boring Paris.'

Nancy was back in London on 6 June 1919: 'My first impression of return – everyone dead, Denny, Edward, Patrick, Raymond, George, Billy and the later, more acute people, the lovers of last year. This <u>disastrous</u> land, much more ravaged by war (to us, naturally) than the great half-ridiculous continent . . . London <u>black</u> with almost extinguished lamps. I'd forgotten about them – and tomorrow – and the new era now, what of all that? Of course it will be Whitsuntide and all the horrors of a newspaper holiday and closed shops . . . this terrible enforced idleness – what <u>shall</u> I do?

'Enter Mother in shining yellow satin and Thomas Beecham – <u>they</u> change not.'

CHAPTER 3

>─┤‹◊›─○─‹◊›┤─<

1919 – A New Era

From her debutante years onwards, much of Nancy's life took place at night, and for most of it she drank too much.

By 1919 a new age had been born – cocktails, nightclubs, dinner and dancing at a restaurant, an uncaringness of what the older generation thought, sports cars, cigarettes in long holders, complaints of boredom that led to an endless search for novelty. In that hectic post-war period fashions came and went: Fair Isle jumpers, diamanté bandeaux and – which might have inspired Nancy's later armfuls of thick ivory bangles – thirty or forty narrow glass bangles in whatever colour you chose, all worn together. As a rule Nancy ignored most passing phases, but she did follow one that she kept all her life: hair cut into a short cap with, in her case, a curl on each cheek.

It was now that she and her friends, night after night, would meet at the Eiffel Tower, which for Nancy had become almost a second home, to be treated as a place where they could behave as they chose: 'Presently Joe* came in and whispered to us that we were making so much noise they had complained of not being able to sleep.† We laughed the louder . . . finally rolled out of Tower.'

'Dined with Hutchy, we really got <u>very</u> blind, wrote to Diana then staggered to the ballet . . . Hutchy furious that I didn't go back and sit with him, a temper that continued until we got to

---

* One of the two elderly, flat-footed waiters. The other was called Fred.
† There were hotel-type rooms above in which people could stay.

the Tower where Basil blew in with two little colourless guardees. He had won at Ascot and we had Lord knows how many bottles of that awful sweet champagne.'

So important was the Tower in Nancy's life that she wrote a poem to it:

> The sound of the clock going wrong,
> The fleet
> Procession of your waiters with their platters –
> Drinks held long
> In one hand, while the other unwinds a discussion . . .
> I feel the mist
> Of the room that mocks the fog in the street . . .
> If ever we go to heaven in a troop
> The Tower must be our ladder

Back in London, she immediately flung herself into a round of seeing friends. Often the day ended with a bolt to the Tower if a dinner party had become dull, there to talk and drink, often to excess. Her diary is full of these partyings and drinkings: 'I was rather buffy and everything seemed something of a whirl.' In the daytime, for Nancy, still living at home, lunch at the Ritz was an almost daily occurrence. Unlike other hotels, which to the mothers of young women had a whiff of impropriety, the Ritz was considered 'safe' – it was the only London hotel that the Duchess of Rutland allowed her daughter Diana to enter. 'The Ritz was more like a club than a hotel; you were bound to see your friends there,' wrote Sir Michael Duff. 'To "meet at the Ritz" was the obvious choice.'

Another reason for its popularity – certainly with Nancy – was that the Ritz also served as a telephone box, which she could use without fear of being overheard; at that time she could not bear solitude. 'I could not find Basil,' records her diary. 'More of that dreadful telephoning from the Ritz and he will not dine. Ring up John and find him, which is wonderful – so I shall <u>not</u> dine alone after all.' Once she called a man she had only met once at almost midnight – he was in bed – and asked him to join her and her friends at the Tower. When he got there he met a woman hung with snaky bracelets, gold anklets, rings and so drunk she could not remember telephoning him. Alcohol figured largely in most evenings: 'Dined with Hutchy, we really got very blind.'

Although the war had decimated the male population, for Nancy there were many admirers, most of them feeling post-war euphoria mingled with a 'whither now?' sensation of confusion. Sometimes there were meetings with old friends, but always the sense that a minute alone was a minute wasted: 'A frantic desire to see Sybil, and with swift decision down to Bexley in a car produced by George Moore 3 [of the Ritz], very hot. Richard [Sybil's husband] vile and sullen, Sybil in a good mood. What an appalling life there.' The next day, Sunday 8 June, was a happy one: 'My clothes all very new and lovely, I fancy I had a very good figure yesterday and was much seen! To Bettina at Richmond and a long and excellent talk of our two husbands the whole afternoon.'

After lunch on Tuesday came the conversation Nancy must have dreaded, with the husband she no longer wanted: 'Having wondered much and long enough on this interview and its result drive round Regents Park talking very clearly tho' constrainedly on all matters. He brings up money questions – odd and out of place, this – otherwise apparently <u>very</u> nice and comprehending – but oh! Why continue the theme of seeing one and treating everything over-cordially? I shall <u>never</u> get this point quite straight and as it should be – but if all this attitude is true it's very very good.'

It was a packed day. After dinner at Claridge's Nancy left for the Tower, accompanied by the Russian who had sat next to her at dinner. Her diary expresses the ennui that all too often overcame her: 'We sit in the Lewis Room and drink vile and ever sweeter champagne – slight buffiness and S getting more and more amorous, infatuated now, a great kissing of hands and feet and curious phrases about "when a woman gives me her lips . . .", a very odd man this, think he must be mad and am considerably bored. Why must the first days in London be like this, and I fresh and hopeful? God keep one from getting <u>too</u> bored.'

Next day, with a hangover, she visited GM, to find her old friend 'extremely wearying, grown very deaf and slow and exacting, but says I have become far more defined a character and am coming into my own, also likes several poems. Very amusing he on the subject of Abelard and Heloise, a grand subject for him, so <u>that</u> afternoon is all to the good.'

Nancy's underlying sense of despair was exacerbated not only by the loss of the man whom she had felt was her true soulmate but by her immense sadness over the death of so many of her friends (as Cynthia Asquith had put it so cogently when she wrote, 'Oh why was I born for this time? Before one is thirty to know more dead than living people?'). For Nancy, while new admirers seemed to spring up on all sides, old ones still pursued her. When she went to stay with the Hutchinsons, she and Hutchinson went for a long walk on the seashore, 'under an uncommonly fine moon. H became rather romantic but I was in a good mood and took it more seriously for once.'

Although she spent most of her time with Hutchinson, usually going out for walks with him alone, Mary, whom she admired, accurately assessed the passion and resentment that lay below Nancy's façade: 'Her character I am sure must be described as deeply disturbed and violent, subject to fierce angers, fierce indignations, fierce enthusiasms.'

Back in London, the roundabout continued, with a visit to a man known only as J, in his apartment at Clarges Street. As he would not come to a party with her she dressed carefully for different escort ('My God, what a help and moral support clothes are'), winding up in the apartment of yet another admirer until 5.00 a.m. Next day, in one of the few overt references to her habit of bedding most of her male friends, her diary records: 'went to Clarges [J's apartment] which culmination always makes things better, smooths down the bitter silences and comforts the nerves, dissipating my shyness'.

Nancy always loved the country, feeling that somehow its peace and quiet would enable her to lead a more fulfilled life and write the poetry that meant so much to her. She hated the social round of luncheons, parties and dinners arranged by her mother which she was expected to attend. The only answer, she felt, was to move out of London: 'I must find a country house – the one refuge and place of content.' Here she knew that Maud, urban to her fingertips, would never follow her; and there could be late-night drinking sessions with friends, careless of whomsoever they might disturb, and no one to report on anything seen as immoral behaviour.

After a careful search she rented Turks Croft, a cottage near Crawley, in Sussex, which had a view into its garden through French windows and a dining room with dark oak beams, dark Jacobean furniture and a table that could seat ten. One of her first visitors was an earlier lover, Ted Ralli: 'He was perfect when he at last arrived, not sad, not depressed as he said he would be. I found it was awfully easy to talk to him and we sat for hours at the table, drank two bottles of old champagne . . . wandered into the moonlight and found a vast oak tree. Ted immediately affectionate, and – so all that's not over . . .'

When Hutchinson arrived two days later, cross at finding Ted already installed, she had to mollify him by spending most of her time with him. The idea of sexual monogamy was not one that Nancy was prepared to entertain: the wild nights in the Fitzroy Street studio, often with near-strangers, her disillusionment with marriage, the death of the only man she felt she had ever really loved and her steady intake of alcohol were, and remained, far too powerful counterweights, so that lovers would often overlap.

As usual, alcohol played a large part ('buffy, rather') in restoring harmony. 'Hutchy was delightful,' records her diary that July. 'We wandered about and walked and read an amazing new poem by Eliot ['Gerontion'], very intense and good. As the afternoon was long, he read aloud from GM's *Memoirs of My Dead Life* – that extraordinary story, 'In the Luxembourg Gardens', where we found much that was typical of him.' Two days later, on 19 July, 'took Hutchy for a long wet walk and founds ourselves at the Ifield Village Peace Celebrations; talked a great deal of GM'. As they did on another occasion, when for the first time Nancy suddenly brought up the possibility (since largely

45

discounted) that as her mother's lover GM might actually be her father: 'During a five-mile walk with Hutchy, discoursed most of the time about GM – but what of my long limbs and general shape of body? – and thought suddenly (which I told him) if I were his daughter, it seems to me I should become quite a different personality and a much more contented one.'

She was also writing. One of her unpublished poems, written that August, even foreshadows what later became a passion, her interest in Africa:

The garden is full of green apples
That I shall never pick. In the evening
I lie in a large field and think of Africa
Teeming with animals, dream of its spaces and mysteries,
Later return unhaunted
By the day into the creaking, haunted house.

Then, on a visit to London to see Marie Ozanne, 'We did the cards and foresaw great journeys for me, and a complete change of existence, which I hoped would be true.'

The weeks passed with much drinking ('we mixed endless cocktails and I could not stop drinking') and its aftermath ('concerned with the buffiness'), lying on the lawn in the sunshine, dancing after dinner, and talks with the various male guests enamoured of her. After one dinner party, they sang songs and danced until finally everyone except Nancy and a new friend, Eddie, were left: 'Eddie and I did some more talking and thought the moonlight looked good enough to go out in.' The two of them then took off their clothes and wandered 'like Babes in the Wood' into the big field next to the house where, in another tacit admission by Nancy of a sexual encounter, they 'lay under a huge oak tree'. Afterwards they were hungry and crept into the kitchen to find some cold remains, where at 3.00 a.m. they were surprised by another guest, holding a huge stick under the impression he had been woken by burglars. 'This was the best weekend of all,' commented Nancy.

Hutchinson was there again when on 20 August there was a difficult and unpleasant visit from Maud, accompanied by GM: 'GM was tightly buttoned into a grey suit, very slow, with buttoned boots of brown, the tabs showing at the top, with a tasselled umbrella that he waves about; he would not sit down and was restless. The mothers [Nancy's friend Marjorie's mother was also visiting] were sour to each other, tea a strain; Her Ladyship apparently in a furious temper; which I did not notice at first though others did.'

When Nancy took GM off for a stroll in the garden, her mother, she said, was working herself up: 'First, over the tea, which she said was so bad that she "wouldn't offer it to a horsethief" . . . secondly, over my supposed friends. All this was said to Hutchy, who was terrified and said "Yes, yes, quite, quite" to everything. It all ended in an outburst to me: "You have *no* sense, knowledge or experience, and *no* plan of life" while GM was in the bathroom. They were both incensed at the time it had taken them to get here from London, and seemed to blame me for that, leaving *at last* in a better temper, having put me into a hot rage and given Hutchy an acute headache. After they had gone, we stamped round fields at a great pace, disclaiming against them, laughing but irritated . . . Hutchy recalled an old expression of mine describing Her Ladyship as a "polished termagant" – very apt for today.'

Back in London, she wrote (on 7 September) of GM visiting her as she lay in bed one morning looking through old letters, her pet dachshund Lynette beside her: 'He talked of love, of erotic adventures, of *his* adventures, citing a very recent one, of a woman who came to see him about a play, lay on a sofa and said "Shall I? Shall I?" Apparently they did! I could hardly believe this. GM was gross at moments but most lovable. He also talked of my ex-husband, saying how awful he had always thought him and how well he understood my point of view.'

Nancy herself was not short of anyone to lie on a sofa with. That summer, the war poet Robert Nichols, twenty-six to Nancy's twenty-three, was one of those who sighed over her. He had returned from America in May and spent much of the summer in and around London, when he fell passionately in love with her but without much response.

By the end of the summer Nancy's marriage was in the past, with a legal separation arranged between her and Sydney. It was back to life at Grosvenor Square,* with the sorting out and labelling of her possessions and life with her mother, from whom even the gift of a superb fur coat 'made no impression on me as I had settled into a complete gloom'. When Maud told her how ill she looked, Nancy was furious 'and more wretched than ever before at not having a home of my own. I must, must sacrifice everything else to it, not drag on as I have done for so vastly too long now. To bed but oh in despair at 10, in a misery that has not lifted . . . I detest that room at Grosvenor, it reminds me of the appalling days when I was ill and mad, it reminds me of the worst days of my life.'

On 10 September, three days after the visit from GM, she left for Paris. It was both a temporary escape from London and a search for a possible new way of life, coupled with the idea that with enough 'fun' and dancing, unhappiness could be kept at bay: 'A delicious lunch at Boulogne, how I love being on French soil.' Marie Ozanne had booked her a room at the old-fashioned Hôtel France et Choiseul, where her little Second Empire salon had a hard, red-plush sofa, a marble console, a gilt clock in a glass case and an antiquated telephone that failed to work. It was too much for Nancy and she swiftly moved to the Ritz, where a tiny room cost her twenty francs a night: 'The Ritz terrible, the whole of the front passage lined with gaping people, no telephones working. I hate everything, waiting for someone to come and wondering when I should really begin to enjoy Paris.'

Although she felt she would know no one, her cousin Edward Cunard was there. Five years older than Nancy, he had joined the Diplomatic Service at the beginning of the war and been sent first to the British Embassy in St Petersburg, and then to the 1919–20 post-war Peace Conference in Paris. Although he had just resigned

---

* After Asquith ceased to be Prime Minister in December 1916 and had to leave Downing Street, Maud could no longer occupy their house in Cavendish Square; she moved instead to 44 Grosvenor Square.

from the Service, this personable bachelor enjoyed the social life that had hinged on the conference so much that he had stayed on in the city, and almost at once he whisked his cousin off to one of the numerous parties given by the couturier Poiret. Based at the Ritz, and with Edward, Nancy was soon being invited out to the Paris version of the social life of her mother which she so disliked. That she often felt ill and disliked or was bored by the people she met did not stop her going almost everywhere she was asked – or her constant intake of alcohol. Her diary is full of references to champagne, cocktails, friends who are 'semi-blind' or complaints if there is not enough to drink. At one weekend house party to which she was invited there was the pejorative comment, 'less wine than at The Wharf!* But a decanter full of water in front of everyone.'

The next time she was asked to the same house she and Hutchinson drank a precautionary bottle of champagne on the way down ('It is really extraordinary how I can and do drink so much champagne, always the best, that is the answer'), and with another man sneaked out later into the garden, where they had surreptitiously stuffed yet another bottle of champagne down a convenient rabbit hole. When they had finished it, they found everyone had gone to bed and the house was locked up, so they had to creep in through a window.

What really cheered Nancy was the arrival of a letter from Austin Harrison, the editor of *The English Review*, saying, 'I like your poem for its intellectual sense of freedom and am publishing it next month.' It was a poem called 'Answer to a Reproof'† and some of its lines set out her stall, so to speak, describing how she viewed herself and forecasting the way she would behave during the coming years:

> I the perfect stranger,
> Outcast and outlaw from the rules of life,
> True to one law alone, a personal logic

---

* The Asquiths' country house.
† It was published in the October 1919 issue.

That will not blend with anything, nor bow
Down to the general rules; inflexible . . .

By the same post came a letter from the neglectful Ted. Clothes shopping – a new black velvet dress from Galeries Lafayette and a couturier-made costume – was also a consolation, as was the arrival of the faithful Hutchinson. They sight-saw and dined together until Ted, smart in his uniform of King's Messenger, arrived on the 29th, his train inevitably several hours late (French trains were then notorious for their unpunctuality): 'We dined happily and well in the Ritz Grill. Then off to Poiret's, same people everywhere, then a nightclub then finally found some curious and obscure sort of brothel, where we had bread and cheese and wine, which was a great help to the things we had to say to each other.'

The idyll with Ted did not last: 'Today was a horror day and no good came of our being in Paris together.' Nor did it balance the lack of steady, dependable admirers, although the constant Hutchinson, with his diplomatic credentials, smoothed their homecoming – their luggage was dealt with, seats reserved on the train and a cabin aboard the cross-Channel steamer, where they had a meal of peaches, sweets, biscuits and the inevitable bottle of champagne. All the same, 'I swore constantly never to go to Paris again without a chap or even several.'

She liked coming home even less: 'I loathe England, one ought never to return to it.' At Grosvenor Square she found Maud delighted over her daughter's success with her poems, but her mother's happy enthusiasm did not stop Nancy going out as soon as she could with a man friend, first to drinks, then the Carlton Grill, then the Tower: 'Mr Stulik in fine form but no one there. I wished to God I had taken the boat back at Folkestone this morning.'

The mad rush to be entertained continued. Anything was better than not going out, so much so that when 'Chile' Guevara saw her in the street and ran after her she let him come to see her, dined with him at the Tower, where they sat smoking scented cigarettes, then unwisely went with him to his Kensington studio, where he 'became too appalling and very violent and I hysterical actually, hating him and his outbursts'. She fled, leaving behind her stick, 'which added to my anger'.

Nancy was not enjoying London. The return to her mother's house was stressful, so she escaped from it as much as possible; when she was there, there always seemed to be tensions: 'Ghastly tea party at 44 where GM was fuming and stamping, also furious with me for taking Ted to see him after lunch.' Her friend Stulik seemed upset – consoling himself by giving them both a glass of Augustus John's brandy – and the streets were packed. Worst of all, despite her convalescence in the South of France her health had not really recovered. Still feeling tired and ill, she took the advice of her doctor and decided on a month's 'rest cure' at Hindhead.

She went there, to a hydro (a spa/nursing home with various water treatments), on 11 October with, first, 'ghastly lunch at 44, ghastly wait, insufferable drive to Hindhead with Mother and TB [Thomas Beecham], she talking the whole time which was exhausting to bear'. Once there, in her ground-floor room, she stayed in bed for the whole of the first two weeks, with a Danish masseuse to work on her every day so that her muscles did not become too weak.

It was a life designed to build up the strength of invalids, with few diversions, not all of Nancy's choosing: 'Every evening the Princess of Monaco comes and sits by my bed, pokes the fire, closes those windows that should be forever open, complains of the cold, talks of Madeira and the S of France and of her literary friends. The days are monotonous, at night I revisualise Paris and long for the impossible journey to the south with T for all the winter. A good dozen of books including GM's *Confessions*, which made me laugh with delight. My first guests were mother, then Marie Ozanne then Sybil. On Saturday Hutchinson came, on Sunday Ted in his new car ... How strange it would be to think of one's life being spent entirely in the country, with never a rendezvous at Ritz or Tower.'

On 10 November she was driven back to London, the doctors

and her mother pleased with her progress – to plunge almost straight away into the old life of parties, late nights, drink, social bad behaviour and juggling her men friends. After lunch with Hutchinson she went home to dress for the Albert Hall Ball, going first to a dinner party, which she and Ted left early, as they did so stealing a bottle of brandy and sticking a grape in it for a cork, then driving wildly to the Albert Hall: 'And there confusion . . . we had a box on the second floor which no one could find. Directly we got into it Ted disappeared for four hours. Hutchy appeared looking like a thundercloud in a huge black cape and wig with a cardboard headpiece trimmed with gigantic plumes of paper. People came and went.' Finally she found Ted again, and after a long and satisfactory talk it was home at 5.00 a.m.

Soon afterwards it was time for an overdue visit to her father. So distant were they now that she always thought of him and wrote to him as Sir Bache, or Sir B. Before dashing for the train there was a quick drink with her friend the poet Robert Nichols.

The visit did nothing to draw Nancy and her father closer together. He was now sixty-nine and what is known as 'set in his ways', constantly playing patience or reading the newspaper, only stopping to roll his own cigarettes and making occasional rather heavy small talk. 'All the old feeling,' wrote Nancy, 'great spirits on arrival gradually sinking into petrifaction and silence . . . one feels more and more remote after an hour or two with Sir B, as if no kind of existence were left one at all – and what's more I believe no one would come to look for one here no matter how long one disappeared for.' After four days she returned to London, her father querulous at such a short visit, and found herself in the midst of a brief love affair.

Robert Nichols had left for lodgings in Brecon in October to avoid spending money and to write. When Nancy wrote to him there he was ecstatic, returning soon afterwards to London, and after her return from her father, perhaps in reaction to the lifelessness of his household, she and Nichols had a short-lived affair. It was to and about Nancy he wrote his *Sonnets to Aurelia*, sending her the full manuscript, with all its corrections, bound in crimson, and imprinted with a large golden 'N' and his own name surrounded by a wreath of bay leaves. This one, Sonnet XIII, contains a hint that he realised her feelings were different from his:

SOMETIMES I think you know not what love is
But only pang of amorous delight:
The terrible resuscitation of the kiss,

Oh, when I so do think, then I could sear
These loving lips with the consuming coal,
Submit these limbs to the machine to tear
And ruin my body to secure your soul.

For rather would I perish as a man,
And hateful as a maniac seem to you,
Than that our joy, which in true love began,
Should, in abuse, turn to its birth untrue.
Wherefore take heed lest, in your passion strong,
Your acts read right but your intention wrong.

Another read:

Who gave you these most terrible of eyes,
That never, never, never know to weep,
That have become my life's unpitying spies,
Nor sleep themselves nor suffer me to sleep?

'These sonnets tell of every kind of lurid occasion that never arose at all between us,' wrote Nancy. 'Poetic licence if ever there was.' She was finding the affair, not to speak of the constant frenzied letters from Nichols, tiresome. On 28 November her diary records, 'Terrible letters from Nicholls [sic], and sonnets that don't scan every morning on the breakfast tray!' At the same time, her portrait was being painted by another man who was in love with her, the painter 'Chile' Guevara. He too was driven to distraction.

For Nichols it was a tortured affair with glimpses of supreme happiness and chasms of despair. During one of these he produced a Colt revolver and threw it at Nancy's feet, begging her to stop him doing something drastic. Her French maid ran from the room terrified as, wrote Nancy, 'the poet screeched that it would be better in my hands than his, for he did not know what he might not do'. Nancy picked up the gun and calmly put it away; immediately afterwards she, Nichols and the rest of the party set off for the Royal Albert Hall fancy-dress ball.

Later, how to get rid of the gun seemed an insurmountable problem. Eventually, she smuggled it across the Channel when travelling to France with GM, who fortunately did not ask about – or did not notice – the bulge in the pocket of her leopard-skin coat, counterbalanced by a half-bottle of good whisky in the pocket on the other side (even more fortunately, neither were spotted by the Calais Customs). As she wrote in her diary, the whole affair was a little too dramatic for her: 'Lord, had I but known what I was starting when I got hold of that young man . . . He is mad, no doubt of it.' As for Nichols, so briefly her lover, a few months later he wrote to a friend: 'It became more than ever evident to me that she had never loved me – she told me so, you know, a number of times but then her acts belied her words.'

To be out and about seemed Nancy's main object then, with lunches at the Ritz, a difficult dinner with Ted, both of them silent and wretched, and the Opera Ball at the Royal Albert Hall, 'Iris in a shining gold armoured St George, Ted in superb Arab clothes and Hutchy an early Victorian mourner, black gloves, large whiskers, hat tied with crepe and holding a wreath, buffy already, so were we.' They wound up in her mother's box, eating the lavish supper prepared there, and got home at five, all 'buffy'.

Many years later she wrote a justification of that time: 'Still extremely unhappy and "lost" after the death of Peter. Still very ill, weak and exhausted by the influenza and pneumonia, hence all the references to feeling like hell, all of which was made worse by the incessant <u>drink</u> (drink, drink, drink, repetitive – God!)

'To think that all these people around me, and Her Ladyship, should have been telling me constantly "<u>Do</u> something! Make good! You're wasting your life" What were the facts? I was then

23 and had married a foul man, Sydney Fairbairn, at the age of 20, in 1916. After shaking off the marriage one day (unfortunately not sticking to that!); I loathed him, knew it was an idiotic thing to do but did it, went through with it all, so as to get away from Her Ladyship and have a home of my own.' She did admit, though, that her mother was giving her the money that she would otherwise have settled on her, so that she was now financially independent, adding that 'I felt I could not count on it . . . and that she could and would have cut it off had she so wished.'

She was still searching for the kind of life she wanted, and where to lead it. Of one thing she was certain: her eventual home would not be anywhere that was in any way under the influence of her mother, and if possible some distance away from her. For someone like Nancy, with her perfect French, her longing for poetry and the arts, her views on sexual freedom and her belief that one should live the life one wants, there was only one place to go – Paris. She already loved the city – in her diary she talked of its 'wonderful and exciting atmosphere' – and if she felt like a spell in London, it was near enough to return to quickly. The decision was easily made and later she believed it to have been a watershed in her life.

'On January 7th 1920, I went to France – alone – "for ever".'

CHAPTER 4

>─┼─◆─○─◇┼─◄

Paris, and Michael Arlen

'For ever' might have been in Nancy's mind when she set off for France in 1920 and in one sense it was true – she no longer felt she had roots in England. But over the next few months she crossed the Channel backwards and forwards several times. Packing to leave a country was one thing, leaving all her friends was another. When she was in London she would attend her mother's parties and regularly visit George Moore, sometimes for dinner, often for just an hour two. Most of the time was spent listening to GM talking, usually of literature. This frequently led to a rant against Henry James – how GM detested him, man and writer.

Sometimes Nancy would dine with GM. She would arrive punctually at eight (later, Nancy became known for perennial lateness) and dinner would start almost at once, with soup, then either fish (which she disliked) or an omelette, then the main course of chicken, a chop or perhaps a pheasant sent to him by friends. Then pudding, cheese and a pear all accompanied by a bottle of wine 'poured out a bit sparingly for my taste', thought Nancy, by now accustomed to drinking a fair bit more. After dinner, the table would be cleared and they would move to two chairs on either side of the fireplace. At eleven Nancy would leave.

Back in France, Nancy would have seen that the difference between the landscape of the two countries was stark. England, of course, had not been fought over, whereas the war had left France almost in ruins, with over 1.3 million of her men dead and the homes, farms, factories, churches and hospitals of north-eastern France destroyed. Bridges had been blown up, forests destroyed and crops laid waste by chemicals.

At Boulogne, where Nancy boarded the train for Paris, the brown French railway carriages were interspersed with captured red German ones and the houses were still damaged from having been battered with shells. Even the nearby trenches had not all been filled in. Widows, orphans and the wounded were everywhere.* And over everything hung what Nancy called 'that frightful melancholy of northern France'.

Paris itself still had its wartime scars: the Germans had come as close as fifty kilometres to the capital, allowing them to bombard it, first with '*La grosse Berthe*' (Big Bertha)† and then, in March 1918, with a new long-range gun, the Paris Gun, so that many buildings were damaged. The worst episode was when a shell hit the roof of a church during the Good Friday service; this fell on those below, killing ninety-one people. But the capital's reputation as *the* place to be if you wanted to write or paint was as firm as ever, acting as a magnet to artists and intellectuals.

Many of those who arrived were American. Some were good-timers simply fleeing Prohibition: America's National Prohibition Act of 1919 came into force in 1920 with a nationwide ban on the production, importation, transportation and sale of alcoholic beverages. It was true that alcohol-related crimes and admissions to hospitals fell by a third, but another, less expected effect was to make alcohol more exciting, especially for the young and partygoing, a glamorous choice because it was against the law, while the profitable bootlegging business fell into the hands of the top gangsters like Al Capone and Johnny Torrio, with Chicago their fiefdom. Here they ran everything from the illegal alcohol trade to brothels and protection rackets. Their victims

---

* At the end of the First World War France was left with 1.327 million dead and a further 600,000 civilian casualties, bring the total number of dead to just under 2 million; and around 4 million wounded.
† German soldiers had named this gun after Bertha Krupp, heiress to the Krupp armaments business.

were often beaten up with a cake of soap at the bottom of a woollen sock which, aimed at the base of the skull, caused huge damage without leaving a mark, the police making little effort to find the culprits,* while home-made alcoholic drinks such as moonshine or bathtub gin usually tasted so disgusting they had to be disguised in a cocktail.

Other American arrivals had first seen Paris as ambulance drivers during the war, been fascinated and come back. When they returned, there were few men but plenty of women – women anxious to be fed, to be entertained, and often to be paid for the pleasure they could give. Any reasonably prosperous-looking young man walking the streets would hear the whispered '*Tu viens?*' from every dark doorway (prostitutes, who had to carry yellow cards, were not permitted to stand under street lamps). Some of these women were the returning prostitutes of Paris who had followed the French army to serve in the 'red lanterns' (for enlisted men), 'blue lanterns' (for officers) or as canteen girls who might 'take pity' on a soldier in return for a cash present. But so well known was Paris's reputation as a city of pleasure and permissiveness that there were not enough of them and young country girls began to flood in.

Many were aspiring writers and painters, who had rebelled against what they saw as the stuffiness, materialism and restrictive puritanism of their own country. Paris, the admitted artistic and intellectual centre of Europe, drew them like a magnet; much of France's determination to recover was expressed through its arts. As the franc plunged – in 1920 there were roughly five francs to the dollar – these expatriates found that money that would only buy them a meal or two at home would keep them in Paris for up to a month, albeit in insalubrious surroundings.

A number of them were young women. In 1920 the ratification of the Nineteenth Amendment granted all American women the right to vote, and the consequent feeling of independence,

---

* By 1928, there were almost twice as many murders in Chicago as in New York.

and the right to run their own lives, was sweeping through young America.*

But as boys and girls launched themselves into what they hoped would be the new freedom, the forces of morality rallied to the attack. The President of the Christian Endeavour Society declared that modern dancing was 'an offence against womanly purity', the President of the University of Florida declared that 'the low-cut gowns, the rolled hose and short skirts are . . . carrying the present and future generations to chaos and destruction'. A Bill was planned in Utah to fine and imprison anyone who wore on the streets 'skirts higher than three inches above the ankle'; in Ohio the proposed legal limit of décolletage was two inches. There was, too, a 'Red Scare', largely caused by the actions of organised labour, resulting in a fear of radicalism in society, so that conformism became ever more important – a clinging to the status quo that liberal youth despised and deplored and found as another reason for leaving home.

Until only a short time earlier, the focal point for these expatriates had been Montmartre but, perennially short of money as these incomers were, Montparnasse had been discovered to be even cheaper. Its narrow streets were packed with small, cheap hotels where single rooms could be rented. In these makeshift studios there was often only a cold-water tap above the sink and beds or mattresses stuffed with straw. Most had a stove, and when the weather became too cold to bear, small bundles of wood could be bought, also briquettes of compressed coal dust, moulded into an egg shape and called *boulets*. Also popular were cat's fur mittens.

The communal toilets were on landings between floors, where the stairs right-angled; these, too, were often primitive in the extreme – mere holes in the floor with cement-moulded footrests and torn-up newspaper instead of toilet paper. These toilets gave straight down into cesspools, emptied at night by being pumped into horse-drawn wagons painted brown and saffron (there

---

* Although legally entitled to vote, black women were effectively denied voting rights in many Southern states until 1965.

were special cafés for the men who operated them because of the odour that clung to them). In the summer, when windows were open, they could be both heard and smelt; often the stench filled the house all day. The only alternatives were the reeking public pissoirs in the streets outside or, for those rendered incapable by the effects of alcohol of reaching even these sanctums, the gutter (peeing in the streets was known as *le pipi sauvage*). If the Seine's water levels rose in winter, nearby cellars were flooded, often with disastrous effect.

At first Nancy saw none of this – the life of the cafés was still ahead. Once in Paris, she remodelled herself into the acme of Twenties chic. Gone were the soft waves that had surrounded her face in her debutante years; her hair was now cut into a gold cap shingled at the back. The sea-blue eyes were encircled with kohl and her mouth was crimson. Her tall, slender figure was perfect for the elegant simplicity of the clothes she bought from Chanel and other designers. Streamlined and chic, she drank when she wanted and smoked freely through a long ivory cigarette holder; though smoking by young women had been taken up after the war and would gradually become more acceptable, it still had a slight edge of the forbidden and was seen as a sign of emancipation.

It was the start of the 'Roaring Twenties', and without television or radio, newspapers and magazines were the main disseminators of information. Many had a social page or gossip column, and the doings of the upper classes, along with the best-known actors or writers, held a fascination for their readers; widespread syndication to local papers ensured that these were soon known all over the country. It was not long before Nancy, rich, gorgeous-looking and stylish in the manner of the times, became one of the icons of the age whose doings could be followed by thousands, and a muse to writers and artists.

One of these was Michael Arlen. Of Nancy's many love affairs, he was the first major one (and the first of my five), in the sense that he was the first to pin her image to the page, most famously in *The Green Hat* (published in 1924 and which made him an international best-seller), in more detail in 'Confessions of a Naturalised Englishman' (published in 1929).

For Arlen, Nancy epitomised the world into which he was desperate to enter – that of elegant women accompanied by men in well-cut suits, emerging from taxis, going to chic restaurants, drinking champagne and dancing to the best bands, all with an aristocratic disdain for what others might think of them.

They had first met at the Eiffel Tower in London at the end of 1919 or in the early days of 1920. Arlen (the name he had just taken) was slight, short and foreign-looking, with dark hair, a long nose and a toothbrush moustache in a dark face, intelligent, talkative and tremendously ambitious. From the moment he could afford it he dressed smartly, with suits from the best tailors, although with a dandified flamboyance that added to his 'foreignness' – a little more padding than usual in the shoulders, a coloured silk handkerchief in the breast pocket.

With her feeling for the unusual and offbeat, Nancy was immediately interested in this oddish-looking stranger who had turned up at the Tower. He was indeed different from most of the people she met: he had been born Dikran Kouyoumdjian, the youngest of the five children of an Armenian merchant family which had fled to Bulgaria to avoid the persecutions of the Armenians by the Ottoman Empire and then, in 1901, moved again, this time to Lancashire.

The young Dikran was sent to Malvern College but refused to go, as his parents wished, to Oxford. Instead, he went to Edinburgh University, ostensibly to read medicine. There, in his own words, 'I only stayed a few months; jumbled months of elementary medicine, political economy, metaphysics, theosophy – I once handed round programmes at an Annie Besant lecture at the Usher Hall – and beer, lots of beer.'

After a few months he left Edinburgh abruptly for London, arriving there in 1913. He was a poor stranger with an unpronounceable name on the outside of this glittering city with his nose pressed to the glass, looking in at the world he longed to join which, of course, took money – and he was virtually penniless – or, sometimes, talent.

Gradually he made friends, though of a rather grubby bohemian kind. 'I do not like lying on the dirty floors of studios with candle grease dripping on me,' he wrote. He lived on an allowance of £2 a week, supplementing this with book reviews and journalism.

When war broke out Dikran's nationality was still Bulgarian, but Bulgaria had disowned him because he would not serve in their army; and because Bulgaria was aligned with Germany, England viewed its citizens with suspicion, meaning that Dikran could neither be naturalised as a British citizen nor change his name.

He found company in literary circles with those who either refused to fight or were not allowed to, like Aldous Huxley and D.H. Lawrence. Although Lawrence thought Dikran 'blatant and pushing because he is *very foreign*, even though he doesn't know it himself,' he added, 'but I find the core of him very good'. Dikran in turn was greatly influenced by Lawrence (who in fact later wrote him into *Lady Chatterley* as Michaelis, the Irish playwright with whom Constance Chatterley has an affair early on in the novel).

It was a hard life and the future did not look very bright. 'Once,' he wrote, 'I wondered if I had not done a very silly thing in being independent, and in not doing as my brothers had done, reading *The Times* in an office every morning from ten to twelve and playing dominoes in the afternoon and auction bridge in the evening, and having several thousands a year when I was forty, and a Wolseley car to take my wife for a holiday to Windermere, because she looked pale, or because we were bored with each other.'

Slowly he moved up in the world, or rather to a better address, leaving Earls Court for Mayfair, where he settled in a small room above a shop in Shepherd Market. Here he wrote his first book, *The London Venture* (1919), making one huge alteration in his life. On the advice of his publisher, William Heinemann, he took as his pen name Michael Arlen, after checking through all the telephone books in the Post Office to see if it was free. Although Arlen, as he was known from now on, received only £30 from

Heinemann for *The London Venture*, it launched him. It was then that he met Nancy, was instantly fascinated and soon began to put his feelings for her on paper. Into his books he poured his enchantment with 'the tall, the fair, the desperate figure of Priscilla', with an almost word-for-word description of Nancy's life and attitudes (the Eiffel Tower, where they met, appears as the Mont Agel).

'What I see, as I sit waiting for her at the Mont Agel restaurant on that first of May, is the radiant countenance of youth . . . I long inexpressibly for the delights of Priscilla's love . . . the delicious moment when Priscilla swept into the Mont Agel, bringing with her the gold of the sun and a profound contempt for the Conservative party, the usages of society, rhymed verse, and her mother.' He describes the golden curl that, like Nancy's, fell down over each of Priscilla's ears, and how 'interwoven with her being was something desperate and self-fatal'.

He talks of how 'Priscilla' was neglected by her mother as a child and a young girl, of how her mother wished to be the premier hostess in London, of how Priscilla at eighteen married a guardee and how she disapproved of her mother as a silly snob: 'Poor Mrs Byrrh grew frightened of her unsociable daughter's relentless attitude toward herself and her friends.' He hints at Priscilla/Nancy's bad reputation ('one had heard stories').

'Of all God's creatures the most contemptible to Priscilla were ladies and gentlemen, and so she could not be at peace but with artists and writers or, failing them, with tarts and mashers.' He sees Priscilla as bewitching and strangely vulnerable, although 'something not to be forgotten' was the influence she had on young men: 'O radiant and melancholy Priscilla, where art thou now?' His summing-up of Nancy is poignantly accurate, with Priscilla's earlier story a mirror-image of Nancy's. As is her influence on men, on whom Nancy's effect was mesmeric.

Her beauty, then at its zenith, was rendered lethal by the aura of fastidious promiscuity that shimmered around her. Although ideas of freedom and change were in the air, especially in bohemian circles, most upper-class young women were still brought up within the straitjacket of conventional morality, and one who appeared to have unbuckled hers and cast it aside was irresistibly exciting.

The writer and critic Raymond Mortimer, who met her on a cross-Channel steamer, was so overwhelmed that he wrote: 'Everybody old, it is hoped, can look back on one person who was incomparably bewitching, and I have never met anyone to equal Nancy Cunard when first I met her.'

'Miss Nancy Cunard is wonderful,' wrote Mary Hutchinson, 'made of alabaster and gold and scarlet, with a face like Donatello's Saint George.' Some thought her eyes brilliant blue, others green, yet others turquoise; all agreed on their effect. Nancy was slender, as Harold Acton put it, 'to the point of evanescence'; the clothes of the day could have been designed with her in mind, from the turbans and cloche hats she favoured to the narrow, easy-fitting dresses and suits. It is not surprising that Arlen was bowled over.

Others at the Tower were not so intrigued by Arlen as Nancy – to whom he was always known as 'the Baron'; he had told her at some point that he and his brothers were all entitled to call themselves barons, but did not choose to outside their own country (he was correct, in that in Armenian the word for 'Mr' is '*Bahr-rohn*').

'Hutchinson,' wrote Nancy later, 'was the one, I am sure, who suffered most from the Baron who, via myself, had suddenly come into his highbrow world like a menacing privateer, at first a mere black sail on the horizon, all too soon a matter of daily, or almost daily occurrence. They used to glare at each other across the napery, until, unable to bear Hutchy's decreasingly veiled sarcasm any longer, the Baron, to the delight of all save Hutchy, would suddenly prick at him with some lordly rococoesque quip.'

Unfortunately for Hutchinson, Arlen was extremely sharp-witted (once, at a party, when the outspoken playwright Edna Ferber said to him apropos of what he was wearing, 'Why, Mr Arlen, you look almost like a woman,' he replied instantly, 'So do you, Miss Ferber'), so that he more than held his own. Hutchinson would later complain to Nancy, 'I really can't see why you like this ghastly oriental rug-merchant – no, no, really, really . . .'

Other men felt rather the same, according to Nancy, who simply stated, 'Men loathed the Baron – at least then.' Later, his literary successes gained him a certain acceptance. His novels were largely about the social strata that fascinated him and into which he was gradually penetrating, that of smart young men about town and beautiful, promiscuous women. Soon he became the archetype of the sort of men he wrote about, one of the symbols of the Twenties, one of the men-about-town who wore fringed white-silk evening scarves and always carried a spare pair of gloves in a pocket when they went to a dance.

Arlen spent most of the summer with Nancy, at a villa she took on the sea near Boulogne. Various of her friends and admirers also visited, from her cousin Victor to the painter 'Chile' Guevara, still wildly in love with her – at one time, the three of them were there alone together. Although Nancy does not say so, it must have been an uncomfortable triumvirate. 'By day the Baron worked,' wrote Nancy. 'In the evening the three of us would settle down to drinking after dinner. And then, at times, there would issue from "Chile" some remarkable remarks. One in particular, though what led to it I can't imagine, made both the Baron and myself very cross (that must have been a very late night). "Huh," said Chile. "Don't you think Dostoevski is like a carthorse in a bowler hat?" Neither of us thought so, as we told him vehemently.'

When Nancy went back to Paris that autumn, followed by Arlen, their affair intensified. They spent most of their time together, any differences smoothed out by drink: 'The Baron was not only good fun and a charming companion. He could be as sullen as distant thunder, as heavy as lead, brooding and brewing for hours. I admit that some of this (as he would point out) was my fault. God, how I loathed him then. It would pass . . . with champagne as like as not.'

By now Nancy was venturing further afield than the Ritz and the circuit of expensive restaurants and dancing places that her cousin Edward and those of her mother's circle frequented; she was beginning to dip a toe into Montmartre: 'Montmartre nights were a delight, that same autumn and winter, my first winter in Paris on my own, the Baron's first taste of France as well.'

Nancy adored dancing – she and one of her men friends had once planned to give stage performances – and Montmartre was full of *boîtes*. Jazz was all the rage and most of the best jazz musicians were black, welcomed in Paris, while looked at askance in London.

For dinner beforehand, Nancy and Arlen had a favourite restaurant: 'We would go generally to La Perle – a most reasonably priced tarts' restaurant, where the obese yet buoyant Madame, dressed in very high, very tight laced boots, now of black and now of white, usually in that astonishingly bright short green taffeta dress of hers, would leeringly whisper to us: "*J'ai connue le Roi Edouard Sept*". It seems to me that she sometimes carried a whip . . .

'In any case, for about twenty francs a head, one could enjoy delicious food while appraising the girls as they came in to eat about ten o'clock, before going off to their work. And then we would go and dance somewhere else in Montmartre. It was always champagne and our heads were often swimming.'

The need for sex – another facet of Paris life that appealed to Nancy – and its many variations was something taken for granted in French culture, so much so that many brothels – *maisons de tolérance* or *maisons closes* – were run by the state. By law, these establishments had to be of discreet external appearance, run by a woman, and display a (lit) red lantern when open for business.*

When Nancy arrived in 1920, the best-known was probably Le Chabanais, run with the same matter-of-fact openness, attention to detail, efficiency and elegance as any of the grand hotels. Its entrance hall was designed as a bare stone cave and its bedrooms were lavishly decorated as Moorish, Hindu, Japanese, Pompeii, Louis XVI and Japanese (this one had won a design prize at the 1900 World Fair in Paris). Among its habitués had been the Prince of Wales (later Edward VII), Toulouse-Lautrec and various diplomatic guests of the French government. Many

---

* Hence 'red light district'.

of these establishments, such as La Fleur Blanche, known for its torture chamber, had walls decorated by famous artists.

There was even a brothel catering for clergymen (l'Abbaye, in rue Saint-Sulpice), with a confessional room lined in red and a Satan's room where the client was received by devils with torture implements of various kinds. A chosen girl would often wear a cassock if her client desired it.

Right at the bottom of the scale were the *maisons d'abattage* ('slaughterhouses'), which catered to the masses and where the girls would service sixty to a hundred clients; these were issued with numbered tickets to tell them when it was their turn. Keeping – or perhaps I should say trying to keep – all these in order were the Morality Police (*Brigade de repression du proxénétisme*), whose job it was to find unlicensed prostitutes and brothels.

As for Nancy and Arlen, they were at their closest ('This too was the time I saw him every day; now he was on my nerves, and now he was not'), an intimacy that led to Arlen making a semi-proposal: 'If I were rich, I should ask you to marry me – d'you see? But as I'm not, there seems no point in doing so – d'you see?' Nancy's response was to remind him that she was still married, having not yet got her divorce, while in her diary she wrote, 'The vanity of some men!'

Arlen was with her during the horrible winter that followed, when she was in and out of hospital for three separate operations. The first was a curettage* in December; with recovery time a mere few days, she was quickly able to return to the joys of that Parisian winter – one of which included spending night after night in Paris's chic new cabaret bar, Le Boeuf sur le Toit, which opened just before Christmas at 28, rue Boissy d'Anglas (in the 8th arrondissement).

In February 1920 Jean Cocteau had put on an opera bouffe, *Le Boeuf sur le Toit*, with scenes set round a bar and clowns as actors. When the opera closed it was reincarnated as a nightclub.

---

* Often a way of – and a euphemism for – performing an early abortion.

It was a huge success from the day it opened, quickly becoming the *ne plus ultra* of Paris cabaret society, who crammed into its one large room that held two rows of small tables with a piano and the bar at the far end. On the tan-fabric-covered walls were the signatures of many of the guests, especially those who were friends of the artist Francis Picabia, whose enormous picture of one large eye dominated the room.

On its opening night its brilliant pianist played Gershwin tunes, with Cocteau providing an accompaniment on the drums to an audience that included Pablo Picasso, René Clair, Sergei Diaghilev and Maurice Chevalier. The social, literary and artistic worlds of Paris would arrive there in evening dress or grey flannels, to dance to music such as 'Ain't She Sweet?' and 'Sometimes I'm Happy', from two pianos, back to back – one of the pianists was so expert he read a detective novel while he played. Other musicians would go to play there after hours. The final accolade was the appearance of the pale, thin figure of Marcel Proust, eyes burning with fever and wrapped in three overcoats against the cold, leaning on the arm of a friend as he arrived for one of his last dinners out in Paris that July (he died a few months later). Nancy adored it. 'I have discovered a new place,' she wrote to Iris. 'There are plenty of friends there. We are not about to go to bed very early.'

Not long after the first operation, Nancy had a second, a hysterectomy, that must have been caused by complications from the first, after which, in February, came a third, caused by a serious infection* and noted by her as 'appendicitis, peritonitis, gangrene, with "a two per cent chance of survival"'. In all, she was in and out of hospital for three months.

For any woman, a hysterectomy is an operation that has a psychological as well as a physical effect – and Nancy was only twenty-four. Although she had always declared she never wanted children, there is a considerable emotional gap between choosing not to have a family and finding yourself unable to. The removal of any possibility of ever becoming, like most of her friends, a

---

* It must be remembered that this was well before the discovery of antibiotics.

mother must have added a certain distance to her view of herself vis-à-vis the world she moved in. Although she often lauded the sexual freedom this offered, now, more than ever, she must have felt herself separate; now, more than ever, she turned to poetry.

Upset though he was on Nancy's behalf over her painful and dangerous operation, for Arlen this trauma – as well as much else in their relationship – was also copy: it went, first, into his novel *Piracy*, published in 1922. Its heroine, Virginia, was a married society woman with what was then known as 'a reputation' – as Nancy had by the time Arlen met her. Like Nancy – as Arlen would have known from their summer in Normandy – she had no hesitation in asking one lover to meet another: 'Virginia loved one and then another, seldom alone but always in a crowd.' Like Nancy, Virginia suffers a gynaecological complaint for which she needs a serious operation while living with the hero in Paris. When recovered, she refuses to marry the hero and they part in anger (as did Nancy and Arlen). But *Piracy* was merely a forerunner to Nancy's appearance in *The Green Hat*, the novel that came out after their parting and that made Arlen rich, and a celebrity.

First, the title. When Arlen wrote his best-seller no woman would have dreamt of leaving the house without a hat (unless in evening dress) and 'a green hat, bravely worn', is the first thing the narrator notices about Iris/Nancy. Iris Storm, the heroine, is a beautiful, twice-widowed woman of many affairs, visiting her alcoholic brother; his flat is above the narrator's, whose help she asks in rousing her brother. They are unsuccessful in this but they end up going to bed together – the one-night stand was a subject barely touched on before. A few days later Iris runs into Napier, the love of her life, who is to be married in three days; they have a brief affair and Iris leaves. Ten months later the narrator discovers her in Paris, deathly ill after having given birth to Napier's stillborn child.

The story, with its beautiful, doomed heroine, appealed on several levels, the daring subject matter, which included extra-marital affairs and syphilis, all wrapped in lushly romantic prose yet with an underlying moral: if you behave badly you are likely to come to a sticky end – Iris finally kills herself by driving her beloved yellow Hispano Suiza into a tree. And in Nancy Arlen had the perfect model for Iris Storm, a woman who met men on their own ground, dazzled them, was to some extent a nympho-maniac, and then usually left them.

Nancy herself said, 'The Baron made a lot of money with *The Green Hat* – and for such nonsense too – but no need to be-grudge him that.' The book received mixed reviews ('a brilliant portrait of a passionate, intelligent, suffering woman', 'mostly tosh', 'the book's theme is that a bad person may really be very good – especially if her hair and other things about her are beau-tiful'), but it sold like wildfire – 250,000 copies in the US alone. Arlen, in the book, describes a commercially successful novelist who 'had observed that the whole purpose of a best-seller is to justify a reasonable amount of adultery in the eyes of subur-ban matrons'. It was a rule he followed successfully for most of his life, although when asked by a Chicago reporter to what he thought he owed his success, he touched the astrakhan collar of his overcoat and replied, '*Per ardua ad astrakhan.*'

CHAPTER 5

Ezra Pound, 1922

Of Nancy's five most important love affairs, the second was undoubtedly that with Ezra Pound (Ezra Weston Loomis Pound, to
give him his full name). Not simply because he was a legendary
figure in the literary world and a founder of the modernist movement, but also because their liaison was one of the few where
Nancy loved more than she was loved. Her letters to him breathe
passionate longing ('Your letters I love . . . your letters and yourself'; 'I want you here'). She went on loving him for five or six
years, and only when it became apparent that his feelings for her
had waned did she 'switch off', although she remained a staunch
friend for years.

They had first met in 1915 at Maud's tea table but giving
her mother credit for the first steps in any of her friendships
was not in Nancy's nature. She had got on well with him and
been impressed by his dashing, poetic appearance, but it was
Maud to whom he had become close, largely through his quest
for financial help for others. Like Nancy, Pound frequented the
Eiffel Tower but they had never met there. Nancy had seen him
again when she was ill in Paris during the winter of 1920–21,
and he had visited her during her convalescence after the series
of operations she underwent in the early part of 1921.

Pound was an attractive personality, highly intelligent and
with a well-developed personal style, although Harold Acton
thought his anxiety to claim attention was almost painful – he
is often recorded as pounding the table or thumping his chest.

71

One of his most engaging characteristics was his championing of other writers he admired; two of these were James Joyce and Wyndham Lewis, whom he had met through the literary circles in which he moved.

Although Pound had been born in Idaho (in 1885), his family soon moved to Pennsylvania, and he first went to Europe with his mother and aunt when he was thirteen. Early on he had determined to become a poet, had specialised in Latin at his school and been admitted to the University of Pennsylvania at only fifteen. Here he studied the Provençal dialect and Old English, read Dante, and from this began the idea for a long poem in three parts – of emotion, instruction and contemplation – planting the seeds for his later work *The Cantos*.

From late 1907 Pound taught Romance languages at Wabash College in Crawfordsville, Indiana, a conservative town that he called 'the sixth circle of hell'. So puritan was it that it tempted him into deliberately provocative behaviour such as smoking (forbidden) and annoying his landlords by entertaining friends, including women. He was finally asked to leave after offering a stranded chorus girl tea and his bed for the night when she was caught in a snowstorm. When she was discovered the next morning by the landladies, his insistence that he had slept on the floor was met with disbelief and he was dismissed.

He left for London almost at once, arriving in August 1908, at the age of twenty-three, with a mere £3 in his pocket; but, clever, audacious and single-minded, he made his mark virtually straight away. He moved into lodgings at 48 Langham Street, a penny bus ride from the British Museum and, having published his first book, *A Lume Spento*, persuaded a nearby bookseller to display it. By October he was already being talked about by the literati.

In December he published a second collection, *A Quinzaine for the Yule*. This helped him secure the vacancy that arose on the death of one of the lecturers at the Regent Street Polytechnic, and at the beginning of 1909 he was giving evening lectures on 'The Development of Literature in Southern Europe'. Mornings were spent in the famous Reading Room of the British Museum, then he would lunch at the Vienna Café in Oxford Street, often meeting the writer Ford Madox Ford there.

One of the things about Pound that had appealed to Nancy when she first met him with her mother was the theatricality, not to say flamboyance, of his dressing; a habit also noted by Ford, who wrote, 'Ezra would approach with the step of a dancer, making passes with a cane at an imaginary opponent. He would wear trousers made of green billiard cloth, a pink coat, a blue shirt, a tie hand-painted by a Japanese friend, an immense sombrero, a flaming beard cut to a point, and a single large blue earring.'

From the start Pound appealed to women. He was enormously energetic and much of that energy went into his pursuit of them. He had met his first serious romance, Hilda Doolittle (later known as the poet H.D.) in Pennsylvania, but when he asked her father, an astronomy professor, for permission to marry her he was understandably refused – it was during the months that his university career was coming off the rails, and he was also seeing two other women at the same time.

Now, in England, less than a year later, Pound received a momentous invitation. It was to the literary salon of the novelist Olivia Shakespear; through Olivia he met not only her beautiful daughter Dorothy (whom he would later marry) but Olivia's former lover, W.B. Yeats, in Pound's view the greatest living poet. Although Yeats was twenty years older than Pound, the two became close friends.

Pound now had the entrée to a hugely distinguished literary circle and, although his next collection of poetry (*Canzoni*) was panned by the *Westminster Gazette* as a 'medley of pretension', he was hired by the editor of the socialist magazine *The New Age* to write a weekly column – giving him, at last, a regular fixed income. He earned a little more – and met many more poets, such as James Joyce, D.H. Lawrence, Robert Frost and Richard Aldington – by contributing to small magazines such as *Poetry* and spending winters with Yeats, whose eyesight was failing, as his secretary.

He was also founding a new literary movement. His former

sweetheart, Hilda Doolittle, with whom his relationship was now one of close friendship rather than sexual love, had arrived in England in 1911. Soon Pound introduced her and Aldington, who eventually became her husband, to the Eiffel Tower. Here they would discuss their work, and the future of poetry generally; like most of the younger poets, they were in revolt against the stirring, patriotic or deeply romantic poetry of Victorians such as Alfred Lord Tennyson and Rudyard Kipling, described by Pound as 'versified moral essays'.

As modernists they focused on the individual and concrete, writing more sharply and tersely, attempting to find new ways of expression that would illuminate the interior mind, often – perhaps usually – scattering literary or classical allusions throughout the poem or work. When Pound signed one of Hilda's poems 'H.D. Imagiste' and it was printed in *Poetry* magazine, this new word entered the poetic lexicon. Soon Imagism was the term used to describe the work of the writers of these short, free-verse poems.

The best description of Imagism comes from Pound himself, who laid down its three tenets: direct treatment of the subject, conciseness and the creation of new rhythms. He picked out as the purest example of Imagism the line by the 1890s poet Lionel Johnson 'Clear lie the fields, and fade into blue air'. Another is Pound's own line from his 'In a Station of the Metro', describing the sudden sight of beautiful women's faces appearing in that crowded spot:

The apparition of these faces in the crowd
Petals on a wet black bough.

Of his contemporaries, there was H.D.'s best-known poem 'Oread' (the name of a mountain nymph who is ordering the sea around):

Whirl up, sea –
Whirl your pointed pines,
Splash your great pines

On our rocks,
Hurl your green over us –
Cover us with your pools of fir.

Pound brought the same persistence and determination to succeed to his love affairs as to his career. He was in love with a beautiful married woman, Bride Scratton, whom he had met in 1910, and had also begun to court Dorothy Shakespear. Her parents were opposed to the marriage, largely because of Pound's meagre income and fairly precarious financial position generally. Finally, though, they consented – Dorothy was deeply in love with Pound and at twenty-seven they must have thought that, as the phrase went, 'she was getting no younger'. The newly-weds moved into a small flat (with no bathroom) just off Kensington Church Street.

Their next-door neighbours were another couple of newly-weds, Pound's old flame H.D., who had married his friend Richard Aldington. Here the Pounds entertained, economically but poetically, the chief refreshment being preserved apricots, which Pound, always conscious of the impression he made, would nip in half with his very white teeth, then lick his fingers before wiping them with a flourish of a silk handkerchief.

The same year as his marriage, through his literary connections, and his nose for talent, Pound met T.S. (Thomas Stearns) Eliot, a young American poet who arrived in England three months before the outbreak of the First World War – and another close literary friendship was formed.

War, which broke out that August, scarcely affected Pound. As an American citizen he did not have to join up; instead, he was appointed co-editor of *Blast*. (War also meant that, with most of the young men away fighting, there was less competition for girls. He made the most of this, something of which Dorothy, still deeply in love with him, was unaware.)

By now, Pound was considered to be the motivating force behind modern poetry, both in his own work and in printing and promoting that of others. He went on publishing collections of poetry, was made London editor of the *Dial* in 1917 and, in

1920, Paris correspondent of the prestigious *Little Review*, so that in January 1921 the Pounds moved to Paris.

A few months later they settled into an inexpensive apartment, the *pavillon* or summer house of 70 bis, rue Notre-Dame-des-Champs, for which Pound built much of the furniture. Here they mixed with the writers and artists looking for new ways of expression; among them were Joan Miró, who had come to join Picasso and was about to hold his first exhibition, and the photographer Man Ray, most of whose one small room in a modest hotel was taken up by the bed and three very large cameras, and who did his developing in his bedroom cupboard. Also in Pound's circle were Stravinsky and Prokofiev, Isadora Duncan, Samuel Beckett and the expatriate Americans Harry and Caresse Crosby and Scott and Zelda Fitzgerald, there on a brief visit.

Fitzgerald's first novel, *This Side of Paradise*, published the previous year, had become an instant best-seller and made the Fitzgeralds famous. At home in New York their behaviour – as of golden spoilt children at a perpetual party where they drank constantly – was regarded indulgently. In Paris, where it did not go down so well, they still maintained this sense of entitlement: Zelda, for instance, kept fastening the doors of their hotel lift back with a rope on their floor, so that it was always at their disposal and no one else could use it, while Scott did not bother to learn French.

Of the new movements, Dadaism* was in full flow. It suited the mood of a world disorganised by the war and ruled, according to the Dadaists, 'by aggressive madmen'. Its founders declared it to mean 'anything and nothing'; its purpose, if it could be said to have a purpose, was to ridicule the meaninglessness of the modern world. Its first *manifestation*, on 20 January 1920, was a piece of performance art by Louis Aragon, André Breton and Philippe Soupault, with a reading by Tristan Tzara of an entire newspaper article chosen at random and accompanied by the clanging of cowbells and the clicking of castanets, so that

---

* 'Dada' was the nursery word for a hobby horse.

nobody could hear what was being said. The manifesto was then read by six people at once. The audience, at first bewildered, quickly grew noisily angry.

The following month, at the Salon des Indépendants, the Dadaists held another performance. There was a rumour – largely put about by the Dadaists – that Charlie Chaplin would be present so the place was packed. Of course he did not appear, so as the Dadaists read out their 'poems' and manifestos, the irate audience began to hurl at them whatever was at hand – mostly eggs, vegetables and small coins. Eventually the lights had to be switched off so that the auditorium could be safely evacuated. After that, whenever a Dada performance was announced, gendarmes patrolled the aisles to keep order and prevent the otherwise inevitable riot.

At another 'play' the eight actors, dressed in cardboard tubes, stood in a row and recited meaningless speeches. 'The equatorial bite in the bluish rock weighs upon the night intimate scent of ammoniacal cradles the flower is a lamp-post doll listens to the mercury,' began one, recorded by the *Times* correspondent Sisley Huddleston, who continued, 'The girl next to me clutched my arm and exclaimed, "One does not know what it signifies, but one feels that there is so much behind it."' This clear case of the emperor's new clothes achieved the Dadaists' desired result, which was to get talked about – and their paintings went up in price.

Nancy's first book of poetry, *Outlaws*, was published early in 1921, and was reviewed at length in the *Observer* (of 27 February 1921) by GM. His review was both laudatory and critical; above all, it was long, a sign of great interest. The book, he wrote, had 'more genius in it than there is in the great mass of her contemporaries, and much less talent. By genius we mean a special way of feeling and seeing that separates a man or woman from the crowd, and by talent we mean handicraft, tact, judgement. Genius cannot be acquired; we have it or we have it not but talent can be.' Perceptively, he added, 'Miss Nancy Cunard is her book: she looks upon it as outlawed, and herself, too: not the apparent woman, perhaps, but the spiritual.' Nancy, who was delighted by GM's review, wrote him what he described as 'a most enthusiastic letter'.

Various friends visited Nancy during the months of her convalescence from the series of operations she had undergone during the winter, among them Duff and Diana Cooper. 'We lunched with Nancy Cunard,' records his diary for 15 March 1921. 'She appears to have quite recovered. She has charming rooms at the very top of the hotel with a wonderful view over the whole of Paris. The Sacré Coeur glittered in the sun.'

Another who came was Ezra Pound. He had visited her during her months in hospital, when poetry had been more than ever her consolation; now, no doubt made more confident by her book's reception in England, she sent Pound a poem that she hoped he would publish in the *Dial*. (At home Maud, proud of Nancy's work, was doing all she could to promote it among the editors and literati that she knew.)

Pound, always fascinated by beautiful women, responded quickly, if rather negatively:

'Lovely Nancy: I will take the poem to the *Dial* this evening, but, my dear, why, why the devil do you write in that obsolete dialect and with the cadences of the late Alfred Tennyson,' began his letter. He went on to say that while he realised she had not sent him her poem in order to hear his criticism, he also knew that he was probably the only person who would give her any. She must not, he said, use overblown language – of which he gave her several examples from her work – and she must keep things simple and concise. 'One must get the speech of poetry even more vivid than that of prose.' In which case, he thought, he might get one of her poems printed. His ending was warmer: 'Vale et me ama Ezra'.

Nancy may have been hurt by his uncompromising words (at any rate, she did not follow his excellent advice) as they did not meet again for several months. She had, also, started an affair with Wyndham Lewis, whose talent she had always admired. 'My dear darling Lewis,' she wrote to him that spring. 'I have found a house, called Les Fresnes, eight miles west of

Dieppe ... if you would *be* there, I would take it for you, any time till September ... I wish I had seen you more; I always do ... You once said I was drunk, when I was sober. Don't do it again!'

She took the rented cottage anyway, in the Normandy village of Saint-Martin-Église, and spent much of the summer there. Here, among other guests like her cousin Edward Cunard, her lover Michael Arlen and Iris and her husband Curtis Moffat, GM came to see her, staying in a nearby hotel for six days. The first two went badly: he was sulky and disturbed when he found that a young man had already arrived and was staying in the cottage, his innate conventionality affronted at the thought of what this might imply to the outside world. Nancy told him that this was the young man of a friend who had wired at the last moment that she could not come and that she, Nancy, had not wanted to put the man off.

Eventually, GM's love of both Nancy and the countryside – they walked through wonderful woods – overcame the sulks and the rest of the visit went well, so much so that in August he wrote to her again about her poetry, offering advice that, if not less critical than Pound's, was expressed more gently and encouragingly because it touched on her way of life rather than her work: 'If you go out and amuse yourself when you can't write, your art life will waste to nothingness. An artist's life in this is like an acrobat's, he must exercise his craft daily, when inspiration is by him and when it is afar. He must not wait for inspiration, he must continue to call it down to him always and at last it will answer him; I should have said, be always with him.'

GM also visited her in Sanary that winter. Here they saw wonderful sunsets and ate *oursins* (sea urchins), caught in the harbour at a depth of nine feet by driving a cleft bamboo pole down so that the *oursin* was firmly gripped by its split ends and then drawn up.

After Sanary, Nancy moved in March 1922 to Monte Carlo, where Maud was also staying – it was still the time when the Riviera was a winter rather than a summer resort. So popular was it among the English escaping their country's weather that most society papers sent reporters there to chronicle the doings of the rich and famous – into which category both Nancy and her mother fell.

The *Sketch* reported that 'Lady Cunard's daughter Mrs Fairbairn – who looks almost more like Lady Cunard than Lady Cunard herself! – is often to be seen tempting fortune at roulette.' As always, Nancy's clothes came in for comment, once for a mauve tulle scarf tied across her eyebrows, with floating ends, surmounted by a big grey felt hat ('oh, so Spanish!') and again, in more demure fashion, 'Nancy Cunard looked charming in black, with a wonderful coral red hat'.

Nancy spent most of the summer moving around, first to Fontainebleau, near Paris, then back to England to a house she took near Hungerford, which she packed with friends – including the faithful Hutchinson and a future lover, the writer Aldous Huxley. During this time Pound, who had tirelessly promoted his friend T.S. Eliot's work, to the point of trying to secure him funds so that he could give up his job in a bank, was editing the manuscript of *The Waste Land*, cutting it drastically in several places and, Eliot believed, improving it greatly.

Nancy had also met Eliot, whose work she admired and which certainly influenced her own (often, in the view of critics, to her detriment). It also seems, to judge by the following, that she managed to seduce him one night at the Tower. In a poem entitled 'The Letter', she later wrote:

We met, you and I, first, that summer night of 1922,
At a ball – you in 'smoking', I in a panniered dress
Of Poiret: red, gold, with cascading white tulle on the hips.
The P of W was there (so polite, lovely face) and we danced
    together . . .
Bored by it all was I. After many dances, we went down
Alone, by the grand staircase to the supper room.
It was then, Eliot, you came in, alone too . . .

The poem goes on to describe how they met the following evening in the Wyndham Lewis room at the Tower and sat by the gas fire all night. 'Not every life's-moment is recalled,' wrote Nancy, 'though all of that night certainly is.' Years later, Eliot wrote to a friend that this night had been his sole fling in a society 'where reasonably discreet adultery was accepted'.*

After the summer came Deauville, then on to Spain and back to Paris in September where she rented a flat on the Quai d'Orsay. She invited Pound to lunch with her – conveniently, Dorothy Pound was on a long visit to her parents in London. As the Pounds had no telephone, Nancy sent her invitation by telegram on 8 September 1922: '*Vous prie de me rencontrer demain samedi matin quai d'Orsay train de Hendaye 11.39 Gardez taxi et munissez vous de 70 francs puis dejeunez avec moi Nancy*'. It is likely that their love affair began then, as by the time Nancy set off on the *Orient Express* to Venice very soon afterwards their correspondence was intimate and in full flow. Nancy's letters† are full of longing: 'Darling, I smoke my last cigarette (maybe) prior to the attempt at sleep in top bunk of the 2nd voiture Orient Express . . . I wish I had the corollary to my last night with me now – you.'

Nancy knew that Pound loved Venice as much as she did and many of her letters to him involved trying to lure him to *La Serenissima*, either then or later. It must have been a temptation difficult to resist: Venice, before the age of mass tourism, was a dream of beauty, with its silent canals, onyx in the moonlight, its sunlit squares with a flower seller on every corner and its ancient buildings lapped by water, the palazzos along the Grand Canal still mainly inhabited by old aristocratic Venetian families. After the war, with the Riviera still considered only a winter playground, Venice had quickly returned to becoming the late-summer social gathering place for the rich and socially elite, its only drawback being the mosquitoes that rose from the canals,

---

* Letter to Emily Hale, 3 November 1930.

† Unfortunately, Pound's letters to Nancy were all destroyed when her house in Normandy was ransacked during the Second World War.

food for the swifts that sliced the warm air above the buildings, so that all who could afford it slept under mosquito nets.

Nancy was quickly involved in Venetian social life, dancing, drinking, partying. Her dazzling blonde beauty, her status as a much-copied, much-photographed icon of the Twenties, made its usual impact, especially on the susceptible Italians. As she told Pound, her mood varied constantly: 'It is dreadful I feel ups and downs since I wrote to you last. Always a feeling of illness. Always a feeling of oppression and generally of depression. Some fifty clutching Italians of a night met, danced with and forgotten immediately after they leave.'

Sometimes her letters are mere scraps, scrawled – as usual in pencil – on small pieces of paper: 'How bloody people are – how nice you are. Dear Ezra, write to me very soon.' Sometimes they are complaints about the people she meets (the real complaint being that Pound was not there with her). Offered an apartment sans any rent by one admirer, she refused it because 'I don't think I can face that as he is one of 50 clutchers, and a bore . . . Truth of it (again) this would be alright if there weren't so many futile people to tire one, a social Piazza.'

All September her letters beg for his company: 'Do come and stay at my apartment. I have taken a floor of the Villa Mainella on the Grand Canal and go to it the day after tomorrow . . . Will you come?' The next one begs 'do come, do come! I can see us at breakfast, splitting a fig, muttering over the foulness of the tea (*chose que je fais seul à present*). Now and then a scandal will raise our laughter. Hours will be devoted to the two typewriters.

'Do come. Come as soon as you get this.

'Sitting on my balcony overlooking the Grand Canal . . . and most of all having been very much thrilled by your letter – my first letter here. Darling, you welcome me, for I have had sourish days in Venice and wished myself elsewhere, in Paris, I think, for all the sun and the glamour as you say, as it is said "*il faut etre a Venise avec l'amoureux*" (I prefer the word "*amant*").'

She told him of the Villa's charms, of the thirteen-year-old girl who had become her inefficient and outspoken maid, of the two roof terraces, of which one should be his: 'I wish that you could be here, and I understand that you can't. Shall I not look for a palace, with one long room, the sala of Venice, empty and waiting to be "done up" by me? Yes indeed, I will look now, this month – and next year perhaps we shall be *Les amants de Venise*, beginning with the spring.

'*Je tiens de te dire que j'aime fort ta facon de m'écrire, que j'apprécie la fréquence de tes lettres* – don't stop, I need them, love them.

'Now I am beginning to long for you terribly, beginning to find it very hard that you can't be here (*pas meme me fuguer**) and when I say "beginning" I suppose the word means an intensification of feeling. But I shall probably never find pasha nor you need the gold-headed cane despite affecting it. Our destinies will proceed otherwise and I hope sometimes together . . . Oh dear me, I wish I didn't wish for you so much.

'Oh, Ezra, do come here. I will be unreasonable about that in every letter – it is so much our life too.'

What Nancy was undoubtedly unreasonable about was the fact that Ezra was married. To Nancy marriage was, if not exactly an irrelevance, something to be discounted where love was concerned. Some of her lovers were married, others were not – *voilà*. With some of the married ones, she knew their wives and, quite often – as with Mary Hutchinson – liked them. What she did not know was that Pound was still conducting his long affair with Bride Scratton. He had earlier written to Bride complaining that she had left Paris: 'Dearest and belovedest . . . I wish you hadn't gone, and I wish you were already on your way back, only it's too much hoping. I love you.'

Nancy's approach to marriage was the diametric opposite of that of her mother. For Maud Cunard's generation marriage was – except in literally a handful of cases – 'until death do us part'. What happened within that marriage was nobody's business provided outward appearances were maintained and discretion was absolute. Being open about a lover was anathema.

---

* 'Not even to run away from me'.

For Nancy, who did not deal in shades of grey, this was the purest hypocrisy, a principle she carried into her life as a feme sole by never hesitating to invite two lovers to stay at the same time or having a fling with a new man while engaged in a relationship. Monogamy was not part of her ethos, or she could not have written as she did to Pound, 'Shall we go to Morocco this winter for tennis? (and what would Hutchinson say to that?).'

In any case, her view of marriage was jaundiced: she had viewed her own solely as an escape route from a life she disliked. Sydney Fairbairn was simply the means – it is notable that nowhere in her diary does she mention even the faintest possibility that his feelings might have been hurt by her brisk abandonment of their marriage, nor is there a tinge of guilt that this man, who had married her in all good faith, now found himself cast adrift for no reason that he could see, at the end of a war in which he had fought bravely, and might have expected to come home to a warm and loving wife. Nancy saw everything, always, from her own point of view – a habit which, while it added a keen extra edge to her own powerful personality, often cut deeply into the emotions of others.

Even though longing for Pound's presence ('Promise me that you will come here next year – write it to me now'), Nancy did not lead a solitary life in Venice. She would slip into one of the black-painted gondolas, poled silently along the canals, to go to a party ('a painter – local John in looks – came in a sublime purple Arab gown') or sit in the piazza on a sunny evening: 'Now I am drinking a very scented Vermouth bianco, again surrounded by people and bells.'

Friends came to stay, the Sitwells and Wyndham Lewis from Nancy's Eiffel Tower circle, the young painter Eugene McCown and the American writer Robert McAlmon, whom Nancy had met in London the previous year. Every day they would gather at one of the great people-watching cafés of Venice, Florian's in St Mark's Square,* where often other friends staying in

---

* Said to be the oldest café in the world.

Venice would spot them or Nancy, always a conscientious hostess, would organise visits to galleries or the art-filled churches. There would be dinner parties with, afterwards, drinking and dancing in the new bars and nightclubs.

Like Pound, McAlmon was also married, although in his case it was a marriage in name only. Eighteen months earlier he had married the lesbian daughter of Sir John Ellerman, founder of the Ellerman Shipping Line and thought to be one of the richest men in England. Winifred Ellerman (always known as Bryher, the name with which she signed her poetry) wanted independence from her family and within minutes of their meeting had proposed the marriage to McAlmon, who longed to go to Paris, chiefly to meet James Joyce, and there lead the life of a writer.

'She faced me with the proposition,' he wrote to his friend William Carlos Williams. 'The marriage is legal only, unromantic, and strictly an agreement ... Bryher could not travel, and be away from home, unmarried.' The unsuspecting Ellerman, delighted that his daughter was at last getting married, gave his son-in-law a lavish allowance – hence the nickname he would earn in the *quartier*, McAlimony – in return for which he and Bryher had agreed that they were both free to lead their own lives as long as they visited Bryher's parents together several times a year.

Bryher managed to keep up the deception by combining it with a good deed. Noticing the semi-chaos in Shakespeare and Company (the small English-language bookshop run by Sylvia Beach), she arranged mailboxes there for those writers who were library members. She herself would give – or later send – Sylvia all her own letters to her mother, which Sylvia would then forward to Lady Ellerman with a Paris stamp on them so that Lady Ellerman, who would not have been happy otherwise, believed that Bryher was still living in Paris with McAlmon.

Robert McAlmon, tall, slim and the same age as Nancy, had pale-blue eyes, an aquiline nose and a good helping of personal magnetism; Nancy had no hesitation in sleeping with him while he was staying with her. But that autumn in Venice, where Nancy had taken the Casa Mainilla, the guest she was interested in was Lewis. In the Tower, she had listened to him avidly as he declaimed his views on war and art; in Venice, she was trying to fix up a studio for him.

On 9 October she believed that Lewis would arrive: 'Up goes the mosquito net but I must find the poor artist a studio as he seems to think I have one and expects some beautiful heads to paint. (After all this, I wonder if he will arrive?)'

She was right to wonder. Lewis only turned up, filthy and unkempt, on the 13th. His appearance had deteriorated greatly since the Eiffel Tower days. Ernest Hemingway, who had arrived in Paris with his wife Hadley in December 1921 to work as a journalist, and who met Lewis a few months earlier, described him as having the face of a frog and 'the eyes of an unsuccessful rapist . . . I do not think I have ever met a nastier-looking man.' To Siegfried Sassoon, who met Lewis on the afternoon of his arrival at Florian's, 'he looked very dirty and untidy, with staring eyes, a three-day growth of beard and a grubby tweed hat on the back of his head'.

Lewis began to draw Nancy at once, 'a pretty drawing in a ball gown begun'; but the one that eventually became known shows her standing by the window of her apartment in a daytime suit, which Lewis sold to the *Sketch* as the second in a series of 'Wyndham Lewis Portraits of Society People'. Sometimes he would sketch the magnificent palazzos that rose out of stinking canals ('the fingers of one hand grasping the pencil, the fingers of the other grasping the nose' was how he described it), but mostly he made drawings of Nancy and her friends.

Now that McAlmon was out of the way – he had left for Florence – Lewis resumed his place as Nancy's lover, although he thought that she did not treat him with the respect that he, a prickly person given to jealous scenes, felt was his due. When the holiday was over they left for the railway station at the same time. Two gondolas were needed; Nancy sat in the first with one of her friends, Lewis in the second with her maid and luggage, which made him so furious that he did not speak to her until they were halfway to Paris.

Nancy still yearned for Pound but understood he could not meet her: 'But that means NEXT YEAR, doesn't it? . . . <u>Promise me</u> that you will come here next year – write it to me now.

'Oh dear me, I wish I didn't wish for you so much.'

CHAPTER 6

Aldous Huxley

When Nancy returned to England in November 1922, what became known as the 'Roaring Twenties' were in full swing. It was a term largely fuelled by the young – to be specific, a group of people too young for the men to have fought in the war, with enough money to do what they wanted and a thirst for constant entertainment.

Dancing was the great craze – of course at balls but also at *thés dansants*, between courses at restaurants and after dinner at private houses with the rugs rolled back. At balls, girls wore silver slippers, waved ostrich feather fans and, if rich enough, wore diamond bracelets outside their white gloves. Fancy-dress parties were often themed, from baby parties to parties held in swimming pools. Another passion was treasure hunts, with the hunters chasing all over London, first by public transport, later in fast cars, in pursuit of such hard-to-obtain objects as a policeman's helmet or the Prime Minister's pipe.*

Though anyone could drink, drugs, much easier to get hold of while Nancy and Diana Manners had been growing up,

---

* The grandest treasure hunt of all was given in Paris in 1927 by the professional party-giver Elsa Maxwell. Items to collect included music-hall star Mistinguett's shoe, a black swan from the Bois de Boulogne and the red pompom from a French seaman's hat. Before the night was over, Mistinguett had to entertain barefoot at the Casino de Paris, two guests were hospitalised by a ferocious swan and the interior decorator Elsie de Wolfe, wife of the British diplomat Sir Charles Mendl, was accused of theft by the French navy.

were now banned under the Dangerous Drugs Act of 1920. But according to the painter John Banting, one of those who later became known as the Bright Young People, drugs were easily obtained in Paris and posted to London. A few of the BYPs famously succumbed, but most remained unscathed, as although many of them would have a sniff of cocaine (known as 'uppies') if offered some at a party, a single sniff was not enough to render them addicted.

Nancy, although she later symbolised the Twenties for so many, was not interested in the BYP shenanigans. To start with, she was a few years older; more importantly, she looked towards the world of ideas rather than that of partygoing. She was also leading a nomadic life: in the past eighteen months she had moved through France, Spain and Italy, going on walking tours before winding up in Venice.

When in London she stayed at her mother's house. Maud had moved the previous year to 5 Carlton House Terrace, one of the grand, white-stuccoed houses designed by Nash that overlooked St James's Park. It was perfect for entertaining, for which Maud's extraordinary gift was now deployed to the full. At a fairly typical luncheon party there was a prince, two princesses and two duchesses among her nineteen guests. While dinner was formal, for such luncheons husbands and wives could be asked separately and numbers between the sexes were often unequal. 'I ask my guests for conversation, not for mating,' Maud would say.

Nancy did not enjoy these parties, although she almost always attended them, usually escaping as quickly as she could afterwards. To Pound she wrote on 11 November, 'Ezra, London is too awful – I feel very ill, rain, kakhi [sic] sky, nerves . . . I go to [Dr] Oreste daily, he says "ca passera" but it is more than ever depressing.'

None of this stopped frequent outings, often to the Tower, where she saw Alfred Orage, one of her friends and editor of the small and highly influential literary magazine New Age, and the Tower's most regular habitué Augustus John ('now very old', as she wrote to Pound). In the same letter she told him that Arlen's book Piracy had just been published: 'Everyone galled by its description of me . . . most of all Hutchinson (not seen <u>him</u> yet), personally have only had time to read a few paragraphs on the Tower (Mont Agel) and Stulik (Mr Stutz) and have heard that the side curls (beavers) I have always worn are therein called Swan and Edgar* – can you beat it? The Baron himself is glad!'

The wistful letters to Pound continued: 'I wish I lived with someone. Is it better not, however?' She told him of travelling to Scotland to see her father, who was ill – and how little it really meant to her. 'The midlands are full of pale fields, cabbages like decapitated heads,' she wrote from the train, 'going across the border to Kelso [where her father was staying] because Sir B is very ill, more or less suddenly, and dying of it I think. I have known anyone better than I have known him – you see how it is then.' However, Sir Bache recovered quickly, and Nancy was able to return to London, soon complaining of dullness there. One sentence (from the number mentioning him) reads, 'Aldous Huxley about (I like him much).'

Huxley certainly was about. Although he had known Nancy for some time, in the spring or summer of 1922 he had become completely obsessed by her. He was part of her Paris life in that she was living in Paris at the time and he attempted several times to follow her there, but this she would not allow. His place as the third of Nancy's major affairs – although the physical connection only lasted a few days – is, I think, assured by her presence in so much of the work of this major novelist (Huxley was later nominated no less than nine times for the Nobel Prize in Literature); let alone the fact that, in order to write at all, his wife had to force him to flee from Nancy to another country.

Huxley's own literary pedigree was impeccable. He came from one of the great intertwined group of Cambridge intellectual families – Darwins, Stracheys, Huxleys, Trevelyans – his father taught at Charterhouse and his mother was a granddaughter of Dr Arnold of Rugby and sister of the novelist Mrs Humphry Ward. She had been educated at Somerville College and obtained

---

* The name of a well-known department store.

a First in English (both extremely rare in those days). She opened
a girls' school, with an emphasis on art and literature, where
Aldous was educated until he was nine, before being sent off to
prep school and then as a scholar to Eton.

Here great misfortune struck. What was mistaken for con-
junctivitis turned out to be an infection of the cornea that left
him almost blind. He had to leave Eton, for eighteen months
could only read by Braille and when he went up to Balliol College, Oxford in 1913 had to use a powerful magnifying glass,
although he could, and did, play the piano for hours. He was of
course rejected for military service when war broke out in 1914.

While at Oxford, he was invited to Garsington Manor, the
seventeenth-century house and estate in South Oxfordshire
bought the previous year by Philip and Lady Ottoline Morrell
(half-sister of the Duke of Portland).

Ottoline, tall, flamboyant, eccentric, with a mass of auburn
hair and an aquiline profile, was one of life's enhancers and she
had decorated Garsington in the same vein. 'Oak panelling had
been painted a dark peacock blue-green,' wrote David Garnett.
'The bare and sombre dignity of Elizabethan wood and stone
had been overwhelmed with an almost oriental magnificence:
the luxuries of silk curtains and Persian carpets, cushions and
pouffes. Ottoline's pack of pug dogs trotted everywhere ...
bowls of potpourri and orris-root stood on every mantelpiece,
side table and window-sill.' The house was full of bric-a-brac,
its walls covered with drawings by Augustus John and paintings
by the young artists of the day. For Ottoline was not interested
in the company of her fellow aristocrats, preferring instead to
entertain those involved in the arts, music and philosophy – one
of her most serious love affairs was with the mathematician and
philosopher Bertrand Russell.

In the summer of 1915 there was an unusual arrival at
Garsington. Maria Nys, a plump, pretty Belgian girl of sixteen
with large blue-green eyes, had been brought over by her mother
with her three sisters to take refuge from the German invasion
of Belgium (the rest of the family found other homes). For this
unsophisticated teenager the Garsington ambiance, with its

emphasis on things of the mind, all spoken of by highly educated older people, in a language that was not her own, was terrifyingly difficult to cope with. Nor had she any money; if she wanted, say, a stamp, she had to ask Ottoline for it. When she went for long walks with Aldous on his visits, it must have been a relief to be with someone nearer her own age. As for Aldous, he was growing much fonder of her than she realised.

When conscription was introduced in January 1916, Garsington became a refuge for pacifists (as were both the Morrells). Before the war, many socialists had also been pacifists, claiming that the main burden of war was borne by the working classes for the benefit of the elite. Others refused to fight for religious or ethical reasons, believing that any taking of life was wrong. Some conscientious objectors (or 'conchies' as they were known) became stretcher-bearers or ambulance drivers, others baulked even at that but were usually let off prison by military tribunals if they were prepared to do 'work of national importance'. Included in such work was farming – and Garsington had a farm.

Here many of the Bloomsbury Group, who had already been Garsington guests, came to work, being entertained, along with other guests, at the house. Soon afterwards, at the end of the summer, Aldous graduated from Balliol. One sunny day, sitting on a rug on the lawn, he proposed to Maria. Both of them knew that marriage at that moment was impossible but they promised to wait for each other.

By now Aldous was visiting Garsington so often that he was almost living there, and one day asked Philip Morrell if he too could work on the farm. From August 1916 he lived in the house, where he met most of the leading intellectual and cultural figures of the day. Of the hot summer nights he wrote, 'I have been sleeping out on the roof in company with an artistic young woman in short hair and purple pyjamas . . . spending most of the night in conversation or in singing folk-songs and rag-time to the stars . . . early in the morning we would be wakened by a gorgeous great peacock howling like a damned soul while he stalked about the tiles showing off his plumage to the sunrise.'

(The short-haired girl was the artist Dora Carrington – always known as Carrington – Iris Tree's Slade friend.)

Working on the farm during the day, Aldous wore fawn-coloured corduroy breeches, with yellow stockings and brogues, and a dark-brown corduroy jacket in which, with his height (he was six feet four inches) and tousled dark hair, he cut an elegant, romantic figure. His main task was chopping logs: Garsington depended almost entirely on wood as fuel.

In October, Maria, who had refused to rejoin her mother and sisters in Florence, moved to a furnished room in London and tried to earn a living teaching French. Aldous went to see her as often as he could, but in December she had to return to her mother and sisters in Florence. To Maria, now nineteen, Florence and Italy were a revelation. She had lost weight; now, slim and beautiful, she had a marvellous time.

With Maria gone, Aldous left Garsington soon afterwards, in the spring of 1917, and began to teach, first at Repton then, in September, at Eton (one of the boys he taught was Eric Blair, later George Orwell). At Eton, says his biographer Sybille Bedford, Aldous 'could be seen walking along the Eton High in so detached a state that he resembled a sleepwalker, a long orange scarf trailing behind him. It was difficult to visualise him keeping the boys in order but they were impressed with his use of language and words.'

From Eton he often went to London, gravitating towards the bohemian society of Fitzrovia. It was during one of these visits that he first met Nancy and her friends at the Eiffel Tower, probably through the Sitwells, as both Aldous and Nancy had contributed to their poetry magazine *Wheels* (it was to the Tower that Aldous went with the Sitwells to celebrate when news of the German surrender came through in November 1918). After this, knowing many of the same people, their paths continued to cross intermittently.

By now Aldous knew that he wanted to earn his living as a writer – he had already published three volumes of verse and one of short stories – but to marry Maria he needed a steady job; equally, he realised that his incompetence in keeping order in class meant that this would not be as a beak (schoolmaster) at Eton. When he was offered a job on the editorial staff of the *Athenaeum* magazine, he jumped at it. Now he could marry Maria, whom he had not seen for over two years.

Maria herself found it difficult to understand the faithfulness of this brilliant, charming and popular man. As she put it many years later, 'Why, why in the world did Aldous choose me out of the many prettier, wittier, richer etc young girls? Why in the world did he come back to fetch me after two long years of running around with more of those pretty and amusing ones of his own world? Knowing all the time that he could never teach me to write poetry or remember what I read in a book, or spel [*sic*] or anything he did set value on . . . And why did I not get for a single moment entranced by the Italian men and easy life and certainly less terrifying intellectual strain of it?'

Sybille Bedford, who knew them both well, believed it was because Maria saw a certain quality in Aldous that it was her duty to serve, although she was terrified of his social world. '*Je tirai son bateau*,' she said. They married in July 1919 and settled in a tiny flat in Hampstead, which Aldous decorated himself. When together, they spoke French – Maria's native language – but English with friends. When their son Matthew was born the following year Huxley, to earn more money, joined Condé Nast at a salary of £400 a year; here he helped launch *House and Garden*.

In 1921 Aldous's association with Chatto & Windus began, with the publication of his first novel, *Crome Yellow*. This thinly disguised satire of life at Garsington, where he had spent so many happy hours, was an immediate success – of it, F. Scott Fitzgerald wrote that 'this is the highest point so far attained by Anglo-Saxon sophistication', adding that Huxley was 'the wittiest man now writing in English'. His mockery ended his friendship with Lady Ottoline, who believed that Aldous had caricatured both her and her hospitality and was bitterly hurt – but it launched his serious writing career.

In January 1923 Aldous signed a contract with Chatto & Windus, agreeing 'to supply them with two new works of fiction per annum (one of which works shall be a full-length novel) written by himself during the next three years', for which he would receive £500 a year (the average weekly wage was about £5), with excellent royalties (twenty per cent after the first 2,000 copies were sold, rising later to twenty-five per cent). He also got the royalties from his previous books. If he was prepared to work hard, it was an admirable arrangement.

The first novel was due that July, but by spring not a word had been written. The trouble was that he had fallen desperately and obsessively in love with Nancy – or perhaps one should say her outward persona, the erotic and exquisite façade: the voice, the look, the walk. 'What struck first was her appearance,' wrote Sybille Bedford. How could it not: Nancy was thin, beautiful and elegant, with short gold hair, a well-shaped head, incandescently white skin and extraordinary blue-green eyes that mesmerised most of those she looked at. She was in the full flood of her rebellion against her mother's way of life and all it stood for; independent, separated from her husband, intelligent, scornful of conventional morality, her aura of sexual power was compelling.

Night after night Aldous would sit at Nancy's table, either in the Tower or some other crowded, smoke-filled café or bar, where everyone drank and talked until the early hours. Then, at three or four in the morning, he would walk home to Hampstead, where Maria lay in bed, usually awake and miserably anxious. When Aldous was at home – he was still working at Condé Nast – his day revolved around whether or not there was a telephone call from Nancy telling him where to meet her that evening. She was not in the slightest in love with Aldous, who had once spent the whole night pacing up and down outside her window, but she much enjoyed his company, so kept him dangling. Again, to Nancy a wife was an irrelevance; she wanted him in her circle as a friend.

Nor would she let Aldous follow her to Paris, which he tried to do several times. She herself was still longing for Pound. 'Ezra, dearest,' she wrote from Naples in early March, 'Italy is for us, you know, we should live in it most of the year. Don't go back to Paris, postpone that as long as you can.' She then set out a tempting list of places they could visit. At the beginning of April she was on the train to Pisa. 'Shall I ever get out of Italy now? I don't care as long as I can go up and down it. But I miss you.'

Whenever she returned, Aldous was there ('a lot of G.M. in London and Huxley', she wrote to Pound). Eventually, out of both affection and irritation, she had a brief affair with him. It lasted only a few days and from Nancy's point of view was disastrous; she later described being made love to by Aldous as 'like having slugs crawl all over you'. On Aldous, predictably, the effect was to increase his passion. Later (in *Antic Hay*) he wrote of that time, 'And once, for two or three days, out of pity, out of affection, out of a mere desire, perhaps, to lay the tiresome ghost, she had given him what his mournful silence implored – only to take it back, almost as soon as accorded.'

At first Maria regarded Aldous's feeling for Nancy in an understanding light. That is to say, she tolerated, and even encouraged these brief, passing loves, believing that they offered Aldous the distraction he needed in order to pursue his work successfully. This attitude may have been helped by the fact that she herself was bisexual and often equally attracted by the beautiful women to whom her husband was drawn.

One aspect of this relationship worried Maria deeply: its effect on Aldous's health, and his safety. His sight was so poor that she hated him being out late, in the dark, without her, in case of an accident or perhaps getting lost. As she also saw, he was getting more and more unhealthy – he hated nightlife, was affected by smoke and stale air and if he drank more than one or two glasses of wine (normally he drank nothing) became queasy. There was, too, the fact that if he broke his contract with Chatto & Windus by not delivering the promised novel, how would they manage financially? Yet how to combat so powerful an obsession?

Maria decided that it was time for an ultimatum that would cut the Gordian knot. When Aldous arrived back from work one fine evening in May (Nancy had returned to London on the 1st), Maria told him that she was going to leave for Italy the following day – with or without him. Aldous, who despite his passion for Nancy loved Maria deeply, had no intention of parting from her. In a word, both of them realised that to free Aldous from Nancy's spell, they had to flee – at once, without a backward glance or second thought, as fast as they could.

They packed all night and, exhausted and breakfast-less, left for Victoria and the boat train for Italy in the morning. Here, in two months flat, Aldous wrote *Antic Hay*.* This novel, published in 1923, depicting the aimless and self-absorbed life of London's cultural circles, has echoes of Nancy in its heroine, Myra Viveash, the woman for whom life, having, like Nancy, lost her real love in the war, was a despairing journey from lover to lover:

'Did you ever know Tony Lamb?' she asked.
'No,' Gumbril answered. 'What about him?'
Mrs Viveash did not answer. What indeed about him? She thought of his very clear blue eyes and the fair bright hair . . . 'I was very fond of him,' she said at last. 'That's all. He was killed in 1917, just about this time of year. It seems a very long time ago, don't you think?

Without Myra Viveash, the book would lack its central core. Even the wound of leaving Nancy is still raw on the page. 'What have I done to you?' Mrs Viveash asked, opening wide her pale-blue eyes. 'Merely wrecked my existence,' responds Gumbril. There are physical characteristics ('Her eyes had a formidable capacity for looking and expressing nothing; they were like the pale blue eyes which peer out of the Siamese cat's black velvet mask'), and even Nancy's walk, described by all her friends, in which she seemed almost to dance along the street while placing one foot directly in front of the other, is depicted: 'He watched her as she crossed the dirty street, placing her feet with a meticulous precision one after the other in the same straight line, as though she were treading a knife edge between goodness only knew what invisible gulfs.'

In *Point Counter Point* (published in 1928) the miseries of

* This means an absurd dance. The phrase comes originally from Christopher Marlowe's *Edward II*.

Huxley's obsession with Nancy are made even clearer, in the description of the agonies of frustrated passion felt by Walter Bidlake, who has fallen desperately in love with the Nancy figure, the sexually aggressive Lucy Tantamount, the rich and fascinating daughter of a highly social peeress: 'Critically, with a kind of cold intellectual hatred, Walter looked at her and wondered why he loved. Why? There was no reason, no justification. All the reasons were against his loving her . . . Lucy smiled, but said nothing. He flinched away in a kind of terror from her eyes. They looked at him calmly, coldly, as though they had seen everything before and were not much interested – only faintly amused, very faintly and coolly amused.'

What Aldous captured completely was Nancy's terror of being alone, her constant hope that something better would turn up, and her restlessness. 'I find it's really impossible to stay in one place more than a couple of months at a time,' says Lucy. 'One gets so stale and wilted, so unutterably bored.' He also put on paper his understanding of Nancy's attitude to him. Here is Lucy Tantamount on Walter Bidlake – but it could just as well be Nancy Cunard on Aldous Huxley: 'All the same, she liked him. Besides, he was clever, he could be a pleasant companion. And tiresome as it was, his love-sickness did at least make him very faithful. That, for Lucy, was important. She was afraid of loneliness.' Aldous also recognised that, like many beauties, she had a strong sense of entitlement: '[Lucy] looked from one to another with a kind of angry anxiety. The dread of solitude was chronic with her. And it was always possible, if one sat up another five minutes, that something really amusing might happen. Besides, it was insufferable that people should do things she didn't want them to do.'

In Italy, under a different sky, and without the constant possibility of seeing Nancy, Aldous's obsession gradually drained away. It had caused both Huxleys much anguish – but it had been a great help to Aldous's novels.

While Huxley was frenziedly writing in Italy, Nancy was spending the summer with Iris at Varengeville-sur-Mer, a small

Normandy town near Dieppe known for its sixteenth-century Manoir d'Ango. Friends, mostly male, came to stay – among them Eugene McCown, Michael Arlen and Man Ray. Ray had begun life as an artist, arriving in Paris in July 1921 with a trunkful of paintings, but when, after an exhibition of them, none was sold, he had decided that he would make his living as a photographer instead: Paris was full of what he called 'the great mass of daubers', but photography was considered commercial. Virtually alone in his field, he soon became well known, was asked everywhere and was able to photograph anyone he liked. One of these was Nancy, whom he photographed again and again.

A few months later, Ezra Pound, still deeply involved with Nancy, was cited as co-respondent by Bride Scratton's husband, who was divorcing her for adultery. By now, judging from the letter she wrote (but did not send), Bride knew that Pound's affections were elsewhere:

> I got your letter this morning expressing surprise that I had not made up my mind to settle in Paris. That seemed the obvious thing to do after the divorce. Yes, so obvious that one saw every step of the way one would take, until one was an old woman. That's why I'm not going. You must remember, in spite of my carrying the letter A round my neck, that I've been married fourteen years and had three children. And am in the ambiguous position of having no lover waiting to marry me ... I can face the barrenness of unwinding years in England but not from a cheap hotel bedroom or café table in Montparnasse.

For Bride, left with little to support herself and her children, it was a sad ending to the love that had given meaning to her life for so long.

At about the same time, now back in Paris, Nancy was healing the breach with Lewis. In December 1922 she wrote to him, 'Dear, dear Lewis, I get warmed when I am with you – you are a sort of black sun, dark earth, rich and full of new things, potential harvests, always dark, *plein de seve*, oil, blood, bread and comfort (among other things). I cannot get a nearer word than Rich. I love you very much.'

Eventually Lewis, compulsively drawn to Nancy but equally fearful of being drawn too much, replied, 'I . . . am thinking as I write "I must see her tomorrow" . . . but I must write in spite of that to say that I do not wish to be involved any more, just now, in your ZEX-LIFE.' Later, he was to claim that their affair had ended because Nancy demanded anal sex. In his diary she was usually referred to as 'Nan' but when, at the end of May, he noted that he was having dinner with her, the word 'Nan' was scratched out and replaced with 'Messalina' in capitals.

Maud came over as usual that spring, staying at the Paris Ritz, to order her spring wardrobe; Nancy herself stayed in the Hôtel Foyot, before leaving for Italy. Here GM wrote to her in February 1923, 'Your letter stirs my longing, always incipient, sometimes very active, for speech with you and sight of you. But you would not be content to journey with me [Nancy, finding that he had never been to Italy, had suggested a visit there]. I should become wearisome at the end of the week, despite the hill villages, their pictures and spires.' Instead she went by herself, booking rooms at the Brighton, in the rue de Rivoli, for GM later when he visited Paris, as he did most years.

On the bedside table she put a vase holding a large bunch of forget-me-nots – flowers more reminiscent of a country garden or hedgerow than the sophistication of Paris. It was a souvenir of the days when, as a little girl of nine or ten, she would walk with GM through the Leicestershire lanes and fields, and he would tell her about the flowers they saw. His favourites were forget-me-nots.

CHAPTER 7

><+>-0-<+>-<

Le Quartier

As 1923 opened, Nancy was still in love with Ezra Pound. In her poem 'I Think of You', from *Sublunary*, her volume of poetry published in June 1923, she wrote of him:

> I go to the feasts adorned
> In a scarlet vestment.
> Bejeweled and hung with many trappings –
> Under these
> Burns the still flame that your hands alone may touch.

Another poem celebrated her friendship with Iris:

> Do you remember in those summer days
> When we were young how often we'd devise
> Together the future? No surprise
> Or turn of fate should part us . . .

Some of its lines seem prophetic. Nancy's life would be nothing if not turbulent, with seemingly a constant quest for the man or way of life that would answer her restless search for a purpose:

> Storms lie around us – shall we ever touch
> The stationary beacon of far flames
> Posed in the distance of an unknown sea?

The reviews of *Sublunary* were satisfactory. Although the *Manchester Guardian* said that her book showed 'promise rather than achievement', the *Observer* was kinder: 'Miss Cunard's poems are most noteworthy for a certain dignified intellectual quality and a determined shapeliness, a gracefulness of form. This latter quality we suspect her of depreciating. She is too often content to be clever in a rather arid way, following those neatly grotesque deities which the Sitwells have so carefully arranged in our modern house of poetry, deities quite unworthy of Miss Cunard's attention or prostration.'

Nancy and Pound still wrote to each other frequently. Although he had expected her in Rapallo in the early spring, she did not come, perhaps because of the constant presence of Dorothy, perhaps because he had also invited the twenty-three-year-old Ernest Hemingway: Nancy, though seldom sexually jealous, liked her men to focus solely on her. Instead, she went to Florence, having written to Pound with a tempting list of places in Italy they could visit. Other letters are full of sentences like 'How I should like to join you!'

In Florence, however, Nancy had one significant encounter. Her friends the Sitwells introduced her to an older man who, like GM, became one of the few who could influence her and someone whom to some extent she similarly regarded as a father figure. This was Norman Douglas, aged fifty-four, a writer well known both for his work and for the various scandals of his private life (his 'peccadilloes', as Nancy would delicately call them). He had left England in 1916 after jumping bail when accused of a sexual assault on a sixteen-year-old boy or, as he later described himself, 'formerly of England, which I fled during the war to avoid persecution for kissing a boy and giving him some cakes and a shilling' (he did not mention that the boy had complained to the police). Soon afterwards, his most famous work, the novel *South Wind*, a fictionalised account of life in Capri, with controversial references to moral and sexual issues, was published to acclaim.

They met in a noisy trattoria, Nancy on edge after warnings from the Sitwells: 'I should be *careful*, if I were you!'. And when

Nancy asked if Douglas was difficult to talk to their response was not exactly reassuring: 'Oh no, not at all, I shouldn't say that, though of course . . . well, you'll soon see.' When Douglas did arrive – he was, uncharacteristically, late – Nancy saw a tall, broad-shouldered, well-set-up man who almost at once drew out a beautiful little snuffbox and offered her some snuff; and for the first time in her life she tried it, managing not to sneeze. It was a good start: she had passed Douglas's snuff test. A month or two later, with Eugene McCown, she visited him in Capri, and their friendship gradually became established.

Hemingway also failed to join Pound in Rapallo, thanks to what any writer would regard as a catastrophe. He had been in Switzerland, covering the Lausanne Peace Conference for the *Toronto Daily Star*, when an influential editor asked to see more of his work. He wrote to his wife Hadley, asking her to bring some pieces; Hadley, thinking that it would help, put everything he had written, including carbons, into a suitcase, to take to him. While the train was still standing in the Gare de Lyon she got out to get a bottle of Evian water for the journey and when she returned to the carriage, the suitcase had gone. For Hemingway, the total and final disappearance of three years' work left him too depressed to follow up the chance of that profitable intro-duction.* For both of them it was a disaster they would remem-ber all their lives.

In March 1923 Nancy wrote to Pound telling him that she was reserving April for him. She was so anxious to see him that, although she had done her best to lure him away from his wife Dorothy, she said that if need be he could bring Dorothy along. But nothing came of the plan, nor did the idea that he, Nancy, Hemingway and Hadley go on a walking tour together come to anything.

---

* Only two stories, 'My Old Man' and 'Up in Michigan', survived, because they were in the mail. It is also possible that this loss helped to account for the honing of Hemingway's prose style. With so much to make up, he must have felt pressed for time and so began to write in the shorter sentences we know today.

In any case, Pound's feelings for Nancy, as for Bride Scratton, were growing less intense. He had just re-encountered the young concert violinist Olga Rudge at the salon of the rich, beautiful and influential Natalie Barney, to whose evenings came both those who, like Olga, now extremely successful, lived in handsome apartments on the fashionable 'Right Bank', and the bohemians of Montparnasse. Olga and Pound had first met briefly when Pound had reviewed a concert Olga gave at the Aeolian Hall in November 1920. When they met again Pound, himself very musical, was composing an opera and, in his usual generous fashion, pushing the work of a young American composer, George Antheil. Through Pound, Olga and Antheil began a long professional collaboration; through the discussions around these, Olga and Pound became lovers. It was a love that would last a lifetime.

Artistic and literary Paris was now focused round Montparnasse ('*le quartier*'). Here Nancy soon became known. 'Since Nancy's return to Paris the pulse of the inner circle of Montparnasse is beating much faster,' said the *Paris Tribune*.

Less known and considered unfashionable, Montparnasse had been found to be cheaper than the previous 'artistic' quarter, Montmartre; now, with the declining franc, it was cheaper still. The result was that more and more people, mainly young Americans, were arriving there. They came because the potent mix of high intellectual discussion and the simple acceptance of carnal desire, shot through with the romance of being young in one of the world's most beautiful cities, was irresistible. Or, as Ezra Pound put it, they thought that in Paris they could 'make it new'.

Of the small, cheap hotels that abounded in the *quartier* a favourite of these incomers was the Hôtel de Lisbonne (at the corner of the rue Monsieur-le-Prince and rue de Vauguard). Each small room that opened off the dark corridors had a washbowl and running water, only hot for half an hour on Sundays, although opposite was a bath-house that provided soap, towels and a certain amount of warm water. What the Lisbonne did have, unusually, was central heating, a reminder of home that may have attracted these expatriates. As so many lived there, it had a certain 'club' atmosphere, with groups gathering in each other's rooms to discuss life, love, work and the novel many of them hoped to write 'one day'.

The streets of the *quartier* were thronged – much of its trade took place on the pavements or in the road itself. First on the scene, early in the morning, might be a man with a herd of goats, usually with a dog to keep them together, who played a pipe to show that he sold milk straight from the udder. People would emerge from their houses with crocks as he passed and he would milk one of his black goats straight into the jug or bowl. Church bells and horses' hooves added to the noise on the cobbled streets; schoolchildren in black aprons and white collars clattered past in their high wooden *sabots* (loose clogs that fitted either foot).

Soon the knife grinders and umbrella menders would arrive, and the waiters in their black alpaca waistcoats and long white aprons put chairs out on the terraces as the first customers arrived for their coffee and croissants. Most of those living in cramped hotel rooms had no cooking facilities, but in workmen's cafés good meals could be had for a few centimes, while for a picnic in one's room there was excellent bread, cheeses, charcuterie, fruit and wine.

Butchers' shops, with their red and white striped awnings, were licensed to sell only beef and lamb – pork was sold at the delicatessen, along with pâtés, rillettes and sausages, poultry at dairy shops and horsemeat at the horse butchers. Vegetables – cheap and good – were sold from barrows in the street. There were markets everywhere, set up at dawn; on Sundays the huge open-air market on the Île de la Cité sold birds instead of flowers.

All along the Seine, and in the heart of Paris, there were fishermen; increasingly these were elderly men: as the franc tumbled, their pensions correspondingly shrank and any free meal was a bonus. At the end of their lines, fastened to long poles, were red-painted wooden floats. Seldom did they catch anything more than small fish, called *goujons*, which were fried and eaten whole, bones and all, rather like sardines or whitebait (when a shell had exploded harmlessly in the Seine towards the end of the war, fishermen had immediately rushed out in boats or used nets from the bank to scoop up the stunned fish).

Policemen, cycling in pairs, often wearing capes and carrying white sticks, were known as *hirondelles* (swallows). They would pounce immediately and ruthlessly on anyone who parked on the 'wrong' side of the street – specific days of the week were allotted to each side and were rigorously enforced – but, as art and literature were so respected in France, they often turned a blind eye to scuffles or alcoholic bad behaviour in the writers' cafés.

These café-bars were where what could be described as the cultural life of the *quartier* took place. Most people had a favourite, perhaps where their particular group gathered every day or which they found conducive to working or drinking, or both, so that they were full from early morning until closing time (which was whenever the proprietor chose).

Nancy was fortunate in having as a guide to this world her old lover and friend Robert McAlmon. He had described her thus in one of his poems, which he often used to recite at parties, sometimes while she was there:

> your straw pale hair,
> Your brittle voice machine-conversing.
> Allotted speeches, no neglect,
> A social sense of order,
> A sharp dry voice
> Speaking through smoke and wine,
> A voice of litheness
> A hard, a cold, a stern white body.

She could not have had a better guide to the pleasures and intricacies of Montparnasse life. Like Nancy, McAlmon, who lived mainly in hotels, was a night person. During the day he would work, either at his publishing business – his father-in-law had just given him $70,000 and he had founded the Contact Publishing Company – or in a newspaper office, then he would appear at the Dôme or Select to start drinking and to 'do nightlife', often with Nancy. Dinner would be followed by more cafés and dance halls, meeting friends on the way or parting from them, and often winding up at a nightclub. With his magnetic personality, whatever bar or café McAlmon patronised at that moment was where you saw everybody. Somehow, he always knew where the action was.

This was important, as telephoning was difficult and expensive. There were no telephones in the hotel rooms in which most of the *quartier* lived, the ones in bars were often broken, and instructions as to when to put in the *jeton* (token given in exchange for money for the call) were frequently complicated; to call long-distance one had to queue at the nearest post office. Much communication was by '*pneu*': people would take their note or *pneu* to a post or telegraph office, where it was placed in a small capsule. This in turn was shot to its destination by air pressure through a network of tubes that went through sewers, along rail and subway lines and across bridges, the capsules inside them speeding along at anything up to thirty kilometres an hour. But most Montparnos – as the inhabitants of the *quartier* were called – relied on bumping into friends in the street or leaving messages at cafés they were known to haunt.

McAlmon knew everyone, and had drunk with most of them, thanks to the largesse from his marriage usually picking up the bill (he also funded his friend Ernest Hemingway's first trip to Spain to see a bullfight). His capacity for alcohol was legendary. Nancy had seen him drink six double whiskies in half an hour and remain sober. By now she herself was a considerable drinker, although this did not seem to affect her appearance, so glamorous that whenever she entered a room heads turned.

In London, most of the literary scene was dominated by men. They were the editors of the small literary magazines for which so many of them wrote, and they led most of the new movements such as the Vorticists. In Paris, by contrast, the great literary hubs, and many of the personalities, were female, and largely lesbian.

For the American and English writers, the throbbing heart

of Montparnasse was Shakespeare and Company, the English-language bookshop and lending library run by the young American Sylvia Beach. Sylvia had first established it in 1919 in a disused laundry then, at the instigation of her friend Adrienne Monnier, owner of a similar but French-language bookshop, moved to larger premises at 2, rue de l'Odéon.

These two women were very different in appearance. Adrienne was plump, a year older than Nancy, with blue-grey eyes, a round face and creamy skin. She was an excellent cook, famous for her chicken dinners. 'Adrienne was mildly spectacular,' wrote the journalist Janet Flanner in the column she wrote for the *New Yorker* magazine. 'Buxom as a handsome abbess, she was a placidly eccentric neighbourhood figure in a costume she had invented for herself and permanently adopted. It consisted of a long, full grey skirt and a sleeveless velveteen waistcoat worn over a white blouse.' Her bookshop, the centre of all that was avant-garde in French writing, was also grey and white.

Sylvia, described by Janet Flanner as thin as a schoolgirl, and in her white blouse with a big white turndown collar 'like one of Colette's young heroines', was short (five foot two inches), slim, and had lively brown eyes, wavy brown hair brushed back and thick below her ears, good legs and usually wore a brown velvet jacket. When she took her shop, she covered the dampish walls with sackcloth, laid white woollen rugs on the floor and had the façade painted. Some of the shelves holding the books had been made by Ezra Pound, who had visited the bookshop almost as soon as he arrived in Paris. During the course of their conversations, said Sylvia, he had asked her if there was anything she wanted mended – he was very proud of his carpentry (he had constructed tables out of packing cases and chairs from boards and canvas for his own flat). 'He mended a cigarette box and a chair,' said Sylvia.

Outside there was a sign with a picture of Shakespeare hung, in un-Parisian fashion, at right angles to the façade like an English pub sign. In the winter the little shop was deliciously warm, with a big stove. There were tables and shelves of books, with new ones in the window and photographs on the wall of famous writers. Inside there were always people borrowing books, talking to Sylvia or each other, even working. 'No one that I ever knew was nicer to me,' said Hemingway of Sylvia. Nancy, who was one of the first subscribers to the library, often visited the little shop; McAlmon, another habitué, used it as a mailing address.

At the same time as opening these new premises, Sylvia had moved into Adrienne's apartment, renting out the rooms above her own shop. Into one of them moved George Antheil. 'I have found a new lodger for my third room above the shop,' Sylvia wrote to her father. 'How lucky I am to have these rooms to help me balance the budget!' When the twenty-two-year old Antheil was late back he would reach his room by swinging himself up via the drainpipe, hanging sign and balcony to avoid the concierge, who would have given him a lecture – concierges were everywhere and knew everything that was going on.

If Sylvia had done nothing else, her place in Paris's pantheon of the arts would have been secured for ever by her publication (on 4 February 1922) of James Joyce's *Ulysses*, which had exploded like a supernova among the Paris literati. After a successful prosecution for obscenity in the US when extracts had been published in the *Little Review* (so ruining the magazine it was forced to close down), no one else had dared touch it. Yet with no capital, no previous experience of publishing and no real idea of whether it would sell or not Sylvia took it on, an act of faith that overcame everything, from the author's almost indecipherable handwriting and constant alterations to the probability of a second obscenity trial.

She had suggested publishing it when Joyce had called on her at the shop, wearing his dark-blue serge suit, grubby white tennis shoes, black felt hat cocked on the back of his sandy-haired head and carrying an ashplant. Sylvia, deeply in awe of him, listened as he sat in the comfortable armchair beside her table and told her of his pressing problems – he had to find somewhere for himself, his wife and their two children to live, he had to feed and clothe them, and he had to finish *Ulysses*. The owner of the flat he had been lent was returning in two weeks, and he had spent all his savings on coming to Paris – if Sylvia knew of anyone wanting lessons in English, German, Modern Greek or Latin, would she send them to him? He also spoke Spanish, Dutch and the three Scandinavian tongues – he had learnt Norwegian to read Ibsen. He wrote at night, he said, after the day's lessons were over.

'Would you let Shakespeare and Company have the honour of bringing *Ulysses* out?' Sylvia asked Joyce, who accepted delight-edly, at once. She planned on an edition of 1,000 copies and, to help finance the book's printing, and assisted by Hemingway and McAlmon, organised a subscription list, sending out notices of its publication to likely subscribers. Most took it up at once, but the response of Joyce's countryman, George Bernard Shaw, was unequivocal.* Having said that he had read a few of the extracts from *Ulysses* that had already been published, GBS launched into a denunciation of the depravity and foul language to be found in Dublin. 'I should like to round up every male person between the ages of 15 and 30 and force them to read [it],' said his letter, concluding, 'In Ireland they try to make a cat cleanly by rubbing its nose in its own filth. Mr Joyce has tried the same treatment on the human subject. I hope it will prove successful.'

GM's verdict was more succinct: 'Joyce has invented a language that only Joyce can understand.'

As it was, the costs she incurred almost wiped Sylvia out. Meanwhile, Joyce, whose attitude to money was that others should provide it, and who believed that as a genius he was en-titled to a comfortable life, was successful in both these aims. Through Pound he met Madame Savitzky, who not only lent him her rue de l'Assomption apartment but also said that she would translate his *Portrait of the Artist as a Young Man* into French, while Robert McAlmon and a surprising number of others gave him money. Nancy was not one of them: although a number of her friends, like McAlmon and Ezra Pound, saw Joyce often, she did not meet him until many years later.

McAlmon, one of whose main reasons for coming to Paris had in fact been to meet Joyce, did much of the typing of *Ulysses* (of

---

* Joyce himself had a bitter dislike of Ireland.

course for nothing). The two would meet for an aperitif most nights, after which the Joyce family could be seen dining in one of the most expensive restaurants in the locality, Le Trianon, at the corner of the boulevard Montparnasse and the rue de Rennes. Never once did Joyce invite Sylvia to join them (she also had to ban dogs from her bookshop as Joyce did not like them).

'I understood from the first that, working with or for Mr Joyce, the pleasure was mine, the profits were for him,' she said, adding loyally that it had been 'an infinite pleasure' to produce this work describing the outer and inner life of three people – Stephen Dedalus, a young Irishman, Leopold Bloom, who collected advertisements for a Dublin newspaper and Bloom's wife Molly – during one single day, 16 June 1904.

After typesetting had begun, in Dijon, Joyce, in a kind of postscript ecstasy of creation, scribbled some 90,000 additional words on the costly, repeatedly reset proofs, making a 400,000-word volume, of which Sylvia had managed to have two copies printed for his fortieth birthday, on 2 February 1922 – one for him, one for her. All the subscriptions were taken up and the book was hastily despatched to English and Americans subscribers before the authorities had time to catch up with the innocent-looking parcels.

One unexpected result of *Ulysses'* success was that many aspiring writers now thought of Shakespeare and Company as a publisher of erotica and would turn up with sheaves of salacious fantasies, often insisting on reading the choicest morsels to an unwilling Sylvia. One of them was Frank Harris, armed with his luridly explicit memoir *My Life and Loves*. He was successfully pointed in the direction of another publisher.

One of the earliest subscribers to the Shakespeare and Company lending library was Gertrude Stein, founder member of the sapphic colony devoted to words. She did not, however, come to borrow; she took, said Sylvia 'little interest ... in any but her own books'. Gertrude had lived in Paris since 1903, amassing a collection of notable pictures (mainly through her brother Leo, with whom she subsequently fell out since he could not abide her writing) by Picasso,* Picabia, Matisse and Braque. Egged on by her brother, she had been one of the very first to buy from Picasso; *Jeune Fille aux Fleurs* was her first purchase, from the atelier Picasso shared with other artists and in which he worked in garage mechanic's overalls. From 1906 onwards she bought more and more of his work. Her patronage was invaluable, contributing greatly to his success; his growing reputation increased the value of her collection.

Gertrude Stein was someone who was both revered and ridiculed but always taken seriously – most of all by herself. She was utterly sure of the genius of her extraordinary, repetitious style of writing – as in this paragraph from her best-known work, *The Making of Americans*:

> There are many that I know and I know it. They are many that I know and they know it. They are all of them themselves and they repeat it and I hear it. Always I listen to it. Slowly I come to understand it. Many years I listened and did not know it. I heard it, I understood it some, I did not know I heard it. They repeat themselves now and I listen to it. Every way that they do it now I hear it. Now each time very slowly I come to understand it. Always it comes very slowly the completed understanding of it, the repeating each one does to tell it the whole history of the being in each one, always now I hear it. Always now slowly I understand it.

Just as Picasso's portrait of Gertrude captured her personality, so did the poet Mina Loy summarise her style in her poem 'Gertrude Stein'.

> Curie
> Of the laboratory
> Of vocabulary
> The crushed

---

* His portrait of Gertrude, painted in 1906, hangs in New York's Metropolitan Museum of Art.

The tonnage
Of consciousness
Congealed to phrases
To extract
A radium of the word

Two of Gertrude Stein's phrases did indeed become famous: 'Rose is a rose is a rose is a rose',* coined in 1913, and 'the lost generation', though Ernest Hemingway gave this one a different genesis. Gertrude owned a small ancient Ford car, which Hemingway took to be repaired one day. The mechanic doing the repair was extremely slow and was chided by the owner of the garage with the words 'You are all a *generation perdue*', going on to explain that men become civilised between the ages of eighteen and thirty but that the war had blotted out that civilising period. When Hemingway repeated the story to Gertrude, she replied, 'That's what you all are. All of you young people who served in the war. You are a lost generation . . . you're all a lost generation, exactly as the garage keeper said.'

Gertrude and her companion, Alice B. ('Pussy') Toklas, swarthy, spider-like and with a wispy black moustache, lived at 27, rue de Fleurus. Gertrude was a big woman with a hearty laugh and legs like pillars (Robert McAlmon claimed that the toes of her sandals were like the prows of gondolas). When she received, her chair was the largest and highest in the room, placed throne-like in the centre; here she would sit, monolithic as an idol, to receive the homage she felt was her due from those younger writers she chose to receive. 'As she scratched her head and fixed you with her eagle eye you felt you were taking tea with a monument,' wrote Harold Acton, now moving between London, Paris and his parents' wonderful villa La Pietra, a mile outside Florence.

Most of the expatriate Americans wangled an introduction and some were asked to return – those she did not wish to see again would receive a postcard from her saying, 'Gertrude Stein

---

* From the poem 'Sacred Emily', *Geography and Plays*.

declines further acquaintance.' Wives, though not welcomed, were tolerated, but talked to only by Alice, who fielded them expertly if they approached Gertrude. The refreshments offered were China tea or fruit liqueurs – framboise or Mirabelle. Nancy's first visit to Gertrude Stein had been when her mother brought her there as a little girl and – as recounted in *The Autobiography of Alice B. Toklas* (written by Gertrude) – 'very solemnly told her not to forget the visit'. She was taken there again by McAlmon, but as a woman was not very welcome.

It was a different story at Natalie Barney's Friday salon. Nancy always got on well with lesbians and the rich,* and gorgeous Natalie was openly bisexual. She was stylish, witty, bilingual – she wrote equally well in French and English – and the centre of a lesbian circle. She lived in the rue Jacob, a narrow, ancient street; her small two-storey house, No. 20, was over 300 years old and hidden behind high walls with a large garden in which stood a little temple dedicated to Eros – sometimes, Natalie and her women friends would dance round it by moonlight.

Natalie rode daily in the Bois de Boulogne dressed in masculine attire, complete with bow tie and bowler, hence her nickname of 'l'Amazone'; living up to this, she would tap her chauffeur on the shoulder with a riding crop when she wanted to give him instructions (she owned an electric brougham). Hers was probably the most famous salon, in the true sense of the word, in Paris. From 4.30 to 8 every Friday during May and June, and again between 15 October and 15 December, Natalie would hold gatherings of fifty to seventy-five people amid the tapestries, gilt and velvet hangings that bedecked her house. For these literary evenings, soft-footed Japanese servants would open the door to guests, leading them into a darkish room – the daylight was filtered through the large trees in the garden – with chairs all around the walls, to where the slim, blonde Natalie, in a white Vionnet dress, waited to receive them. Here tea, cakes, triangular cucumber sandwiches and ices were served, and reputations made

---

* Born in Dayton, Ohio, she was the heiress to the Barney Railroad Car Foundry fortune.

or shattered. Sometimes there were plays, pageants or cultural readings, by writers of both sexes.

Natalie was a close friend of Ezra Pound, with whom she often played tennis, and they schemed together on how to support T.S. Eliot so that he could leave his job and concentrate on writing, but he refused the grant raised. It was Pound who introduced Natalie to George Antheil. Hers was above all a literary salon to which everyone came – Nancy, Somerset Maugham, Janet Flanner, André Gide, Gertrude Stein, Ford Madox Ford, William Carlos Williams, Louis Aragon, Sylvia Beach – while Ezra Pound introduced his friends T.S. Eliot and James Joyce. Two days before one of these evenings, Natalie would send her chauffeur to Shakespeare and Company to borrow the books of writers who had been invited, so that she could welcome them knowledgeably.

One of Natalie's closest friends was the American writer Djuna Barnes – in Barnes's later satiric chronicle of Paris lesbian life, *Ladies Almanack*, Natalie would be the central figure. Djuna too was bisexual; her fervent belief was that 'one fell in love with the person, not the gender'. She had arrived in Paris in 1921 on a lucrative assignment for *McCall's* magazine and, once in the city she admired for its freethinking and innovative arts scene, she had decided to stay on, earning her living by interviewing her fellow expatriate writers and artists for US magazines. Her literary reputation was already high, largely on the strength of her short story 'A Night Among the Horses', which had been published in the *Little Review*. Soon she was a well-known Montparnasse figure, chic in her black cloak and crisp, tilted hats. Her capacity for alcohol was also a good fit in the *quartier*; as she put it, 'After all, it is not where one washes one's neck that counts but where one moistens one's throat.'

Typical of those who had first seen Paris during the war and been drawn back to it was Ernest Hemingway, who had arrived as a foreign correspondent with his wife Hadley and almost no money. The Hemingways first lived in a two-room flat at 74, rue du Cardinal Lemoine, with a mattress on the floor as a bed; it was reached by a stinking spiral staircase with, on every floor, a cold-water tap and a crude pissoir. Their flat had no running water and an antiseptic portable container as a toilet, to be emptied every morning. Rubbish was carried down four floors to the courtyard. They subsisted largely on the cheapest vegetables from the nearby market plus, of course, plenty of cheap *vin ordinaire*.

Where Hemingway differed from most of his compatriots was in his capacity to rewrite his past and make of his outward persona a construct in which both he and others believed, notably that he was a war hero, victim of a tragic past and a man whose virility was barely held in check by the conventions of the day. In the latter he was helped by his appearance – he was tall, good-looking and well built – and a forceful personality garnished with what seemed an engaging modesty and pleasant manner.

He managed to convince Sylvia Beach, with whom he became great friends, that when he was a mere schoolboy his father had died suddenly and tragically (at the time he told her this, his father was very much alive), and that he had received his war wound fighting in Italy ('they thought I was done for'), rather than as an ambulance man handing out chocolates and cigarettes to the troops. Later he claimed that he had had an affair with Mata Hari, who was executed well before he had arrived in France. By 1924, he was telling the barman at Dingo's that he had fought bulls.

Gertrude Stein was very taken with him and soon told him that he could come in any day after five in wintertime – in the winter, the glazed-in terraces of cafés filled up with those who, like Hemingway, had no heating in their hotel rooms; here one could sit for hours behind a single glass of wine or *café filtre*. As there was a carpenter's shop beneath the Hemingways' flat (they were now living at 113, rue Notre-Dame-des-Champs) the noise was intense, so Ernest had taken to working at the nearby Closerie des Lilas café with its elderly moustachioed waiters, setting off each morning with the blue notebooks in which he always wrote, pencils in one pocket and a rabbit's foot in the other for luck. A visit to the Stein household, where he was an accepted acolyte and always given eau de vie, was very welcome on the way home. He knew, too, exactly how to treat Gertrude with the necessary reverence, admiration and total focus on herself – she seldom spoke well of any other writer unless they had written favourably of her own work. Joyce, in particular, was anathema. 'Mention Joyce twice and you would never be asked to come again,' said Hemingway.

Naturally, Gertrude regarded the attention surrounding the publication of *Ulysses* as direct competition with herself – which to her was, of course, forbidden – and was outraged. There was an immediate breach with Sylvia; Gertrude, who wished to formally record her displeasure at this *lèse-majesté*, called one day with Alice at Shakespeare and Company to announce that they were transferring their allegiance from her lending library to the American Library on the Right Bank. The response from Sylvia, who did not fear Gertrude's disapproval, was, 'Yes, a thorn is a thorn is a thorn.'

In the autumn of 1923, Nancy was put in touch with the two women who would become her greatest female friends in Paris, Janet Flanner and Solita Solano. One bond was that all three of them had failed marriages behind them. The thirty-five-year-old Solita, born Sarah Wilkinson (she changed her name when she became a drama critic), was pretty, with eyes of deep blue and a glossy dark bob – after George Moore met her, he wrote to her that 'I shall never forget the beauty of your very white teeth'. The petite Janet, thirty-one to Nancy's twenty-seven, had thick chestnut hair, small hands and a largish head that with its clear-cut features and emphatic jawline caused her friend Ernest Hemingway to call her 'The Great Stone Head'.

It was a time when female friendships, especially among the women of Paris, were forming and solidifying. The surge in independence of this post-war generation of women had given them confidence in themselves: no longer was it necessary to rely on men for entertainment, to beguile some man into taking them to a restaurant or café or, if none was available, having to stay at home. They felt in charge of their lives and acted accordingly, valuing the companionship and artistic insights they got from other women, and feeling able to confide in a female friend in a way often impossible with a man.

Nancy's new friends were a couple: Janet had fallen in love with Solita, the drama critic of the *New York Tribune*, and the two had settled in Paris in the autumn of 1922. They had first looked at the unheated, vacant apartment above Sylvia's shop, at 500 francs a month, linen included, but the thought of cold winters put them off; instead they chose a large room in a small hotel in the rue Bonaparte for less than a dollar a day, where they stayed for the next sixteen years, mingling with their fellow expatriates. 'We were a literary lot,' said Janet. 'Each of us aspired to become a famous writer as soon as possible.'

The three, introduced to each other through Eugene McCown, had met in a Montparnasse café one rainy evening. Nancy, typically, was late but only, as Solita later wrote, by an hour, 'which was quite early for her to be late': 'How could I have said, but I did, "You are late," to that golden head set with sapphires. "But of course, darling," she said kindly. We "got along" indeed. The three became a fixed triangle, we survived all the spring quarrels and the sea changes of forty-two years of modern female fidelity.'

CHAPTER 8

><+>-O-<+><

The Life of the Cafés

In early 1924 Nancy took an apartment on the Île Saint-Louis, 2, rue le Regrattier, at the corner of the Quai d'Orleans. This, her first real home of her own, was more than anything else the sign that Paris was where she felt she belonged. The ground-floor apartment she chose faced south and overlooked the Seine flowing deep below the high-walled embankment on which grew poplar trees – sometimes their feathery seeds blew in when the two tall windows of her salon were open on warm nights. Although small, her flat had great charm: the narrow dining room had an old oak table, a scarlet lacquer cabinet between two doors and green-panelled eighteenth-century walls on each side of the bookshelves – when GM came to dine, he could see in them a handsomely bound row of his own works. In one of them, given a couple of years earlier, was the inscription, 'To Nancy, with much affection, from her "first friend", George Moore, April 5th, 1922.'

Then they would chat in the beautifully proportioned little salon, its walls painted a smoky red above black wainscoting, looking across the river at the view of Notre-Dame, GM sitting on a comfortable settee covered in plum velvet. Here Nancy had installed her suite of Boulle furniture, Gaudier Brzeska's *Faun*, which she had acquired after reading the Pound memorial to the sculptor, and her pictures – two Chiricos, two Tanguys and a large Picabia gouache of a man with four pairs of eyes and a vermilion-spotted body.

Moore in his seventies was direct as he always had been. 'His speech was deliberated and clearly articulated, faintly Irish salted with homely expressions, apt but often astonishing in their context,' said Harold Acton, another constant friend. 'His opinions were dogmatic, intolerant and often perverse. He was given to sudden rants – against "those odious dogs that made the street so filthy", hooting taxi drivers, callers when he did not want them.'

Once, walking back slowly to her flat on the Île Saint-Louis after he and Nancy had lunched in Montparnasse, GM began to talk of love, breaking off in the middle of a sentence to gaze upwards to the third floor of a white and grey house; here had lived a woman with whom he had been deeply in love a long time ago. 'I was a great dab at making love, you know!' he told Nancy. As they continued their walk, he told her of other conquests and his 'prowess' in the art of physical lovemaking. He was now in his early seventies; earlier, he had written in one of his books that he believed his virility had declined after the age of fifty. Nancy realised, though, that he still appealed greatly to women, perhaps because he was a romantic. 'I am penetrated through and through by an intelligent, passionate, dreamy interest in sex, going much deeper than the mere rutting instinct,' he wrote. '[I] turn to women as a plant does to the light, as unconsciously, breathing them through every pore, and my writings are but the exhalations that follow the inspiration.'

It was at about this time that Nancy finally consented to a strange episode taking place. GM had always been fascinated by women's naked bodies; he once told how, when women fans wrote to him begging for a rendezvous, in his reply he would request a nude photograph. Many responded with just such a shot, which he would put in an album only (he said) if he had seen the originals. Reminded as always in Paris of the physical love he had enjoyed there in his youth – and probably also of the many nudes he had viewed as an art student – he had for some time been asking Nancy to allow him to see her naked. 'I am sure you have a lovely body – now why won't you let me see it? I am an old man,' he would say. One night, after dinner at the hotel where he had taken rooms, she agreed.*

'Suddenly, something within me said "Do this!"' she wrote in *GM: Memories of George Moore*,† 'and without more ado, facing away from him, I took off all my clothes, standing motionless a few feet from where he sat. How lightly, how easily it came about. My clothes left me, lying in a graceful summer pool on the floor as if they had slipped away of themselves. The night was warm and the mood serene. Without hesitation, my long, naked back and legs were at last in front of him and the silence was complete ... at length came a low murmuring sigh "Oh, what a beautiful back you have, Nancy, it is as long as a weasel's. What a beautiful back."'

That was all – except for the appearance of the phrase 'as long as a weasel's' describing a woman's back in GM's next book. His loving affection for Nancy never wavered. He admired her mind, he adored her beauty, she was above all the daughter of the woman he had loved for so long. They continued to write to each other regularly, GM often saying how he missed her: 'Dearest Nancy, here is a book you will enjoy reading [it was Longus's *Daphnis and Chloe*]. Do come back. I am still thinking of the two pleasant hours we spent together, for I love you very dearly.'

When Nancy was not out, she entertained, cooked for by her Breton maid, Anna Calloch. She had begun the collection of African ivory bracelets for which she became known, largely at the instigation of Curtis Moffat, the husband of Iris Tree, now living nearby. There were, too, new friends, made largely through Robert McAlmon, Ezra Pound and at Natalie Barney's salon. Other neighbours on the Quai d'Orsay were Ezra Pound's friends Harry and Caresse (formerly Polly) Crosby, one of the

---

* Three years later, Lady Diana Bridgeman told the diarist Chips Channon how she went to tea with GM in Ebury Street, where he described in detail of the novel he planned to write, to do with a Venus looking backwards over her shoulder. Eventually he asked Diana to undress and take up this pose, saying that it was so long since he had seen the posterior of a beautiful girl; 'it was the roundness, the colour, the contours he wished to study'.
† Published in 1956.

most extravagant and outrageous couples of the era, who had arrived in Paris in mid-March 1922, moving into their flat near Nancy in June 1923.

Harry and Caresse were *haut* Wasp, from Boston, with a background where morality was strict, divorce meant a steep drop on the social – and therefore often financial – ladder, and anything smacking of a bohemian life devoted to the arts was viewed with mistrust. Harry was another who had first been to France during the war, in which he had been a volunteer in the American Field Service and then served in the US Ambulance Corps, narrowly escaping with his life, and becoming one of the youngest Americans to win the Croix de Guerre for his bravery under fire. He was profoundly affected by the terrible sights he had seen during the war and could not settle in 'dreary, drearier, dreariest Boston', deploring all that went with it, its attitudes and especially 'Boston virgins who are brought up among sex-less surroundings, who wear canvas drawers and flat-heeled shoes', one of whom his parents would have undoubtedly ex-pected him to marry. In many ways, he was the male equivalent of Nancy: like Nancy, he had left his country; like Nancy, he believed in the kind of sexual freedom that allowed him to sleep with others while in a strong bond with one person; both he and Nancy wrote poetry; both travelled frequently, both looked wonderful, both bought what they wanted – in short, did ex-actly what they pleased, something for which both of them had enough money.

When Harry fell in love with Polly Peabody, a married woman seven years older than himself, the moment he met her, and the two became lovers within a fortnight, puritanical Boston was scandalised. When he eventually persuaded her to divorce her alcoholic husband and to marry him, the two felt the only escape from the clouds of disapproval surrounding them was the freer, more liberated air of Paris. Here Harry immediately flung him-self into a life of self-indulgence – fortunately he had an income of $12,000 a year, so that work simply wasn't worth it. During the brief period that he did have a job in Paris, Caresse (as he renamed Polly) would row him along the Seine to a landing stage

Nancy as a debutante, her style not yet fully developed.

Nancy's father Sir Bache Cunard, Bt, and her mother Maud at 'Black Ascot' in 1910. Although King Edward VII had died only a month earlier, his love and support of racing were so well known that it was decided not to cancel the meeting. Instead, everyone wore black.

Emerald Cunard at the
Strauss Ball, held at the
Savoy in January 1931.
She is accompanied by Sir
Jai Singh, the free-spending,
brilliant and charming
Maharajah of Alwa.

Nancy Cunard, painted
by Ambrose McEvoy, a
painting so considered
to evoke the spirit of the
Twenties that prints are
still available today.

George Moore, Maud Cunard's lover and Nancy's 'First Friend',
as a young man.

The Armenian-born novelist Michael Arlen, who became internationally famous with his novel *The Green Hat*, its heroine based on Nancy.

Ezra Pound, flamboyant red-haired American poet and founder of the Imagists, with whom Nancy was in love for years.

Aldous Huxley, who became so obsessed by Nancy that he could no longer work. Although not in love with him, she found him such an engaging companion that she kept him dangling.

Nancy and Henry Crowder working in the Hours Press.

Louis Aragon, novelist, poet, one of the three founders of Surrealism and later the leading intellectual of the Communist Party, was Nancy's lover for a turbulent two years.

near his office. On the way back it was to a chorus of whistles from the workmen who had been admiring Caresse's voluptuous figure in her tight scarlet bathing suit but who had earlier been restrained from expressing this approval by the sight of Harry in smart suit and bowler hat.

But work in a bank was not for Harry and, away from the inhibiting influence of Boston and all it stood for, he left his job. To the puzzlement and dismay of his strait-laced but loving parents, he told them he wished instead to spend his life as a poet. As they knew, he had written poetry from childhood, although they did not know that his twin obsessions were the sun – to be mystically worshipped and to serve as a focus for poems and dreams – and death.

Thereafter the Crosbys' life became one of excess, of sex, drugs, drink and high-roll gambling, spun from a belief that nothing was worse or more alien than convention and orthodoxy – one of their parties had a skeleton, with a black-bordered condom for a tongue, standing like the butler at the door. Nor did Harry allow his devotion to Caresse to preclude him from having affair after affair.

Nancy was out a lot, often meeting her new friends Janet Flanner and Solita Solano for lunch at Janet's favourite restaurant, La Quatrième République, in the rue Jacob, just below the Place Saint-Germain. When Janet asked the proprietor, who was also the cook, why it was so called, since at that time they were in the Third Republic, he replied gloomily that at the rate the government of France was running downhill, a Fourth Republic would soon be unavoidable: 'So I have named my bistro for it in advance, to be ready for the future without having to paint a new sign over my door, which would cost money.'

La Quatrième Republique was avant-garde in its décor, with a *trompe l'oeil* design of false steps, painted in Cubist style, running up the wall surrounding the narrow spiral staircase that led to the dining room on the second floor – their distorting effect treacherous for anyone with poor sight or a bit tipsy. The menu and the price, however, were fixed: hors d'œuvres, including a slice of Jura pâté flavoured with wild thyme and, as the main dish, a succulent stew or an escalope of veal, a salad, and goat's cheese, plus a small carafe of wine and a demi-tasse of black French coffee which, said Janet, 'tasted like death'. The price was about thirty cents, plus a ten-cent tip for the waitress.

Janet and Solita lived nearby, on the fourth floor of the Hôtel Napoleon Bonaparte, a building that could more properly be described as a rooming-house. Solita's description of it gives its flavour (and that of many other similar small 'hotels'):

> A narrow hallway ... served as reception room and was furnished only by a bench. A half-room off the hall held a chair, a table and the hotel telephone. The stairs began opposite the bench and continued upwards for five floors. At each turn was a landing, the *palier*, from which opened four doors, two on the street side two on the court ... 6 was where Jean Cocteau later held his levées and smoked opium, the third [floor] held 9, 10, 11, 12; then our floor, with rooms 13, 14 (a room of constant drama, marital and otherwise).

Room 15 was Janet's and 16 Solita's; these cost the equivalent of a dollar a day. Their rooms, with their dark-yellow wallpaper and faded roses, were steam-heated (at extra cost) and got the morning sun. To hers Janet added a large yellow armchair – known as 'Ernest's chair', as it was the one Hemingway always sat in when he visited them – leopard-skin throws and a small antique table for writing.

> The top floor was important to us all for next to room 20 was the hotel's only bathroom, containing a tub and a chair. The bathmat was five attached wooden slats. To have a bath it was necessary to notify the hotel's one and only servitor – the *garcon de tous les étages* – the hotel employed no maid. He drew the water, laid out a small towel and marked down the equivalent of 20 cents in his little black book. From 11pm the front door was locked and after that one had to cry '*Cordon, s'il vous plait!*' or ring a bell. This bell was at the head of the

garcon's bed and woke him, and he had to pull the cordon and ask who it was before allowing them in.

Only a block away, on the Place of the oldest church in Paris, Saint-Germain-des-Pres, were the Café de Flore and Janet Flanner's favourite, the café Les Deux Magots, where the two breakfasted every morning at nine (cooking was not allowed in their rooms). Here Janet would meet Ernest Hemingway for an evening of drinks and talk – on Stendhal, on detective stories, on how to write – sitting at a table at the back, near the toilets; here Nancy would join Janet for Janet's preferred aperitif of fruit juice and Cinzano.

Sometimes such evenings were spent at the Montparnasse cafés.* The *quartier* was the epicentre of *Les Années folles* (the 'Roaring Twenties'), and the cafés were where this seething life took place. Here those drawn to the city known to be the centre of intellectual and artistic life argued, sometimes fought, endlessly discussed the questions of the day and each other or poured out their life stories to strangers over glass after glass of harsh white wine.

Paris cafés usually had a long zinc bar – they were in fact often called *les zincs* – a few tables, sometimes marble-topped, with bottles stacked in shelves behind the bar and a terrace outside, often with a green and white striped awning above, on which customers sat when the weather was warm enough. As it got colder and the *terrasse* grew chilly, charcoal braziers were placed there strategically. The saucers in front of you indicated how many drinks you had had.

At the beginning of the Twenties Le Dôme was *the* café. It had originally been a small bistro for working men, but sudden popularity came when one sunny morning the manager of the Rotonde, opposite and then much busier, and favoured by artists such as Modigliani and Picasso, had seen a young American girl

---

* The 'mountain' from which Montparnasse took its name was a grass-covered heap of rubble from an old quarry then on the edge of Paris, to which seventeenth-century students from the Latin Quarter would go for some fresh air and which they ironically named 'Mount Parnassus'.

sitting on his terrace who was smoking and, almost worse, not wearing a hat – hats were then worn by virtually everyone and few 'respectable' women smoked in public. He went up to her and asked her to sit inside if she wished to smoke. 'But why?' she said. 'The sun is lovely. I am not causing any trouble. I prefer to stay here.'

As the argument continued a crowd began to gather, with most of the English and Americans championing the girl. Finally she stood up, saying that if she could not smoke on the terrace she would leave. And she did; and, like the queen bee leading the swarm, she was followed by all the English and Americans in the Rotonde as she crossed the street to the Dôme, where she asked the patron if she could sit on its terrace without a hat and with a cigarette. He agreed immediately, and from then on the Dôme was frequented by most of the English and Americans as well as artists. (Tourists were more apt to go to the Rotonde, newly revamped to become more upmarket, with a large dance floor and higher prices.)

Would-be artists' models – young girls up from the country, drawn by the glamour of Paris or simply to earn a living – came to the Dôme hoping some artist would ask them to pose. One of them was Kiki, who had become one of the most famous women in Montparnasse, with a regular table, seating about ten, at the Dôme. A voluptuous creature with a cropped black bob, porcelain skin and huge cat-like green eyes, Kiki had haunted the cafés from the age of sixteen onwards to try and meet young artists from whom she could earn money by posing or singing. As she wrote in her memoirs, when that failed she could 'get two francs by showing my bosom' to old men behind the Gare Montparnasse: 'Sometimes I got five francs. I have a terrific bosom.' From time to time she would burst into some highly improper song, always in French, for which she would be wildly applauded. Then she would snatch a hat from one of the café's customers and pass it round.

By the time Nancy and her friends arrived, Kiki was one of the sights of Montparnasse. She lived with Man Ray, whom she had met one night at the Rotonde. When he asked her to pose for him (then, 'posing' almost invariably meant in the nude) she refused at first, saying this would reveal her 'physical defect'. When he finally persuaded her this 'defect' turned out to be that she had virtually no pubic hair: 'I have to make myself up with black crayon.' Fortunately, this cosmetic camouflage enabled her to overcome her embarrassment and she soon moved in with Man Ray. After he had finished work, Kiki would take a bath, after which she would spend hours getting ready to go out – for her each evening was a performance. Often Man Ray would design her a face for the evening – eyes embellished with blue, copper, silver or jade-green eyeshadow, eyebrows shaved so that he could draw new ones.

So well known was the Dôme that on nights when a big celebration was taking place among the journalists who staffed the various American papers, one or two policemen would be stationed outside whatever venue they had chosen, ready to help anyone who stumbled out to the taxi rank or, if they were too drunk to remember their address, send the taxi to the Dôme, as someone there would be bound to know where they lived.

Often when Nancy, Janet and Solita went out for the evening they would wear some of the exquisite dresses, perhaps from Poiret or Vionnet, sent to Nancy by her mother, who came over every year to replenish her wardrobe, invariably buying more than she needed; she once told an interviewer that her dress-maker's bill frequently ran into thousands as she was usually in such a hurry that she would order ten or twenty dresses at once, wear perhaps two or three and give the rest away.

The three young women were a striking trio, Solita small, dark and pretty, Janet chestnut-haired and handsome, Nancy, in Solita's words, 'with Nefertiti's proud eyes and fine taut mouth painted scarlet [a certain lipstick of the period was called A Scarlet Wound]'. Sometimes they would dine first at 'the Grattery', as Nancy's flat in the rue le Regrattier was known, before spending an evening dancing at one of the bals musettes to be found in a winding street leading down to the Panthéon – le fox (the fox-trot, a recent import from America) was beginning to catch on.

These *bals musettes* were dances open to all, with a modest band, sometimes only a violin and an accordion (the *musette*), places where a young workman, shopgirl or student might go for an evening's enjoyable dancing. Dress was informal – men often kept their hats on or their cigarettes in their mouths – and entry was free, but anyone who wanted to dance had to buy a dance token, usually a metal tag, collected by a man with a large bag who moved among the couples on the floor. Often, especially if it was the woman who had asked the man to dance, it was she who paid. Most were highly respectable, so much so that you did not speak to your partner – that would have been considered an invasion of privacy – yet the French danced so close together that women's arms frequently encircled the men's necks, and men often abandoned the conventional ballroom position for something more like a hug.

There were also *boîtes à la musique*, like Nancy's favourite, Le Jockey, at the corner of the rue de Chevreuse and the boulevard Montparnasse. This was decorated on the outside with brightly coloured figures of cowboys and American Indians; inside, its central pillar supported many of those on the way to full intoxication. Here too Kiki de Montparnasse reigned. From time to time, while the black pianist was thumping out *le jazz hot*, she would sing here as well, drawing as usual from her repertoire of filthy *chansons* (when Chanel gave a dinner for eighty to honour Diaghilev at the end of the decade, Kiki, drunk, chanted ballads of such obscenity that a government minister's wife stomped angrily from the room).

At the smart end of the scale was Le Grand Écart, which had opened under the auspices of Cocteau, after the success of his novel of that title and his other bar, Le Boeuf sur le Toit. This chic *boîte de nuit* had a brilliant jazz pianist, pale, golden-yellow walls and warm gold lighting, a perfect setting for the golden-haired Nancy, who arrived there one New Year's Eve wearing a close-fitting dress of cloth of gold.

There was also the newly arrived chanteuse Ada Beatrice Queen Victoria Louise Virginia Smith, better known as Bricktop (for her flaming-red hair), who sang and danced at a Montmartre club called Le Grand Duc. Her personality was what drew people. She would welcome visitors to the club with a handshake and often say goodbye to them the same way – sometimes finding a good tip in her hand afterwards. Tips were what turned survival into living – they meant a new dress, a good meal. 'Always let the customer raise his hand first,' she was advised 'and never set too long at a table – if you become too intimate, they get embarrassed about tipping you.'

Bricktop's breakthrough chance came when the extremely rich songwriter Cole Porter and his wife Linda, who lived in a grand house, all platinum wallpaper and chairs upholstered in zebra skin, discovered her performing in this small, half-empty club. Soon she was singing for them at lavish parties. To earn enough money for the club she planned to open she also taught the new dances like the black bottom (which you could dance solo or as a couple) and the Charleston, often at the Porter house near Les Invalides.

It was from Bricktop that Nancy, passionate about dancing, learnt the Charleston, and when Bricktop did open her club, the Music Box (but always known as Bricktop's), she was one of its most regular visitors, entering through its leather-covered door studded with brass nails and guarded by a black man in a scarlet and gold uniform. It was for Bricktop that Cole Porter later wrote his song 'Miss Otis Regrets'; the idea for the song emerged when Bricktop, who originally came from West Virginia, told Porter of a lynching in the American South: 'Well, that man won't lunch tomorrow.'

'Everybody belonged, or else they didn't bother coming to Bricktop's more than once,' Bricktop wrote in her autobiography. Dressed by Schiaparelli, wearing diamonds by Cartier, she would begin a number still standing at her cashier's desk, keeping track of her accounts. With her eye on every facet of the club's operation, she would pause a song to coax a reluctant customer to pay his bill or prevent others from coming to blows.

Another of Nancy's favourite café-bars was Dingo's, because its popular barman Jimmie Charters had just arrived there. Jimmie, a former boxer, was known as the 'Father Confessor' of Montparnasse and whatever bar he was behind was always full. Dingo's was small, with only six tables where the black filter coffee was served in thick sherbet glasses. But that did not matter, as everyone wanted to stand at the bar and talk to Jimmie, a man of infinite discretion and the fine judgement that allowed him to know when to extend credit, when a fight was about to break out and to nip it in the bud (he had been a good amateur boxer), and who genuinely liked all his customers. The trouble came when they occasionally persuaded him to go out on the town with them when Jimmie, normally extremely moderate in his drinking, would get so completely pie-eyed he would be sacked the next day. Nancy liked him so much that she offered to set him up in a bar of his own, but he refused politely on the grounds that it would then become merely a club for Nancy and her friends (the intention behind her offer), whereas he liked a wider spectrum of people.

The most riotous celebration of the year was the Quat'Z'Arts Ball, a night so wild that it made its opposite number, the Chelsea Arts Ball, look sedate by comparison. At the end of April or early in May each painting academy held a party to which the students were allowed to invite as many friends as they chose, but who would pay for admission. The profit from these went to organising the Quat'Z'Arts Ball, to which all the students were invited. Male students had to be genuine but, as no Frenchwoman with the remotest claim to respectability would have dreamt of attending, the women who did go were generally artists' models. Added to these were others who paid the price of admission – twenty francs for women, fifty for men – and were prepared to dress (though perhaps undress would be more accurate) the part.

The theme of the ball, always taken very seriously, was announced several weeks beforehand. In 1924 it was early Phoenician, involving the purchase of bottles of skin dye and the composition of elaborate headdresses, looked up in reference books – these were important as men wore little more than loincloths and women short tunics.

That night, Jimmie Charters recalled that his party of about one hundred and fifty, all in costume, met at about six o'clock for drinks and dinner. After dinner, they set off arm in arm up the boulevard in a procession that filled the whole width of the street. In front and behind were a number of police who were there not to prevent the band of partygoers causing trouble but to protect them should trouble start. For as Jimmie explained, on this one night of the year the students had the right to do whatever they chose, short of causing extensive damage to property or bodily injury, with full licence from the authorities.

And so as we marched up the boulevard we stopped every car that came along, removed from it any girl who seemed attractive, kissed her all round, and then proceeded to the next car. The girls so addressed took it in good part, though they were probably not so pleased when they found their faces literally covered with red paint!

His party tore through Claridge (in the Champs-Élysées), snatching drinks from guests or pulling their noses, and rushed screaming through corridors, flinging doors open.

Finally they got to the Luna Park venue for the ball, where men went through one door and women through another, their costumes checked for authenticity. In the hall were about 2,000 men and girls – before the evening was over most of them were completely naked except for red paint. The first event was a parade around the hall as costumes were judged, then came drinking, love-making and dancing to two orchestras.

One American couple, who had mistakenly turned up in full evening dress and been let in, were instantly surrounded by a howling mob of students, who stripped off all their clothes. 'They fled naked and naked got into a taxi,' recorded Jimmie, 'and naked rushed into their hotel, the Crillon, where the doorman quickly lent them raincoats to reach their room, their clothes, money and jewellery gone for ever. They left Paris the next morning.' When the ball finally ended the last few hundred survivors followed the tradition of nude bathing in the fountains of the Place de la Concorde to wash off the paint.

There was more partying on the national holiday of 14 July.

'Chinese lanterns hung in rows among the trees; bands played at every corner; everywhere people were dancing in the streets,' remembered the writer Malcolm Cowley. 'Paris, deserted for the summer by its aristocrats, bankers and politicians, forgetting its hordes of tourists, was given over to a vast plebeian carnival, a general madness, in which we had eagerly joined. Now, tired of dancing, we sipped our drinks and talked in loud voices to make ourselves heard above the music, the rattle of saucers, the shuffle of feet along the sidewalk.'

There were ten in Cowley's party. Flown by wine, they decided to cross the road and attack the unpopular proprietor of the Rotonde. The group set off, Cowley in a workman's blue shirt, old trousers and rope-soled shoes, Nancy's future lover Louis Aragon elegant in a dinner jacket, some of the girls in bright evening dresses, others in tweeds and all hatless – the crime for which the Rotonde's proprietor had earlier despatched the American girl to the Dôme. The attack began with insults until Cowley pushed himself through the crowd and hit the patron on the jaw. Unsurprisingly, he was thrown out – but the group felt they had made their point.

By now Nancy was a well-known figure in Montparnasse and a muse to many. Eugene McCown, with whom she had maintained a friendship, had painted her portrait, in which she wears a white shirt with turned-up collar, waistcoat and her father's top hat (she always said it was her favourite portrait of herself). T.S. Eliot had savaged her in an early version of *The Waste Land* as a spoilt, promiscuous society girl with literary pretensions ('The same eternal and consuming itch/Can make a martyr or plain simple bitch . . . But women intellectual grow dull/And lose the other wit of native trull'), and Robert McAlmon had edited her out. The future Nobel Prize winner Pablo Neruda celebrated her 'lovely sky-blue eyes', and the poet Mina Loy wrote a poem about and to her:

Your eyes diffused with holly lights
of ancient Christmas

helmeted with masks
whose silken nostrils
point the cardinal airs,

The vermilion wall
receding as a sin
beyond your moonstone whiteness,

Your chiffon voice
tears with soft mystery
a lily loaded with a sucrose dew
of vigil carnival,

Your lone fragility
of mythological queens
conjures long-vanished dragons —
— their vast jaws
yawning in disillusion,

Your drifting hands
faint as exotic snow
spread silver silence

As a fondant nun
framed in the facing profiles
of Princess Murat
and George Moore.

It was now that Arlen's *The Green Hat* came out; that Nancy was its putative heroine only added to her éclat. She herself was not pleased, complaining to Janet Flanner that a complete stranger had come up to her at a party and begun questioning her as to whether she was Iris Storm.

Everyone spoke of her looks. 'She was famous for what is called in French *son regard*,' said Janet Flanner. 'For her intense manner of looking at you, of seeing you and seizing you with her large jade-green eyes, always heavily outlined top and bottom with black make-up below her thick, ash-coloured hair.' When Ezra Pound's university friend William Carlos Williams, whose father was English and mother a Puerto Rican with French blood, arrived in Paris with his wife Flossie, he too was bowled over.

Williams was a man who successfully pursued two careers: that of family doctor specialising in paediatrics and prolific writer of poetry, novels, short stories and plays. With Ezra Pound, he had become involved in the Imagist movement while they both studied at Pennsylvania University. When he had arrived in Paris towards the end of January 1924 Pound was still in Rapallo, and it fell to the invaluable McAlmon to organise rooms for the Williamses in the Hôtel Lutetia and, in the main, to introduce them to the literary figures they so wished to meet. One, of course, was Nancy, about to set off for a few weeks in the South of France, but who would see them frequently on her return in May. The Williamses too left for the south and were visited one day by Nancy, who came, as Williams wrote, 'to invite us for a walk ... and to talk, of writing, of anything that was in her mind; and if there was anything that was not in that courteous, cultured and fearless mind, I have yet to discover it'.

Back in Paris, Williams took advantage of all Paris could offer, from exhibitions to meeting the various Montparnasse personalities. The first was James Joyce, through a dinner party on 22 January arranged by Robert McAlmon, almost inevitably at the Joyces' favourite restaurant, the Trianon. For Williams, who had hoped for an absorbing, in-depth literary discussion, it was a disappointment; instead of fascinating aperçus, Joyce got drunk and insisted on singing Irish songs – his wife, the red-haired, earthy Nora, always believed that he should have been a singer. It was, however, noteworthy for Nora's comment on her husband's best-known work: 'I guess the man's a genius, but what a dirty mind he has, hasn't he?'

McAlmon also took Williams to meet Gertrude Stein, although this too did not go as well as hoped. Williams, a busy and successful doctor who had had to deal with most aspects of human emotion and behaviour in his practice, as well as being a well-published author, had little time for what he saw as pretentiousness or self-promotion. So when he met Gertrude, it was out of interest rather than to sit at her feet like many of the other writers and aspirant writers who attended her salon. Gertrude, who believed that whatever she said was of interest to everyone, asked his opinion on what she should do with the numerous accumulated manuscripts of her work (she wrote and rewrote constantly). 'Oh, if they were mine, having so many,' replied Williams, 'I should probably select what I thought were the best and throw the rest on the fire.'

This sensible reply was heresy to someone so egotistical they felt that even their detritus was worth preserving. In that gathering, the shock of someone saying something so outrageous to the presiding deity produced a moment's stunned silence, until Gertrude pulled herself together and replied, 'But of course, Doctor, writing is not your metier,' to receive the immediate response, 'But Doctor Stein' – Gertrude had studied medicine at Johns Hopkins University – 'are you sure it is yours?' The visit did not end well. Gertrude was, after all, the woman who had once told Robert McAlmon that 'the Jews have produced only three originative geniuses, Christ, Spinoza and myself'.

The Williamses' last days before their return to the US in mid-June 1924 were crowded. On 28 May Williams, after playing tennis with Hemingway, who was also one of Nancy's tennis partners, spent the evening at Nancy's flat, talking with Iris Tree, Clive Bell, Robert McAlmon and Bryher from ten at night until five in the morning, when he went to a taxi drivers' stand, ate some fried eggs and watched the dawn. He and his wife slept until noon and then visited Mina Loy. After several more dinners at Nancy's apartment – and clearly, a front-row view of some of their goings-on – he wrote of Nancy and Iris, 'Depravity was their prayer, their ritual, their rhythmic exercises: they denied sin by making it hackneyed in their own bodies, shucking it away to come out dirtied but pure.'

When Pound returned from Rapallo, delighted to see his old friend, he took him to one of Natalie Barney's Friday salons. In his diary Williams wrote:

I admired her and her lovely garden, well kept, her laughing doves and her Japanese servants. There were officers wearing red buttons in their lapels* there and women of all descriptions. The story is told of some member of the Chamber of Deputies, a big, red-faced guy who had turned up there after a routine social acceptance. To his annoyance, as he stood lonely in the centre of the dance floor, he saw women about him, dancing gaily together on all sides. Thereupon he undid his pants buttons, took out his tool and, shaking it left and right, yelled out in a rage, "Have you never seen one of these?"'

At Natalie's, of course, few of the women would have been interested.

By now the Hemingways, who had moved with their baby son to cheaper lodgings at 113, rue Notre-Dame, were appallingly short of money. Hadley dressed in shapeless, long-lasting clothes, and Gertrude Stein taught Hemingway how to cut his wife's hair. Hemingway himself, who often skipped lunch as unaffordable, would occasionally manage to kill one of the Jardin du Luxembourg pigeons with a home-made catapult, taking it back hidden inside his jacket to roast on the fire for supper. When Williams realised their financial state, he offered as a friend to use his paediatric knowledge to check over their seven-month-old son Jack (always known as Bumby) and told them the baby needed circumcising. This he did for them on 4 June, noting that 'big, tough' Hemingway nearly fainted at the sight of his son's blood.

The operation was followed by another evening of heavy drinking at Nancy's, where Williams met Cocteau, before catching the boat train next morning. His final verdict on Nancy was, 'Nancy was to me as constant as the heavens in her complete and passionate inconstancy. Out of passion, to defy its domination [she] . . . kept herself burned to the bone.'

Ezra Pound, moved by the Hemingways' plight, managed to get Hemingway a job on one of the small magazines that constantly sprouted, bloomed for a while, then fell by the wayside.

---

* Presumably the red ribbon of the Légion d'Honneur.

This was the *Transatlantic Review*, that was to last for twelve issues, one every month of 1924. Before it finally folded, it published work by Hemingway, Djuna Barnes (whom Janet Flanner thought the most important woman writer in Montparnasse) and early extracts of Joyce's *Finnegans Wake*.

Its offices were at the top of an ancient wine cellar on the Quai d'Anjou; here also was Robert McAlmon's Contact Editions and Bill Bird's Three Mountains Press, later sold to Nancy. The *Transatlantic Review*'s editor was Ford Madox Ford, a large man with flaxen hair, pale-blue eyes and a habit of pulling a pack of cards from his pocket if he suffered from writer's block and playing patience until he felt words beginning to flow again. Hemingway's job was as his editorial assistant. For Hemingway it was purgatory: he disliked Ford intensely, largely because he had bad breath and smelt. Ford was a large man, and his odorous physical presence was overpowering in their cubbyhole of an office. 'I always had to go out of a shop as soon as I could when Ford came in,' said Hemingway. But thanks to working there, and guest-editing the August issue, he was able to do his friend Gertrude Stein a favour: sections of her magnum opus, *The Making of Americans*, began to appear in the *Transatlantic Review*.

Nancy, of course, had no financial worries. When she felt like writing poetry she wrote, compiling material for the collection that would appear the following year, 1925. Although it was clear to those around him that Pound's feelings for Olga were growing, Nancy was still emotionally enmeshed with him, as much of her poetry shows:

And . . . You and I,
Propelled, controlled by need only,
Forced by dark appetites;
Lovers, friends, rivals for a time, thinking to choose
And having chosen, losing,
. . . How long shall we last each other?*

---

* From *Parallax*.

CHAPTER 9

⊱┤◆⟩•○•⟨◆┤⊰

The Birth of Surrealism

Nancy's Paris was expanding rapidly. When she had first arrived in 1920, there were only about 5,000 or 6,000 Americans living in the city; by 1924 it was home to almost 30,000. Several factors accounted for this huge increase.

The first was that while tourists had been coming to Montparnasse for some time, attracted by the idea of the spectacle of artistic life, by now they were beginning to outnumber the resident colony and the natives. The introduction this same year of new cheap transatlantic steamship fares put the French capital more easily within reach of both tourists and those would-be artists and writers for whom Paris was a magnet; once arrived, thanks to the ever-descending value of the franc, they could live on a mere few dollars a week – a complete dinner could be had for as little as fifty cents.

Such a dinner naturally included wine – another great draw. The effect of Prohibition on the American urge to travel was profound. And Paris, where wine was cheap, often excellent, and drunk before, during or after every meal, was alcohol heaven, so much so that anyone comparing the delicious drink they were enjoying with the expense and often filthy taste of the bootlegged stuff at home would be likely to feel that the only possible answer was to have another glass. (Prohibition was such an alien concept to the French mind that the waiter at one of Janet Flanner's local restaurants asked her if it was a new religion.)

The third and possibly the most compelling reason was that

138

for anybody creative, the only place was Paris. There was no censorship, so that here books or articles forbidden by the obscenity
laws of other countries could be safely published. Here were the
small magazines, publications made possible by the economic
situation, that would print poetry or fiction that at home would
be greeted by a baffled stare – or in at least one case tossed on the
fire – and which gave new writers a chance not only to be heard
but, often more importantly, to declare themselves as published
rather than would-be writers.

And in this most romantic of cities, where lovers kissed
openly under the chestnuts on the banks of the Seine, they might
even find themselves enjoying love in a garret. John Glassco, a
young Canadian poet who had arrived in Montparnasse when
he was seventeen, wrote nostalgically of his studio apartment
with its skylight and large window looking out over the roofs
of Paris: 'Here I met the woman with whom I at last fell in love
and whom, however miserable the outcome of that love, I shall
always remember in this setting as she undressed one night in
a luminous haze of gaslight and moonbeams before we threw
ourselves in ecstasy on one of the ... straw-stuffed beds. It was
the theatre of my youth.'

There was sexual freedom of all kinds, taken perfectly for
granted rather than whispered of in corners disapprovingly,
catered for efficiently and treated with a sophisticated matter-
of-factness that enhanced Paris's reputation as the place to go
to for pleasure – sometimes wealthy young men would come
over from England for a night simply to visit one of its elegant,
upmarket brothels. One that opened that year was the One-
Two-Two, one of the most luxurious that even Paris had seen. Its
rooms were beautifully decorated, it was open from 4.00 p.m. to
4.00 a.m., the girls had a mere four sex sessions a day and there
was even a restaurant, staffed by waitresses wearing only high
heels and a camellia in their hair. Many who visited this deluxe
establishment came only to dine, smoke a cigar afterwards in
the salon and chat with the girls. All in all, the boulevards of
Paris could not have been more different from Main Street,
Smalltown, USA.

The unrest among young Americans interested in the arts was expressed by one of them, the talented Harold Edmund Stearns, author, journalist and literary critic, in *America and the Young Intellectual*. 'Something must be radically wrong with a culture and a civilisation when its youth begins to desert it,' he wrote:

> Youth is the natural time for revolt, for experiment, for a generous idealism that is eager for action. Any civilisation which has the wisdom of self-preservation will allow a certain margin of freedom for the expression of this youthful mood. But the plain, unpalatable fact is that in América today that margin of freedom has been reduced to the vanishing point.
>
> Rebellious youth is not wanted here. In our environment there is nothing to challenge our young men; there is no flexibility, no colour, no possibility for adventure, no chance to shape events more generously than is permitted under the rules of highly organised looting. All our institutional life combines for the common purpose of blackjacking our youth into the acceptance of the status quo; and not acceptance of it merely, but rather its glorification.

Handing the manuscript to his publishers, the thirty-year-old Stearns put his belief to the word and left immediately for France, arriving, like the Hemingways, Murphys (two rich Americans who were great friends of the Fitzgeralds) and Robert McAlmon, in 1921. His book was published soon after his arrival, not only giving him a halo of renown but encouraging more and more of those who saw themselves as the young he was writing about to follow him, a trickle that soon became a flood.

Stearns himself, with the kudos of an influential book already published, soon became known as the 'Quintessential Expatriate'. He moved into cheap lodgings in Montparnasse and, as he put it, an agreeable existence among (mostly American) 'students, newspaper men, artists or plain serious drinkers'. The latter description was the most accurate where he was concerned: he quickly settled down to the life of constant and continual imbibing that occupied so many.

By 1924 he was not a prepossessing figure. Typically, he would be unwashed and unshaven, in a dirty raincoat and battered felt hat, an outfit exchanged for a grubby white shirt and black suit in warmer weather, sitting drunk in some Montparnasse bar or, as one friend put it, 'screwed into his chair at the Select or the Rotonde as the saucers rose before him'.

Just as his money was about to run out, he was told there was a job for him at the *Herald* – many new arrivals took up some form of journalism on one of the two main Paris-American dailies, the *Paris Herald* or the *Paris Tribune* (the Paris offices of the *New York Herald* and the *Chicago Tribune*), or perhaps the *Continental Daily Mail*, from England. Although there were few staff jobs, owing to quick turnover through inefficiency or drunkenness, there were often vacancies for proof-readers, translators and general dogsbodies that paid the pittance needed to live on. Those thus employed would do anything from fetching another bottle to answering letters – Ezra Pound's alone were almost a full-time job. 'Daily the *Herald* received from Pound a letter or postcard, and some days both, laden with maledictions, obscene and scatological, upon persons and events reported in the paper, as well as upon the paper itself,' wrote Martha Foley, a young woman who had secured one of these poorly paid jobs. 'I was instructed, if I found nothing printable, to toss them in the wastebasket, which I did with the great majority of his angry scrawls.'

At the *Herald* Stearns worked as a reporter while filing a weekly Paris-letter column for the *Baltimore Sun* and *Town & Country*, achieving critical success with articles and essays. In 1925 he left the *Herald* for the *Tribune*, where he covered the races under a pseudonym – although his choices were eccentric, he was successful as a tipster (although often so drunk that he saw racehorses flying over the stands).

The eight-page *Tribune*, described by its staff as a 'front page of news backed up by several pages of rewrite and reprint', that emerged from an office at 5, rue Scribe was an extraordinary mixture of talent, incompetence, address bureau and sometimes sheer invention, staffed by a few regulars and a revolving-door cast of extras. Henry Miller (later famous for *Tropic of Capricorn*) was summarily fired, James Thurber – who worked on it for a year – was admired for his ability to spin a fifty-word cable from Chicago into an entire column. American tourists could register with it, so that their names and where they were staying appeared in next day's 'Arrivals' column, thus alerting friends of their whereabouts.

At the *Tribune*, the copy-readers sat round a large table, with the rewrite men and reporters at desks on either side. Through the tall windows of this upstairs room drifted the scent of plane trees, the smell of urine from the nearby pissoirs, the noises from the street of taxi horns, whistles and the chatter from the cafés. Cigarette smoke wreathed around the yellowed ceiling and liquid refreshment was never far away. Many of the staff kept bottles of wine in or under their desks, and even the paper's managing editor acknowledged that the *Tribune* had 'a fairly liberal attitude towards drinking', while Stearns declared that on any given day the editors could assume that a number of the staff would be useless because of drink, 'half because it was not there and the other half because it was'. Stearns himself was given to making up stories if he thought the ones he was told to write were too dull, such as an entirely fictitious tale about how the respected elder (whom he named) of a religious commune had had his beard caught in the automatic wringer of a steam laundry where he was working incognito.

Another deskman, when drunk, was unable to tell the difference between the real and what he imagined or hoped had happened. In the summer of 1924 Paris hosted the Olympic Games – no German athletes were invited – attended by the Prince of Wales, (later Edward VIII). While in Paris, the prince also laid a wreath at the tomb of the Unknown Warrior and dedicated an orphanage. When our deskman was given a handout on the dedication to rewrite into a news story, he produced the following: 'Stopping before one manly youth the Prince enquired: "What is your name, my lad?" "None of your goddammed business, Sir," the youngster replied. At that, the Prince snatched a riding crop from his equerry and beat the boy's brains out.'

The story went through copy-editors and proof-readers – all presumably half cut – and appeared on page one under the headline 'Prince of Wales Bashes Boy's Brains out with Bludgeon'. Fortunately, the prince accepted the paper's apology and did not sue. The rewrite man was fired and lived happily for a while on the free meals and drinks bought for him by those who wanted to meet the man who had accused the Prince of Wales of murder.

Thanks largely to the huge number of these American arrivals and their uninhibited downing of glass after glass, one prominent Methodist churchman suggested to the US House Judiciary Committee that too many young American males, veterans of the European campaign, had been corrupted by what he called the 'free moral life of France'. They had gone, he alleged, as innocent country boys and been infected by what the *New York Times* called 'conditions of vice such as they had never seen before' – conditions that they embraced with such open arms that the French Academy of Sciences soon announced that alcohol consumption had doubled since 1920.

Paris was a place, said the *Washington Post,* * where the average taxi driver had been involved in five separate accidents, where they fought with their fists in parliament and where luxury and extravagance combined in a fashion that could only be called titillating – look at Mistinguett, the popular actress famous for her risqué routines at the Folies Bergères, who bathed in champagne and owned 320 pairs of shoes.

But so far the drinking of the tourists was nothing on what those who had settled in Montparnasse consumed. Sometimes an almighty binge† might lead to a disappearance of weeks instead of days, with someone working steadily for months at a time then dropping out of sight. The well-regarded novelist Elliot Paul, stocky and black-bearded, who had the closest ties with literary and artistic Paris and was a legendary carouser, would disappear for months when his royalty cheques arrived. One day, recalled the *Tribune*'s managing editor, 'he rose from his desk,

---

* On 1 March 1924.
† To go on such a bender was known as *faire la bombe*.

stretched and went out to get a sandwich. That was the last we saw of him for several months.' As a star, he was welcomed back as if nothing had happened.

James Joyce was another notorious for over-indulgence, or, as Janet Flanner put it, getting 'fastidiously intoxicated'. On one bender described by his drinking partner Robert McAlmon they were turfed out of the Gypsy Bar at 5.00 a.m. when it closed, and decided to finish the night at a small bistro on the boulevard Saint-Germain, where they bought cigars and decided to drink their way through the list of French drinks. Joyce kept dropping his cigars, and when McAlmon was no longer able to pick them up without falling on his face they lit them, after which they burnt cigarettes. 'At ten in the morning we sat alone in that small bistro,' wrote McAlmon, 'the floor covered with some twenty cigars, innumerable cigarettes, and the table with the forty glasses which had held the various drinks we had taken.' Finally, with the aid of the patron, they took a taxi to Joyce's hotel, after which McAlmon returned to his 'to sleep, to die, to know agony, to curse Joyce, life, drink and myself . . . it took me three months to get mildly into order with health after that night'.*

The alcoholic leitmotif of life in Paris suited Nancy perfectly, as it was already so much part of her own behaviour. Although dependent on alcohol and often half tipsy, she never became a *poivrotte*, as female drunkards were known, and almost always could talk and argue clearly. Occasionally her excesses left a mark, as when at one lunch party she appeared with a black eye and scratches, having tried to climb a tree the night before and fallen, but these could be explained away by high spirits or a dare. Perhaps the most accurate summing-up of her usual state was through the assessing eye of the experienced doctor William Carlos Williams: 'I never saw her drunk; I can imagine that she was never quite sober.'

Although she was constantly making new friends, Nancy was good at keeping in touch with old ones – especially her beloved GM, whose views on her work were valuable to her. 'When you

---

* Neither Joyce, Stearns nor McAlmon reached the age of sixty-one.

were a little girl I used to talk to you about an anthology of pure poetry,' he wrote to her at the beginning of March 1924. 'But you were too young to understand objective poetry and now the anthology is completed. Would that we had searched out the lovely flowers together but we cannot go searching for poetry whilst a sea is between us. I propose to cross the sea in May and to spend a month near Fontainebleau. Shall I see you or are you going to spend the month of June in London?'

Shortly afterwards, anxious for her company, he wrote, 'I see now that to be intimate with you I must study free verse else resign my post as critic of your verse and an exponent of your talent, and so I propose to read some of Eliot's verses with you when you come to London in 10 days or a fortnight. You shall be guide.'

Like GM, Nancy was immensely supportive of her friends. When Solita Solana's first novel was published, she wrote not only to Solita but also to Janet Flanner: 'I am reading Solita's book and am very much impressed. I think it's almost astounding. I shall make Mortimer read it and perhaps he will write a review, though it seems to me that the better the book the less important it is that it has a review.'

Settling in Paris had not removed the restlessness that was so much part of Nancy's nature. Always attracted by the new, the avant-garde, the distant, she still travelled constantly. In March 1924 she went to the South of France – to Sanary and Monte Carlo – and in the summer to the country, near Dieppe. Here, as she told Janet Flanner, she had intended to work very hard on a translation of *Faust* for her new lover, Tristan Tzara.

Although still yearning for Ezra Pound, Nancy had begun an affair with Tzara, a Romanian-born poet, essayist and performance artist of Jewish extraction – he was born Samuel Rosenstock – who had come to Paris in 1919. Quiet and reserved in person though quite the opposite on stage, he was the same age as Nancy, slim and pale with large, dark intense eyes, over one of which he wore a monocle, and he was the high priest of Dadaism. Tzara, along with the faithful Eugene McCown, accompanied her when she met Norman Douglas in Bologna – Nancy remembered the great 'spread of dishes and wines', both of which meant a lot to Douglas.

It is easy to understand Nancy's involvement in Dadaism, a seemingly nonsensical movement. The underlying theme of Dada was revolt – revolt against what had gone before, notably the 'reason' and 'logic' of bourgeois capitalist society that had led people into war, a revolt expressed in a rejection of such logic and the embracing of chaos and irrationality; all paralleled in a sense by Nancy's own life, with its rejection of ordered days, its somewhat chaotic spur-of-the-moment decisions to do this or that, or visit a place not yet known, and its deliberate refusal to be part of the highly capitalist society into which she had been born.

One of those Nancy met through Tzara was the Romanian sculptor Constantin Brâncuşi, one of the pioneers of modernism with his smooth, geometric yet symbolic forms. To Brâncuşi Nancy seemed the embodiment of the Twenties and her style and beauty captured his imagination. 'Everything about the way she behaved,' he recalled, 'showed how truly sophisticated she was for her day,' and it was not long before he wanted to sculpt her. He would have had plenty of time to study her: unlike the other Montparnos, Brâncuşi never entertained in the cafés but always in his studio, which was filled with his sculptures. He was famous for his chicken dinners, cooked on his open wood stove, and his cold bean purée, served with garlic mayonnaise. Although Nancy never posed for Brâncuşi, several sculptures of her by the great Romanian artist appeared later.

Nancy found Dada's revolt against the conventional entirely sympathetic. From the days when she had fought shy of the debutante circuit and all that it had involved, she had sought a new way of living, and a new circle of friends, something that required enormous determination and the ability to disregard the views of those around her. Today it is difficult to realise how much in thrall England was then to the idea of a distinct social order; and that if you were born into a particular stratum, that is where you stayed. Nancy had deliberately left hers, although through her cousins Edward and Victor Cunard and her mother she continued to return from time to time, and the manners and mores of her upbringing and background gave a gloss of distinction and elegance to her personality. As for the irrationality, she watched with amusement as Tzara delivered the Dadaist manifesto with a croissant dangling from his left nostril or arranged a reading of a poem in several different languages simultaneously.

Tzara himself wanted to create an art free of logic, to expose the absurdity and deficiency of 'knowledge', specifically that which had led to the First World War. It was an approach with which Nancy, who had lost not only her great love but so many of her friends in the fighting, found herself in agreement. The fact that the Dadaists' antics caused crowds to gather and pelt them with fruit and vegetables while shouting insults, thus drawing the police, only appealed further to the revolutionary in her, an instinct that was steadily growing and that would, in the next few years, flower into outrage, and action, against anything that she perceived as an injustice.

The liveliness of Dada, with its irreverence and unexpectedness, in contrast to the serious and intense discussions on art, literature and the life of the intellect that hung as thick as the cigarette smoke in most of the cafés, created an atmosphere that is best described as fun. For Nancy, this light-heartedness was something that she enjoyed almost as a holiday.

She and Tzara would spend whole evenings at Le Boeuf sur le Toit where Cocteau, one of France's leading intellectuals, was also in time-off mood. In red tie and opera hat he would play the drums, or the pianist would play jazz versions of Bach fugues while Nancy and Tzara danced, or sat at their favourite table under Picabia's painting *L'Oeil cacodylate*, which had the same eye and spotted torso as the Picabia in Nancy's flat. Or she and Tzara would spend evenings with Solita, Janet, Brâncuşi, Man Ray and Kiki and Eugene McCown.

Tzara continued to write, as in this Dadaist instruction on how to write a poem:

Take a newspaper
Take a pair of scissors

Choose from the paper an article as long as you are planning
    to make your poem
Cut the article out
Next carefully cut out each of the words that make up the
    article and put them in a bag
Shake gently
Next take each clipping out one after another in the order in
    which they left the bag
Copy conscientiously
The poem will look like you
And there you are – an infinitely original author endowed with
    a charming sensibility though beyond the understanding of
    the vulgar.

Another of the Dadaists' acts was to have a dozen men move
to the front of the stage and declaim mournfully, 'No art, no
literature, no politics, no republic, no royalists no philosophers,
no nothing – dada, dada, dada . . .'

The original Dada impetus was, however, declining and its
leading lights were beginning to quarrel among themselves. The
crunch between the two factions came when Tzara's original play
Le Cœur à gaz (first shown for one night in 1921) was restaged
in 1923 in a more professional production, when it provoked
a riot in the theatre initiated by André Breton, one of the three
founders of the movement that was to become Surrealism. Even
the previous year, in one of his columns for the *Transatlantic
Review*, Hemingway had pronounced 'Dada is dead'.

Tzara now turned his writing towards the theatre, turning out
Dada plays, in one or two of which Nancy appeared – she had
always had a slight penchant for the stage. In *LECMOM 3rd
Diens* she had a dancing role, in another she was accompanied by
Eugene McCown. The most important was the 1924 *Mouchoir
de nuages*, which Tzara claimed he had written after a sneezing
fit from eating a whole pot of mustard to show off to Nancy.
Mouchoir was soon included in the repertoire of the impresario
Sergei Diaghilev's Ballets Russes.

This play of fifteen (very short) acts had been commissioned by the immensely rich Comte Étienne de Beaumont, patron of most aspects of modern art and noted party-giver famous for his annual costume balls where guests dressed as eye-catchingly as possible – at one the Marchesa Casati, already famous as a spectacle in Venice, went as Eve with a live snake coiled round her shoulders. Nancy had attended many of his balls during her early visits to Paris; now he was staging *Soirées de Paris*, a five-week-long series of commissioned ballets, plays and performances that he financed at the Théâtre de la Cigale in Montmartre. It was timed to coincide roughly with the Olympic Games, for which so many had come to Paris and, de Beaumont being de Beaumont, included many evening festivities. There is a widely published photograph of Nancy and Tzara at one of them, Nancy's slender figure emphasised by a narrow silver trouser suit by Poiret.* She wears a mask over her eyes and her father's top hat on her head (this was often lent to Janet); at her feet kneels Tzara, kissing her hand. He also dedicated *Mouchoir* to Nancy.

Like much that the Dadaists, and later the Surrealists, did, it created outrage as well as admiration. 'In our world in the early Twenties, to be "Avant Garde" was considered strange and Bolshie,' wrote Alannah Harper, the young author and publisher who the following year founded the journal *Echanges* to give British and French writers an audience for each other's work – among those she introduced to the French were T.S. Eliot and Virginia Woolf:

> To like contemporary art estranged one from one's friends and made one feel oneself to be a superior person. I remember returning from Paris full of enthusiasm about the *Soirées de Paris* in which Parade and Salade were given and other ballets, and recitals of modern poetry, and the music of Les Six. It was the first time I had come in contact with the contemporary movement in the arts and it was a revelation to me. These

---

* The catastrophic drop in the value of the franc had inspired, noted Janet Flanner, a bizarre fashion trend: clothes made from various metals, 'cloth of gold, cloth of silver, or cloth of copper, at least, or lead, and pewter maybe'.

manifestations had the same reception as the Sitwells' Facade, they were greeted with howls of vulgar laughter, tomatoes and eggs were hurled at the artists, instead of the bouquets they should have received . . .

The affair with Tzara was light-hearted and fun – Nancy wrote of how much they laughed. They danced, they visited the small Surrealist galleries that were opening up – Tzara and indeed the Dada movement itself were turning more and more towards the Surrealists. It is also possible that it helped increase her feelings for something for which she soon became famous: her love of African art and artefacts and, later, her involvement with and campaigning for the rights of black Americans. From almost its beginnings, Dadaism had lauded African culture – or what it saw as African culture – not so much for what it was as for being outside mainstream European thought.

It was probably in Les Deux Magots, and certainly through Tzara, that Nancy would first have seen the man who would become her next great love (and the fourth love of my title): Louis Aragon, a poet, novelist and editor, although they did not meet for another eighteen months.

In 1924 Aragon became a founding member of Surrealism, along with André Breton and Philippe Soupault. Dreams, imagination and the subconscious played a large part in their ethos as Breton's *Manifeste du Surréalisme*, published that year, pointed out: 'Psychic automatism in its pure state, by which one proposes to express – be it verbally, by the written word, or in any other way – the actual functioning of thought, in the absence of any control exercised by reason, exempt from any aesthetic or moral concern.'

The group was also quite fond of a little violence. In their early days there was such an aggressive row at the Closerie des Lilas – chairs flying through the air, crockery crashing through the windows – as they fought those they considered their critics that the police had to be called to restore order. As the *Times* correspondent Sisley Huddleston pointed out, 'They are as ready to express their dislikes with fists as with words. Their manifestoes always create an uproar. They are violently opposed to bourgeois conceptions.'

Described by some as talented literary clowns, they were strongly drawn to Freud, Rimbaud, Marx and Lenin (Aragon later became the leading intellectual of the French Communist Party). Breton, their leader, defined Surrealism as a pure state of mind that allows someone to express thoughts freely and without the encumbrance of a belief in reason and societal rules, pushing artists to look into their unconscious minds for inspiration, without influence from the outside world.

The first Surrealists were a group of thirty-odd young men. Several were painters and the rest writers or poets. This core wrote, painted and signed collective manifestos, and met daily – sometimes twice a day – at the same Paris café. When Nancy first encountered them they had their own table at Les Deux Magots; later they favoured the Café Cyrano in Place Blanche, Montmartre.

Their rules were strict and seemingly designed to cause trouble. They told the editor of a leading literary periodical (*Les Nouvelles littéraires*) that they would not allow their names to be mentioned in his paper – an extraordinary order to give to a magazine that specialised in talk of new movements and new authors. They were, of course mentioned, upon which a group of them armed themselves, burst into the editor's office, broke all the furniture and created such mayhem that again the police had to be called.

'In films and photography there was a new vision and a new technique,' wrote Nancy, 'writing bent on lassoing dreams and coralling the subconscious into strangely evolved sentences. As for Painting! Painting was as it had never been before in the whole history of art.' Nancy defined Surrealism as being 'an intellectual revolution, which began in 1924–5'; they honoured 'love and emotion, and inventiveness and fantasy. The most admired writings were revolutionary, not only in a socio-political sense, but in the aesthetic-iconoclastic one too ... All the jingo values of La Patrie and La Gloire, the militarism so real to official France, were anathemised and colonialism was consistently denounced.'

It is easy to see how this appealed to Nancy. From being against the status quo into which she had been born, she had become ever more against anything she felt had no compelling *raison d'être*, thus she tended towards movements or ideas that were anti something she thought to be mistaken rather than promoting anything she believed in.

Her closest friends saw this clearly. 'It was impossible for her to work quietly for the rights of man; Nancy functioned best in a state of fury in which, in order to defend, she attacked every windmill in a landscape of windmills,' said Solita Solano.

CHAPTER 10

⊰━◈━◯━◈━⊱

Of Writers and Writing

At the beginning of 1925 Nancy visited England to attend the opening of what was possibly the most glamorous nightclub ever. Lord Glenconner's son, the twenty-two-year-old David Tennant, just down from Cambridge, had taken a fifty-year lease of an elegant Georgian house in Soho's Dean Street and transformed the three upper floors into a brilliant setting where bohemia and the upper echelon of society were equally at ease. He called it the Gargoyle; it had a very large ballroom, a Tudor Room, coffee room, drawing room and a 350-square-yard flat roof with a garden for dining and dancing, around which the neighbouring chimneys were painted brilliant red. All were reached by a rickety external lift which held a mere four people at most and was located round the corner in Meard Street.

By contrast, the interior was designed by the best-known architect of the day, Sir Edward Lutyens, and two of the most famous painters, Augustus John and Henri Matisse. The result was theatrical – a fountain on the dance floor, log fires in the dining room, wooden gargoyles suspended as lanterns, a coffered ceiling painted with gold leaf. Matisse himself designed the stunning entrance staircase in glittering steel and brass, while two of his paintings, bought by Tennant in Paris for £600, hung on its walls: *L'Atelier rouge* over the bar and *Studio, Quai Saint-Michel*, featuring a voluptuous nude, on the club's stairs.*

---

* In 1941 this was offered to the Tate Gallery, which declined it, for £400; in 1949 it went to the MOMA in New York, where it still hangs. The *Studio* is now in The Phillips Collection in Washington, DC.

David Tennant, handsome, rich and clever, had enviable social connections and the Gargoyle immediately acquired 300 members, many of whom turned up for the opening night on 16 January; as well as Nancy, these included Somerset Maugham, Noël Coward, Virginia Woolf, Adele Astaire, Edwina Mountbatten, Gladys Cooper and Nancy's former lover, Michael Arlen, now, thanks to *The Green Hat*, a celebrated author. After this, whenever Nancy came to London and dined at the Tower, she and the friends she met there would often go on later to dance at the Gargoyle, sure of meeting others of their coterie – perhaps Iris and her husband Curtis Moffat, Sybil Hart-Davis or Michael Arlen (who once remarked, 'I should be kicked out of any club in London, the Gargoyle excepted – and rightly so – for I am a born cad').

After the Gargoyle opening, Nancy was soon back in Paris, where the cult of '*les noirs*' was sweeping through the city. Never was jazz more popular than in the Twenties, and nobody could play jazz like black musicians. More and more of the chic *boîtes* began to feature black bands, usually of three or four of the enterprising young men who had managed to save enough for their passage to France.

Ever since the war, tales had begun to filter back to the US that here was a land where they could expect different treatment from that which they got at home. At first these stories came largely from returned servicemen who had served with the French army. For of the 350,000-odd African-American troops who had served with the US army in France in the war, between 30,000 and 50,000 had been placed under French commanders.*

The difference between the daily life of those black US soldiers serving in their own army and those under French command was striking. At home these men were segregated and treated as a subservient race – in the South they could be lynched if there was even a hint that they had approached a white woman. In the US army they were similarly kept completely apart, never

---

* These men saw more combat than any other black American troops.

serving alongside white troops, and forbidden to mingle with local people on pain of severe penalties.

But for the African-American troops under French command there was none of this. They fought beside the French; they could go into a shop or a bar just as a Frenchman could. France's acquisition of a sub-Saharan empire and the interflow between the mother country and its colonies, with many of the educated elite of the latter acquiring not only the language but the culture of the former, resulted in an acceptance of *les noirs*. With many of these colonials conscripted into the French army to fight in the war (the Senegalese were credited with having saved Paris in the second Battle of the Marne), feelings towards them were warm.

In short, there was little or no colour bar in Paris, where these black soldiers could visit the same restaurants – or brothels – as everyone else. Protests from the Americans had no effect, although the moment the war ended, these same African-American troops were put under severe restraints by the American high command, even being excluded from the victory parade along the Champs-Élysées.

When they returned home, to the same segregation as before, stories of how well they had been received by the French trickled out, and to many Paris began to seem like the promised land. Another incentive to leave was that at the same time, the power of the dreaded Ku Klux Klan (famous, among other things, for lynching blacks) was growing; membership, which had declined after the Civil War, was almost a million, producing fo the Klan an annual income of $3 million. The Klan boosted its popularity by giving money to charities, hospitals and welfare organisations, and hosting picnics and barbecues to put across the notion that its main interest was the wellbeing of the community. Only once its hold had been established did it begin targeting immigrants, political opponents – and blacks.

Although by 1925 the Klan's membership had dropped and its influence was minimal, the stories of Paris had lost none of their power and now there was a new springboard – jazz. The popularity of jazz (not for nothing were the Twenties often called the 'Jazz Age') had largely sprung from black American communities.

Many black jazz musicians had learnt by ear, picking up tunes on the streets of New Orleans, improvising on Negro spirituals they already knew or simply playing for sheer enjoyment.

The post-war young, who loved both jazz and dancing, began to visit the bars and cabarets where these black musicians played. Many were in Chicago – by the mid-Twenties it had over 10,000 speakeasies, nightclubs and bars with music compared to the 800-odd cabarets in New York, mostly in Harlem, then a self-contained 'city' within a city, some of which were so expensive and popular that almost all their clientele was white.

But the legend of Paris, and the lure of social acceptance, persisted. If they wanted to go to France, earning their living through their music was the obvious way. Gradually, those who could raise the money for their fare, often through the brilliance of the jazz they played, arrived in the French capital as entertainers. Along with their popularity came an interest in African art and culture.

For Nancy the two blended perfectly. She loved dancing and she was increasingly interested in the African peoples, adorning herself with their jewellery, from bangles to huge earrings – all of which helped define her image and stamp her yet more firmly on the public consciousness as a personality who embodied the spirit of the age. As a little girl she had dreamt of Africa, vivid dreams of which she wrote as being 'full of movement . . . Africans dancing and drumming around me, and I one of them, though still white, knowing, mysteriously enough, how to dance in their own manner'.

She still had not given up on Ezra Pound. She must have felt that if they could see each other alone, she could win him back. Pound, now firmly ensconced in Rapallo, had invited her there and on 17 March she wrote hopefully, 'Ezra, Ezra – I hope there will be no one at Rapallo but our good selves.' It was not to be: Dorothy was very much present and Nancy herself was accompanied by a friend. Instead, she went to Italy with the poet and publisher John Rodker, with whom she began a sporadic affair.

The great literary excitement of Nancy's spring was the publication of her long narrative poem *Parallax* in April 1925. When

Sublunary had come out two years earlier, the *Observer* had said: 'We wish Miss Cunard would try her hand at a long narrative or dramatic poem; with larger scope and the need continuously to submit to the discipline of imaging others' lives and thoughts, she might do something far more remarkable than and as beautiful as some of the poems in this volume.' Now she had done exactly that.

It was beautifully produced by Leonard and Virginia Woolf at their Hogarth Press, a publishing company that had begun more as a hobby than anything when the Woolfs had bought a hand press in 1917 for £19, set it up in the dining room of their Richmond home, Hogarth House, and taught themselves how to use it. Their first publication was a booklet containing two stories, one by Leonard and the other by Virginia. The Press was not really a money-making concern as their profits were tiny; when they printed T.S. Eliot's *The Waste Land* – the first UK printing – in December 1922 they made just over £10. For Nancy they hand-printed 420 copies of *Parallax*, its cover designed by her friend Eugene McCown.

Several reviewers noted similarities between *Parallax* and *The Waste Land*. According to *The Nation*, 'Miss Cunard's poem would never have been conceived without the example of Mr Eliot. But even when this is recognized, Miss Cunard's poem shows the individuality of its author.' 'T.S. Eliot is the first who heard the new music in its full harmony,' said *Outlook*. 'Miss Cunard has caught strains of it too. She is not piping over again Mr. Eliot's tune [but] adding her own motifs and orchestration to the general theme.' The *Times Literary Supplement* hailed it as 'the creation of a resilient mind'. Others were more dismissive, regarding it as an imitation rather than a response to Eliot, and even today it is still being re-evaluated and argued over.

At the same time, the new-(ish) movement of Art Deco was becoming mainstream fashion. With the opening in April of the *Exposition internationale des arts décoratifs et industriels modernes* (International Exhibition of Modern Decorative and Industrial Arts), 'Deco', as it was called, was appearing everywhere. Its geometric shapes, smooth curves that were often almost circular and straight lines that reflected aspects of modern technology – albeit with a nod to Cubism – were used in buildings, furniture, mirrors and jewellery, often in expensive materials. Ebony, ivory, silver, crystal, jade and lacquer were a glamorous answer to post-war austerity.

Modernism was everywhere. The Paris apartment belonging to Gerald and Sara Murphy was painted white, with glossy, lac-quered black floors splashed with white Mexican rugs. Red an-tique brocade curtains framed the huge windows with their view of the Seine, chairs and sofas were upholstered in black satin, coffee tables had mirrored tops and instead of flowers there were stalks of pale-green celery in black or white opalescent vases.

Nancy herself became the subject of a modernist portrait. Brâncuşi, who had wanted to sculpt her for some time, now pro-duced *La Jeune Fille sophistiquée (Portrait de Nancy Cunard)* in polished wood, an oval shape with a small neck and a thick twist of hair, on a cylindrical base. Other versions followed, with the final one, in 1932, light and elegant in polished brass.

Many of the Montparnos had books out that spring. Robert McAlmon had torn himself away from the bottle ('If bread is the staff of life, whisky is the staff of night life' was his motto) suf-ficiently to produce *Village*, much admired by Hemingway, who wrote from Austria that it was 'absolutely first rate and damned good reading', and who told Sylvia Beach, 'McAlmon's book *Village* came and is damn good. If anyone asks for it tell them it's recommended by E.M. Hemingway, the famous Austrian skiing authority.'

Back from Austria just after the publication of *The Great Gatsby* and its glowing reviews, Hemingway, having a drink in Dingo's, was tapped on the shoulder by the book's author, F. Scott Fitzgerald, who introduced himself. Both loved to drink, both were writers – though compared to Fitzgerald, who had published three novels and two volumes of short stories, Hem-ingway, with a mere eighty-eight published pages to his credit, had barely started. They became friends so quickly that soon Hemingway was introducing Fitzgerald to Gertrude Stein, with whom he was still on excellent terms.

The meeting was a success. Gertrude was charmed by Fitz-gerald's admiration and behaviour and, for once, gave unqualified approval to another author's work: 'Here we are and have read your book and it is a good book . . . You write naturally in sentences and one can read all of them and that among other things is a comfort.' The only person who did not enjoy the encounter was Zelda. Accustomed not only to being the centre of attention but, as a Southern belle, for that attention to come mainly from men, she was not pleased to be corralled into a corner by Alice B. Toklas.

A month after the meeting, Hemingway and Hadley left for Pamplona – the Hemingways had originally gone there in 1923 at the suggestion of Gertrude Stein. They planned to be there in a party for the fiesta and the running of the bulls; there would be two old friends of Hemingway, Don Stewart and Bill Smith, over from New York, and Harold Loeb, with whom Hemingway played tennis, often dined and discussed their mutual writings. There would also be Duff Twysden, in the process of divorcing her second husband Sir Roger Twysden, a naval officer and baronet, and Lady Twysden's lover Pat Guthrie.

From the start the likelihood of drama, rows, drunkenness and sexual tension hung in the air. Hemingway was strongly attracted to Duff Twysden, a tall, slim, stylish blonde with short hair who often wore a fedora tipped at a rakish angle and who exuded a casual sensuality; Hadley, who had realised this, withdrew into her shell. Loeb left Paris two weeks early without telling Hemingway that he was taking Duff to Saint-Jean-de-Luz for a romantic fling, nor did Duff tell him when she returned alone to the *quartier*. Inevitably Hemingway found out and his mood soured. At Saint-Jean, Loeb received a letter from Duff, telling him, 'I am coming on the Pamplona trip with Hem and your lot. Can you bear it? With Pat of course . . . I'm dying to come, and feel that even seeing and being able to talk to you will be better than nothing.'

The Hemingway party left Paris on 25 June. Next came an unsuccessful fishing trip, then the arrival of Duff, Loeb and Pat Guthrie, the last two barely civil to each other. The situation was complicated by the fact that Hemingway had begun to behave as if he owned Duff, who in turn had not guessed that Loeb would fall in love with her instead of treating their fortnight in Saint-Juan as just a bit of fun, as she did.

Once in Pamplona, the serious drinking began. There were fireworks, tipsy parades through the streets, balloons, brassy music all day and most of the night, and goatskins full of wine. Guthrie was a drunk and Duff saw most things through an alcoholic haze. Hemingway had arrived in a bad mood, jealous of Loeb who, with no wife and a certain amount of money, could take Duff away with him. When Loeb became the hero of the crowd and the photographers by grasping a bull's horns and riding on its neck, it was too much. Second to not being reverential about bullfighting, the surest way to antagonise Hemingway was to take the limelight away from him. Loeb, who did not know this and who was not aware of Hemingway's thwarted desire for Duff, could not understand why his friend was turning on him and making him feel like a rich Jew who did not belong in the party (Hemingway did, however, later send him a note of apology for his awful behaviour).

When the party did leave on 13 July, Duff and McGrath could not pay their share of the bill – they had come to Pamplona confident that someone else would pick up the tab. Don Stewart had to 'lend' them the money.

Even worse was to come. Hemingway had been steadily filling his blue notebooks with the raw material of what was to become *The Sun Also Rises*, the book that was to make his name. In it would appear these friends, easily recognisable with the details of their failed past marriages, college sporting activities, speaking idiosyncrasies and assorted indiscretions. Loeb would become the hapless, insufferable Robert Cohn. Duff would be translated into the glamorous but anguished Lady Brett Ashley, a caricature that branded her as an alcoholic nymphomaniac, for Guthrie it would be Mike Campbell, another drunk. Stewart and Smith came off best, combined into the wry Bill Gorton. None of them, of course, had any idea that within a year they would find themselves unwillingly immortalised.

*

The reputation of Montparnasse as the place that drew every young artist and writer of promise had spread so widely that the number of tourists arriving in the summer months was overwhelming, so much so that most of the real Montparnos took themselves off for the summer. Picasso went to Juan-les-Pins, the Joyces to Normandy and Matisse to Italy. Nancy herself went to Le Lavandou, where Solita Solano and Janet Flanner had rented a small house near a group of fishing huts, with a view of mimosa trees and olive groves. Nearby was Eugene McCown, and the four would meet in a café to talk of the books they wanted to write – or, in Eugene's case, the paintings he wanted to paint – and went for long walks along the coast in the evenings. After this, Nancy rented a house deep in the Corrèze countryside (in south-west France) with John Rodker, where they went boating, fishing and for long walks.

While Nancy was away, Ezra Pound's daughter Mary, by Olga, was born on 9 July. Then came the problem of what to do with the child. Pound, whose marriage was shaky, could not take her, nor did he want to, while Olga knew that an illegitimate child might fatally stigmatise her career. Fortunately – for the couple – a woman in the next bed to Olga who had lost her own baby at birth agreed to bring up Olga's. There was no formal adoption, but Olga paid to have Mary looked after by this family of peasant farmers in the German-speaking South Tyrolean village of Gais. This birth now determined Dorothy Pound to have a child of her own, perhaps in an attempt to win her husband back.

Towards the end of August, GM, who clearly wanted a spell in Paris but not in a hotel, wrote to his 'dearest Nancy' with the bizarre suggestion that a house-swap would improve her writing style:

When I was your age a French writer said to me: you are missing your chances of becoming an English writer by living in France. On looking back I cannot avoid the conclusion that I should not have done as well as I have done if I had not returned to England. We must live a great deal in the country we address. Now what do you think of this: well you can live in my house in Ebury Street for six months of the year and let me live for six months in your flat? . . . You will pay my servants and I will pay yours. The arrangement from a literary point of view will be highly beneficial.

Nancy did not take up this offer.

While Nancy was at Le Lavandou, Gertrude Stein had spent the whole summer correcting proofs of her mammoth work *The Making of Americans*. She had originally asked the Woolfs to publish it – perhaps having been impressed by their production of Nancy's *Parallax* that spring – but once they learnt the length of *Americans*, which Gertrude put at 560,000 words, they jibbed. Eventually, at her urging, Robert McAlmon agreed to publish the entire work through his Contact Editions.

Although McAlmon was known for his consumption of alcohol and busy nightlife, he was extremely professional when it came to work. The list of those modernist writers published by Contact Editions is impressive: Hemingway, Ford Madox Ford, Mina Loy, and the two he was most impressed by, Ezra Pound and William Carlos Williams. 'Brighter than most,' he would say of them, his ultimate in praise.

For Gertrude, McAlmon's agreement was a coup. It would get the book 'out' and its size and very impenetrability – though she would never have put it this way – were a riposte to her bête noir, James Joyce. McAlmon agreed to a print run of 500, with Gertrude confident she could sell fifty copies, these to be specially bound and more expensive.

McAlmon knew that he would make a loss on it, but he was concerned that this should not be too large. Because *Americans* was about three times the size of any other book he had published it was correspondingly expensive to print, with the final costs between $2,000 and $3,000.* It was thick – at 4.2cm almost as

---

* These costs could have supported two households in either the UK or the US for a year.

thick as *Ulysses*, but about half as long again – and very closely printed in dark print. McAlmon had kept the selling price of the main body of copies down to £8 by keeping the paper thin.

The trouble was that it proved almost impossible to shift. Gertrude had counted on selling fifty copies but sold only ten and gave the other forty to various friends; and the other 450 were left on McAlmon's hands. Gertrude wanted them distributed in America, there to establish her reputation as a leading modernist, but it was difficult to sell books that had been printed in Paris in the US because they were so often believed to be obscene and therefore were confiscated by the authorities on arrival; and McAlmon was maddened by Gertrude's attempts to set up deals through her friends, often without letting him know. Accusations flew thick and fast. Eventually, a number of the remaining copies were sent to bookshops, from only a few of which McAlmon received payment. By the end of the year the two were not speaking to each other.

McAlmon, however, got his own back when he was later asked to review *The Making of Americans*, writing, 'Unfortunately Miss Stein, a naïve, fairly childish person, has had thrust upon her a legend as a leader of modern literature . . . one feels that Miss Stein triumphs within herself to think that she can put words together, and having done so feels charmed enough to repeat them again and again.' And in a portrait of her finally published by Ezra Pound in 1928, in *Exile*, he compared her thought processes and mode of expression to an elephant laboriously heaving itself through mud.

Nancy, still with John Rodker, went on a walking tour with him in the Dordogne before going on to Venice. Here, in one of the big Lido hotels, she met the Labour Party member (and in 1929 MP) John Strachey, who had accompanied his friend the Labour politician Oswald Mosley, later the British fascist leader. For Strachey, meeting Nancy was something entirely new to him and he was mesmerised by her. '[He] was intoxicated by the free world in which Nancy lived,' says his biographer Hugh Thomas. 'He was delighted by the endless breaking of conventions, the relentless desire to experiment and the heady mixture of racial and sexual freedom which she administered to her admirers.' Many years later, Nancy wrote to Solita that Strachey 'was one of mine – Ah! So very much'. They did indeed continue seeing each other for some time, once spending an entire afternoon on the River Thames after lunching at Eel Pie Island.

In the late autumn, Nancy went to London, where she saw old friends, persuading Raymond Mortimer to review Solita Solano's just-published novel, seeing Michael Arlen from time to time – and disliking it intensely when tackled about her role as protagonist in the novel that had brought him celebrity, *The Green Hat*. 'Went to an appalling party,' she wrote, 'where a perfect swine, an ex-guardsman, tried to find out once and for all whether I was the Green Hat! Can you beat it? As for the *Hat*, it is indescribable.'

In September, Janet Flanner was hired by the *New Yorker* magazine, founded six months earlier in February 1925, to send a fortnightly 'Letter from Paris'. Her brief was to write about Paris from the point of view of what the French, rather than Americans, would find interesting; her pieces, ironic, sparky, up-to-date and well informed, were signed 'Genêt'. The first of these appeared on 10 October 1925. She was the magazine's only foreign correspondent, as its editor considered Paris to be the sole place of interest other than New York to his sophisticated, or would-be sophisticated, readership. Her style suited this perfectly: of an elderly French aristocrat she wrote, 'She came from an era when men were not men but dukes.'

Janet's new job involved not only culling the eight daily French papers for the most striking, glittering and revealing pieces of news but also covering gallery openings, film premieres, fashion shows, auctions, the weddings and funerals of the political and cultural elite, the trials of swindlers and serial killers, new books and restaurants. It also had the incidental effect of widening even Nancy's social horizons as Janet took her and Solita to new exhibitions, *boîtes*, plays or parties in the search for copy, of which she remarked, 'I act as a sponge. I soak it up and squeeze it out in ink every two weeks.'

One of the first 'events' Janet covered was the arrival of a spectacular new star on the Paris stage. The advent of the nineteen-year-old Josephine Baker caused a storm. After her first appearance in *La Revue nègre* at the Théâtre des Champs-Élysées on 2 October 1925, those lucky enough to have seen her were surrounded in the cafés as they expatiated on her stunning performance.

'She made her entry entirely nude except for a pink flamingo feather between her limbs,' wrote Janet, in one of her most famous columns. 'She was being carried upside down and doing the split on the shoulder of a black giant. Mid-stage he paused, and with his long fingers holding her basket-wise around the waist, swung her in a slow cartwheel to the stage floor, where she stood, like his magnificent discarded burden, in an instant of complete silence. She was an unforgettable female ebony statue.'

When a reporter asked Josephine the following morning what had been her most vivid memory of her triumph, she replied, 'After the show, the theatre was turned into a big restaurant. And for the first time in my life, I was invited to sit at a table and eat with white people.' She became the instant rage of the capital, her bronze skin increasing the fashion for suntans that had started to become chic two years earlier when Coco Chanel had disembarked from a cruise with her lover the Duke of Westminster 'brown as a cabin boy'.

By the following year, Baker was the most successful American entertainer in France. After a sell-out tour of Europe, she had broken her contract and returned to Paris to star at the Folies Bergère. Here her erotic dancing and her insouciant near-nudity on stage were show-stopping: she performed her *Danse sauvage* wearing a costume consisting only of a skirt made of a string of artificial bananas, dreamt up by her great admirer Jean Cocteau. She would wear this with nothing else but a rope of pearls. (In later shows she was often accompanied on stage by her pet cheetah, equally scantily dressed in a diamond collar. The cheetah frequently escaped into the orchestra pit, to the terror of the musicians but adding another frisson of excitement to Josephine's performance.)

Ernest Hemingway, who spent hours talking with Josephine in bars, called her 'the most sensational woman anyone ever saw. Or ever will', and Picasso depicted her alluring beauty. What she also did was to stimulate and renew interest in non-Western forms of art, including African, to which Nancy would soon begin to take a more ideological approach.

In the late autumn Nancy returned to England. Her father had become ill and she went to his home, Haycock House, a large and gloomy building, to nurse him during the sad last days. 'It has all been rather terrible,' she wrote to Sybil, 'to see someone die.' But then, although both had held great affection for one another, there had seldom been any real closeness and certainly no meeting of minds.

Most of the fortune Sir Bache had inherited had disappeared. What was left, apart from the appurtenances that reflected his sporting life – his guns, hunting prints and so forth – which went to various male relatives, he left everything to Nancy, who received a total of £14,418 13s 2d* and a life-size silver figure of a fox that had been presented to him by his hunting friends. Maud was nowhere mentioned in his will, though after he died GM wrote to her, perhaps in would-be consolation, 'I loved you in the beginning and shall love you to the end.'

During her time in England, Nancy had taken a small house in Sussex. Sometimes she went to London, where she visited her 'first friend'. 'Nancy called here,' wrote GM to Maud at the beginning of January. 'We had a long talk and walked to Hyde Park Corner together, and would have walked farther if the rain hadn't come on. The subject of our conversation was her prose story. I told her the lines I wrote about you and she seemed to like them.' At other times friends came to stay. To Janet Flanner she wrote to say 'I would rather hear anything from you than from any other teller,' asking her to come and stay and promising 'cat for lap and

---

* Around £95,000 in purchasing power today

dog for walk – a yard and a half of books – plenty of wine – sleep without dreams and baths without shudders – do come'.

As well as acquiring a capital sum, Nancy was now completely free again. Neither she nor Sydney Fairbairn had done anything about a divorce, but when Sydney wished to remarry it became essential and in 1925, six years after they had separated, they were finally divorced.

Nancy was not 'single' for long. When she returned to Paris in the spring of 1926 she started a new love affair with a man she had met earlier, Louis Aragon. So intense and so passionate was their relationship that towards the end of her life she said that he was probably the only man who had ever really loved her.

CHAPTER II

Louis Aragon

Louis Aragon was the sort of man anyone could fall in love with: tall, dark, slim, good-looking and well dressed, with a pale and rather intense face, great intelligence and a reputation among those who knew him of being a magnet to women – his friends used to complain that he could go into any bar or café and walk out with any woman he chose, whether or not she had been accompanied. Where women were concerned he was a romantic; he once gave an old beggar woman fifty francs and an orchid on condition she would never forget, for as long as she lived, the name of the woman he loved. He had been involved in Dadaism from 1919; as it splintered on internal dissensions he had supported Tzara, both turning towards Surrealism.

Aragon's story was in itself almost surreal. His mother had become pregnant by her much older lover, a married right-wing politician. Her pregnancy and Aragon's birth were concealed, with the support of her well-connected but poor family, and he grew up believing that his young mother was his older sister. He was only told the truth at the age of nineteen, as he was leaving to serve in the First World War, from which neither he nor his family thought he would return. When he did, he lived until 1923 at Neuilly in a household of women – aunts whom he had believed to be sisters and the grandmother he had believed to be his mother.

He first studied medicine, a career of which his conventional, hard-up and Catholic family thoroughly approved. It was highly respectable, it did good and it would give him a comfortable living. But while working as a medical student in the Val-de-Grâce hospital, near the Sorbonne, he met André Breton, the second of the trio (with Philippe Soupault) who would lead the new, emerging movement of Surrealism. This made an irresistible appeal to the young man who had already determined to write as well as to become a doctor and who, like most of his generation, believed that it was essential that the status quo be changed.

When Breton decided to throw up medicine in order to fling himself into the ferment of art and letters in post-war Paris, Aragon – now writing poetry – followed him from Neuilly, to the horror of his family. They were only slightly mollified when he got a (poorly paid) job editing a small literary magazine, *Paris-Journal* – but in 1923 he suddenly resigned. His family blamed Breton, who after all had led him away from home and a comfortable medical career, and indirectly they were right: he had left because of the Surrealist veto on all forms of journalism, and in particular literary journalism.

For Aragon had not only become a journalist; he was writing a novel. To do this without the open disapproval of his Surrealist friends, he buried himself in the country; here, thanks to a small advance, he was able to live and work. When most of the novel was written he returned to Paris, to plunge into the activities of the Surrealists, from the writing of manifestos to the twice-daily conferences at the Café Cyrano under the aegis of André Breton. By these regular companions he was regarded with a certain awe, in part because of his closeness to the formidable Breton, but largely for his looks, intellect, sharp wit and a certain air of mystery. This in fact covered a form of social embarrassment, something that had begun with his belated discovery of his illegitimacy. As he expressed it once, 'For a very long time, shame for me was a social feeling directed against my family – the notion that it was inferior.'

Nancy and Aragon were aware of each other for some time before they met. Frequenting the same bars and with friends and acquaintances overlapping, both so good-looking that they stood out from the crowd, it was only a question of time until they actually met. One evening in January 1926, Aragon ran into a young poet and publisher he knew. It was John Rodker,* who was with Nancy and – though Aragon did not know it – her then lover, although after that evening he would cease to be. 'As soon as I saw him [Aragon] I set my sights on him,' Nancy told Aragon's biographer Pierre Daix† many years later. Aragon in turn was fascinated by Nancy's looks and elegance, self-assurance and perfect French spoken with a caressing intonation.

After the evening ended, the three of them shared a taxi to go home. In the darkness Nancy, never hesitant at making the first move, put her hand on Aragon's knee.‡ They dropped off Rodker first, after which she kissed Aragon and, taking advantage of what two of Aragon's biographers describe as 'the legendary discretion of the drivers of fiacres as to what went in in the back of their vehicles', their affair began then and there. At first Rodker suspected nothing, even offering to lend Aragon his flat in London should he wish to go there, but thanks to the gossip that ran round the *quartier* almost as fast as the pouring of wine into the drinkers' glasses, he soon realised the position – Nancy was never worried that others should know who she was sleeping with.

Whether she realised it or not at the time, taking the initiative that first night was the right tactic with Aragon. He found Nancy's brand of predatory glamour irresistible. For Aragon, a romantic, wished always for a woman who met him halfway, if not nearer; not for him the shrinking violet, the chase, pursuit and eventual capture; a woman's open expression of admiration and desire quelled the uncertainties engendered by his upbringing and answered his longing for love. 'I have a horror of virgins,' he said later. 'I have only had relations with real

---

* During the First World War Rodker was a conscientious objector. In 1919 he started the Ovid Press which, although it only lasted year, published T.S. Eliot and Ezra Pound. He spent most of the Twenties in Paris, largely working on the second edition of *Ulysses*, then continued publishing on occult subjects.
† Daix was a French journalist, a friend and biographer of Picasso, and a friend of Aragon's.
‡ This may be a euphemism.

women who know what love is and who make no bones about it.'

Nancy described him as 'beautiful as a young god, but terribly shy'. His story and brilliance enthralled her. This was a man who, like her, had broken free from his background and the expectations of his family. They were drawn together like two balls of mercury, each dazzled by the looks, style, intellect and wit of the other. Both were poets, both believed in commitment to a cause (though Nancy had not yet found hers). Although Aragon seemed quiet and reserved beside Nancy's burning vitality, this carapace hid an intense energy, a quality admired by Nancy. 'A is delicious, in perfect training always ['always' was underlined six times] to write at will, any place, of anything,' she wrote to Janet Flanner.

Like Nancy, Aragon was very much a night person, as was fashionable in the *quartier*; he loved brothels, dance halls and early morning bars. Like Nancy, too – but unlike most of the other Surrealists – he was at ease in, and enjoyed, smart society and good clothes. Like her, he was fascinated by African art and culture, then thought strange and ugly by most of their contemporaries. (During the coming summer, while she and Aragon were travelling, Nancy wrote to Janet Flanner that she planned to travel from Paris to Southampton* with Aragon 'to look for African and Oceanic things – because that is the most recent and now very large interest in my life – ivory, gods, masks, fetishes'.)

At the time they met Aragon was living in a small attic room in the rue Malebranche that had in fact been found for him, almost as a goodbye present, by the married woman with whom he had been in love. Here, as he wrote later, 'my poor, my darling Nane [as he always called Nancy] you would arrive in the evening. At no matter what hour.' It was a noisy house but 'we were always quiet, Nane and I, in the bed at the far end of the apartment, from which nothing could be heard at the other end of the landing'.

---

* Many sailors brought back carvings and jewellery from Africa either as mementos or to sell, so that curio shops selling them grew up in large seaports.

Their affair quickly became one of the talking points of the *quartier*. Many of the younger members of the group, now shifting more and more leftwards, lived in a large converted warehouse, No. 54, rue du Château, an area of dark, narrow streets and shady hotels. Just beside it was a bridge over which caravans of animal-drawn milk trucks rattled as they crossed the uneven cobbles – a racket that heralded the approach of dawn or the first subway train. The decrepit building had been rented by one of the Surrealists who had more money than the others and who refurbished it, installing running water, electricity and a certain amount of furniture. The bedrooms, all with large beds, were luxurious, with velvety beige pile carpets and alabaster bedside lamps; on an upper gallery there were four black-leather-covered mattresses for casual drop-ins and blackish linoleum on the floor. Most of the walls were hung with cheap, unbleached canvas. Anyone who had money bought food for the evening and, of course, wine. It was, in effect, a commune.

Shortly to arrive there was the twenty-year-old André Thirion, a dedicated Marxist, from a family who were well off and intellectually distinguished, as was that of his friend Georges Sadoul, whose father was the founding publisher of *Le Pays Lorrain* and curator of the Lorraine Museum. Together the two young men had put on festivals of modernist art and literature in Nancy, where they lived, and where they had become fascinated by the writings of Louis Aragon in particular and André Breton, which they had seen in *La Nouvelle Revue Française*. On their hikes through the mountains and forests of the Vosges, discussing the latest writers – Proust, Gide, Cocteau, Morand – the allure of Paris and Surrealism became so strong that they agreed they must go there. When Thirion arrived he visited the rue du Château; through its inhabitants, inevitably, he met his hero Aragon with whom, despite the ten years between them, he would become a close friend.

Most of the Surrealists were, if not communists, sympathisers with the party and many of them, who were naturally against capitalism in any form, were, said Thirion, 'disturbed because of Nancy's fortune'. However, they recognised what one younger member called her 'striking allure'. One of them noted her eyes, 'which were very blue and quite strange, her fine, bony face, her lion-like mane of fine blonde hair; then one was amazed to see how her thin arms were covered from wrists to shoulder with African ivory bracelets'.

It was quickly apparent that this affair would be different from others enjoyed by the Surrealists. For a start, Nancy took Aragon away from his usual life – the routine of meeting twice a day at the same café, dining together and doing everything as a group. Not to follow this pattern was considered suspicious and disloyal, with its implication that you were no longer a true believer – at the least, it was a mark of disrespect. 'To the Surrealists,' recalled Aragon many years later, 'their group life and regular visits to the Café Cyrano, were the barometer of fidelity. In their eyes, one's presence at midday and at the hour of aperitifs was a given, and by not being there one was suspected of disagreement with the cause or at the least a lack of interest in everything we did together.'

This aspect of her lover's life had no effect upon Nancy who, with her innate sense of entitlement, was as usual determined to do things in the way she wanted. At the beginning of February she whisked Aragon off to London, where they stayed at the Tower – to buy his plane ticket, he had to ask for more money from his future publisher. In *Le Roman inachevé* Aragon wrote of that time:

> One evening in London I walked through the yellow fogs of
> February,
> Alone with a love that had just begun.
> Will she come?

After ten days, Aragon returned to Paris while Nancy stayed on, partly to welcome Janet Flanner, who had come to England anxious to see Stonehenge with Nancy. But Janet found her friend in bed with flu; instead, when well enough, Nancy took her to meet GM in Ebury Street. That first meeting was not altogether successful: GM was in what Nancy called a 'typical' mood and

Janet, who was expecting some wise and illuminating comment from the great writer, was nonplussed when he remarked of *Ulysses*, 'It cannot be a novel, for there isn't a tree in it!'

That spring, Nancy's looks – perhaps because she was newly in love – dazzled. One of her friends, John Banting, remembered seeing her in an emerald-green velvet dress at a party: 'I priggishly avoided joining the hive around her as she was a celebrity but at another party where she wore pale shell pink with plunging back and beautiful heavy African bracelets up to the elbows I could not resist asking her to dance. I made the bracelets clack and click in rhythm to the music. Until we drifted apart years later she remembered both occasions but not me.' And on 3 March Virginia Woolf was writing in her diary of missing the fancy-dress party given by Raymond Mortimer: 'Raymond telephoned . . . and said how lovely Nancy had looked, that I had missed the greatest sight of the season.'

A week later Nancy celebrated her thirtieth birthday at the Eiffel Tower ('through several bottles', she wrote), staying there for three days, with her appearance once again noted in the gossip columns. 'One thing Nancy Cunard did while in London was to start a new fashion in ivory bracelets,' wrote one society columnist. 'Each time I saw her she was wearing three or four huge ivory bracelets, each of them extremely thick and two or three inches wide.' Nancy usually wore more of them in the evening, one of them frequently a four-inch-wide cuff; this she would also use as an aide-memoire, writing a note to herself on it that she could easily wipe off with a piece of cloth. A few days later she left for Paris, where she and Aragon were reunited in mid-March.

Nancy was still writing, prose as well as poetry; *Vogue* had asked her for an occasional letter from Paris. In this she covered anything from bicycle races, the Surrealist art galleries, the forthcoming Paris concert season of her mother's lover Thomas Beecham and plans for new ballets by Cocteau and the Ballets Russes to the troubles of the many Russian taxi drivers in Paris. In May 1926, for example, she contributed an article on avant-garde Parisian culture in which she wrote of the now indisputable African influence in modernist painting, and glowingly reviewed a Josephine Baker performance at the Folies Bergères, in her new show *La Folie du jour*. After eight scantily clad girls were shown the wealth of Paris, leaving the stage more fully dressed than when they had appeared, Josephine came on as Fantou, wearing only her famous girdle of bananas. Nancy wrote of 'the perfect delight one gets from Josephine Baker, most astounding of mulatto dancers, in her necklets, bracelets and flouncing feathered loincloths' as she 'contorts her surprising form through a maze of complicated rhythms . . . [and] The wild-fire syncopation of Josephine Baker's beautiful brown electric body'.

In the spring Nancy and Aragon were off again, first to Brittany, then to Fontainebleau. Hardly had they got back to Paris than they packed their suitcases for Spain – here their open sharing of a room caused scandal in this Catholic country – then there was a long trip through southern France, where they stayed for a while at Souillac, in the Dordogne. 'Souillac was good,' wrote Nancy to Janet Flanner, 'but a certain amount of petty annoyance came to me from not knowing how to dispose of the days. Essentially a place for work, from dusty dawn to dewless dark, very little work got done. An idea came, however, a long one, for a poem.'

Nancy, as always, soon found herself anxious to move on: 'My hair is long and I am unkempt, and irritated by I don't know what – the damp, the light, night to hold nothing of vicissitude or peregrination. No high spots. Flea bites, sun burn, rheumatism.' Although Nancy always packed what she described to Janet as her 'travelling mousetrap', these other irritations were not so easy to combat.

It was back to Paris briefly, where most of her friends were away. 'Well, back to the Gratterie,' she wrote to Janet on 14 July 1926. 'The effect is loneliness, a good thing I suppose twice or thrice a year, but for what purpose? Oh, were it a poem . . .' There followed a complaint about the editing of her second letter for *Vogue* ('Well, Vogue ain't the world'), before she and Aragon set off again, through Marseilles and Cagnes-sur-Mer to Antibes.

Here they were seen by the communist writer Yvonne Kapp (later to be involved with Nancy) dining in the summer dusk by the sea wall in the garden of the Pension Josse, where Yvonne was staying. She was so struck by her first sight of these dazzling creatures that she recorded it: 'Oblivious to all around them, absorbed in one another, the glamorous pair could not fail to excite attention. They stayed on until the skies darkened and Madame Josse came out to place a little lamp on their table. When next I looked, they had vanished, leaving behind an impression of magical beauty.'

Aragon had little money so Nancy paid for almost everything, but it did not matter to either of them; they were deeply in love and Nancy was at her most affectionate and gentlest. 'He is a very sweet person,' she wrote of Aragon, 'were I not myself so irreductible I should be very happy. I am, as far as can be.' When she introduced her lover to George Moore the two got on well. It seemed Nancy might at last have found the right man for her. In the late summer, it was Italy, with visits to Assisi and then Florence.

In Florence she was able to introduce Aragon to Norman Douglas, as she had to GM; it was important to her that these two older men, in particular her 'first friend', knew and approved of her lovers and intimates. The meeting was a success, although both Nancy and Aragon were made uneasy by the growing influence of fascism in Italy, frequently brought to their attention because Nancy had a mackintosh that turned from a rust colour to communist blood-red in the rain, provoking unwanted hostility.

After Florence she planned that they should go to Venice, although, as she wrote to Janet, 'Her L is to be there abouts late August. So that much is certain, that I shan't.' Nancy had now reached the stage of wishing to avoid her mother at all costs. They went to Venice without seeing Maud; Aragon, conscious of his desertion of the others, wrote to his friend Thirion, 'I am the prisoner of love and I think it is the real thing,' adding, 'Through a thousand daily worries I remain continuously happy for the first time in my life.'

In Paris, a musical storm had broken that summer while most of the Montparnos were away. The young American George Antheil was going to give a concert featuring the avant-garde composition on which he had been working for so long, the *Ballet mécanique*. 'Paris, at the time, was full of violent infant prodigies, designing death for the Louvre and the French language,' said one of his contemporaries.*

There had already been a taste of Antheil's music: the previous autumn it was played in a private concert to an invited audience in the Conservatoire. Antheil had done everything he could to promote himself, even engineering his supposed 'disappearance' while on a visit to Africa, to get media attention. The publicity stunt worked: the press were avid to know any details about Antheil, turning to Sylvia Beach, his landlady, for information. Sylvia fended them off as best she could and sent a frantic telegram to Antheil, saying it was time for his return, but a friend, clad unconventionally for the podium in an orange mackintosh, had to stand in for him. The effect of his music was immediate: Adrienne Monnier, who was there with Sylvia, recorded that when at 10.30 the first notes of the *Ballet mécanique* were played, three people stood up 'crying out with fright and pain' and made for the door, slamming it behind them with all their might.

This summer, Antheil's concert would be the real thing, a proper public performance. The official Paris premiere took place on 19 June 1926 at the Théâtre des Champs-Élysées, sponsored by an American patroness. The theatre was packed; the 2,500-strong audience included Surrealists with wild hair, respectably dressed concertgoers and many of Antheil's Montparnasse friends, including celebrities like James Joyce and Ezra Pound. Man Ray was there with Kiki, her eyes painted in large triangles to match her triangular earrings, Sergei Diaghilev, Brâncuşi and, over from London, T.S. Eliot. The performance began late because Antheil, who had found a moth hole at the front of his trousers, had to wait while a friend darned it.

The first piece played was a Handel concerto, followed by Antheil's unexceptionable Second Symphony, a combination that must have lulled the audience into a false sense of security and

---

* Waldo Frank, novelist and political activist.

allowed them to relax in their seats. Then, as they watched, the 'instruments' for the *Ballet mécanique* were wheeled or carried on to the stage – pianos, pianolas, xylophones, hammers, bells, car horns, loudspeakers – and the raucous sounds began, soon to be drowned out by the reaction of the listeners. As always, the Paris audience was not hesitant in expressing its views. Some noisily supported this new art form, others objected even more loudly, until the theatre was pandemonium. Ezra Pound, in a blue shirt, stood up and shouted, but such was the din that only a few words ('Imbecile!' 'Ignoramus!' 'Philistine!') could be heard.

Then an even louder noise drowned the yells – the score called for aeroplane propellers, which were now set in deafening motion, gusting over the audience so that women pulled their wraps tightly round their shoulders, men turned up their coat collars and a man in the front row had his wig blown off. Another stood up and opened his umbrella, focusing it against the cold draught from the stage, to be copied by several more. Sporadic cheering broke out, and after twenty-eight minutes of raucous hubbub and riot the *Ballet* was over. At the end of the concert the American sponsor was tossed in a blanket by three baronesses and a duke.

The audience was so bitterly divided as to the *Ballet mécanique*'s merits, or lack of them, that they took to physical action to support their views and the nearby streets were filled with rioters. No Dadaist could have wished for more. Janet Flanner described the music in her 'Letter from Paris' as the sounds made by three people, 'one pounding an old boiler, one grinding a model 1890 coffee grinder and one blowing the usual 7 o'clock factory whistle and ringing the bell that starts the New York fire department going in the morning'.

For Ezra Pound, it was a tribute to modernism and the importance of machines. 'Machines are musical,' he said. 'They are not literary or poetic. I doubt if they are pictorial or sculptural: they have form but their distinction is not in form, it is in their movement and energy . . . Music is the art most fit to express the fine quality of machines. Machines are now a part of life; it is proper that men should feel something about them; there would be something weak about art if it couldn't deal with this new content.'

The next morning the concert and its aftermath were all over the front pages of the Paris newspapers. Some had cartoons of the event; one showed Antheil dressed in overalls, standing before a piano that had a small steam engine attached, controlling a system of indicators, gauges and levers instead of a keyboard. The caption below read: 'Last night's music of the future at the Ballet Suédois'.

When Antheil and a friend went to the Dôme that afternoon he realised that 'most eyes present followed us to our table. I was pointed out from every hand. I knew that almost everybody was talking about me.' It was a heady sensation for a young composer struggling for recognition.

Scarcely was the aftermath of the concert over than it was time for the Bal des Quat'Z'Arts. The Crosbys, for whom no excess was too great, were going, thanks to their adoption by one of the student ateliers, generously repaid with food and drink, and were planning the evening in true Crosby style. 'Costumes are being prepared and C tries on hers and is passionate with bare legs, bare breasts and a wig of turquoise hair,' wrote Harry Crosby on 18 June 1926. 'Many people undressing and painting for the ball . . . two or three students and Mortimer and myself all naked rubbing red ochre all over ourselves (my costume a frail red loin-cloth and a necklace of three dead pigeons).'

The party started at eight o'clock in the Crosby library, when eighty students arrived for supper and punch ('forty bottles of champagne, five whiskey, five gin, five cointreau'), then on to the ball, where Caresse won the prize for their atelier (another twenty-five bottles of champagne) as the most beautiful, riding around the ballroom in the jaws of the giant serpent that was that year's motif. Caresse herself put her victory down to her sizeable breasts.

Nancy and Aragon, both creatures of cafés, bars, *boîtes* and the night, were seldom in. La Coupole, with its bar that stretched the whole length of a long, narrow room and its ceiling an unusual fifteen feet high (designed to cut down on the usual smoky atmosphere), was a favourite, then came the Dôme, the Select – the first café to stay open all night – the Jungle and Bricktop's, where they went so often that later, whenever Aragon (known to Bricktop as Louis) entered, Bricktop would greet him warmly and order the band to play 'St Louis Blues'. To Nancy and Aragon, jazz seemed not only to exude eroticism and sheer animal abandon but also to express a humanity submitting blindly to the machine, a demoralisation born of the war.

Yet, despite their obvious passion for one another, already there were times when evenings ended badly: Nancy, with her endemic restlessness, her feeling that there might just be something more exciting round the next corner, would drag the two of them from *boîte* to *boîte* until she was near-drunk and Aragon had to half persuade, half carry her home.

What made their affair even more unusual in Surrealist circles was that Nancy clearly was, and so regarded herself, the equal of everyone in the group. First, she had taken Aragon away; then, in Paris, she would join them at their daily meetings, drinking drink for drink, sometimes the only woman there; although a number of the Surrealists had wives or steady girlfriends (known as *légitimes*), these played little part in the movement. For the Surrealists – in spite of their outlandish pranks and clownish behaviour, their desire to shock and break down barriers – were curiously traditional in their idea of female behaviour: women should stay at home, remain faithful, cook and look after any children – a mode of life unimaginable to the restless, footloose, hard-drinking, promiscuous Nancy.

'Sleeping around was just not done,' said André Thirion. 'The golden rule was passionate love, preferably faithful, between two individuals of opposite sexes . . . the beloved woman became an object of total veneration.' Yet the group did not object to prostitution or brothels, and indeed quite often visited them, despite posters which had arrived that year warning against syphilis and which now blazed from every public pissoir. '*Défendez-vous contra la syphilis*' ran the message above a list of the horrible things that could happen to one infected by the dread disease, which was represented on the poster by a menacing, skull-like and unmistakably female face.

Aragon's life had become so different, though, that rumblings were beginning among the comrades, who started to ask how one could be a communist writer and at the same time the lover of a millionaire's daughter. There was also jealousy – Aragon was clearly leading a much better life with Nancy than he had with them, and she was a beautiful woman whom all of them would have seen as a trophy. She had given Aragon a wonderful black cape that she had had made in Venice for him, from the same material used by gondoliers for their costumes, and when he arrived unexpectedly at a café at which Thirion was sitting with a group of young Surrealists, swathed in this romantic garment that added to his air of mystery and enhanced his dark handsomeness, he now seemed more than ever a figure from a different world.

In October 1926, Ernest Hemingway's novel *The Sun Also Rises* was published in the US to immediate acclaim, with its portrait of the disillusionment, the aimless drifting and drinking, with no moral compass, of the many of his age who had lived through similar experiences.

Its title came from verses in Ecclesiastes: 'One generation passeth away, and another generation cometh; but the earth abideth forever. The sun also ariseth, and the sun goeth down, and hasteth to his place where he arose.' Hemingway wished to express the idea that while one generation fades into another, his – the lost generation – had been shattered either by what they saw or experienced in the war, or by its effects afterwards. All they could do was drift, their lack of direction or purpose shrouded by the mists of alcohol.

As for their homeland, many of them were anxious to leave it. 'Red drug stores, filling stations, comfort stations, go-to-the-right-signs, lurid billboards and automobiles swarming everywhere like vermin,' Harry Crosby wrote during a visit home from Paris in 1926. 'How I hate this community spirit with its civic federations and its boyscout clubs and its educational toys and its Y.M.C.A. and its congregational baptist churches and all this smug self-satisfaction. Horribly bleak, horribly depressing.' Or as Gerald Murphy reported to Hemingway from New York, 'everyone in America is discontented, unhappy or complaining'.

Back in Paris, they were also complaining – but about Hemingway rather than the effects of the war. All the characters in his book were easily recognisable, pinpointed by the expedition to Spain he had taken with them the previous year. Harold Loeb, in particular, who had done so much to promote his friend's work and who was so generous with money, was cut to the quick to see himself portrayed as the Jew disliked by everyone else on the trip and told to go home because he was not wanted. At one time all Montparnasse, said the well-informed barman Jimmie Charters, was talking of the 'six characters in search of an author – with a gun!'. After his book was published, Hemingway prudently stayed away from his usual haunt, Dingo's, of which the originals of his cast of characters were habitués.

He was also in the midst of domestic troubles. During the last months of 1925, he and Hadley had met a rich and attractive *Vogue* editor called Pauline Pfeiffer, then thirty, the daughter of a wealthy Arkansas landowner. Pauline's sister Jinny had joined her for a visit and at first Hemingway was interested in her, thinking she was better-looking than Pauline, but she proved to be a lesbian. All four became great friends and would go out to cafés and *bals musettes* together. After Jinny went back, Hadley, stuck at home most of the time with a small child, welcomed the companionship of Pauline, with her beautiful clothes, her sophisticated polish, the gossip she brought from the world to which her job at *Vogue* gave her the entrée. Pauline, she felt, had become *her* particular friend.

Hemingway, without their small child Bumby to keep him at home, also began to see more of Pauline. They took afternoon walks together, were seen eating in obscure bistros, and he began to visit her flat in the rue Picot, on the Right Bank. Hadley thus knew nothing of these meetings and the three remained so close that Pauline joined the Hemingways for a skiing trip in Schruns, Austria, over Christmas 1925.

There, however, Pauline began an affair with Hemingway, who no doubt contrasted her fresh, vivacious appeal with the more careworn, matronly look of Hadley, now thirty-four to his twenty-six. Pauline's wealth in itself held a special glamour for him; the Hemingways were so poverty-stricken that they often could not afford to have the holes in their shoes mended, while Pauline's emerald earrings, furs and chic couture creations made a stark contrast to the clothes worn by the impecunious Hadley, who was in any case uninterested in fashion. For Hemingway, always conscious of his own image, to be accompanying someone so stylish could have only added to Pauline's allure.

At first the two kept their liaison secret. But such a change in the relationship between two of a close-knit trio could not go unnoticed by the third, and by the spring of 1926 Hadley was conscious of the changed dynamics. At first, she must have hoped that nothing would come of it, but gradually she grew to realise that Pauline was determined to stay in Hemingway's life. He in turn suggested a *ménage à trois*, a proposition flatly rebutted by both women.

Hadley grew more unhappy, and angrier, and the arguments between her and Hemingway increased. When the three came back from the Hemingways' annual trip to Pamplona, Hemingway, who now had to choose between them, moved in with Pauline and asked Hadley for a divorce. She finally conceded, but with the proviso that the couple agreed to a 100-day separation to test their love; this was to begin in September 1926. To fill in the time Pauline returned to Arkansas, where she edited several of Hemingway's manuscripts.

Hemingway now had no money at all – the couple had been living on Hadley's small trust fund which she, naturally, now kept for herself. Gerald Murphy came to his rescue, lending him a small studio and giving him $400 for living expenses. Although he had left Hadley, they still moved in the same social circles – where many of their friends sided with Hadley – and once ran into each other at a café, a meeting that ended with Hadley slapping him twice in the face. Hemingway, alone, broke and since

his book friendless, began suffering again from the depression*
that plagued him from time to time. It could not have been a
more miserable few months for him – though, as the living cast
of characters in his book would undoubtedly have thought, he
had brought it on himself.

In the autumn of 1926 Maud Cunard, staying as usual in Venice,
announced at a dinner party she was giving that she had decided
to change her name from Maud to Emerald, as these were her
favourite stones. It would be as Emerald that she became most
known to future generations. The only person disturbed by this,
through a misunderstanding, was George Moore, to whom she
wrote soon afterwards, signing herself 'Maud Emerald', no doubt
to make him aware of her change of name. His instant reaction
was that his beloved, without his knowledge, must have married
a Mr Emerald.

   One of his friends, the famous art dealer Sir Joseph Duveen,
to whom GM showed the letter that had caused him such anguish, remembered Moore 'spending the morning pacing up and
down the room like a caged animal'. Only when he received a
letter from Emerald (as she must now be called) explaining her
new signature did he relax, although he himself never ceased to
address her as his 'Dearest Maud'.

   In November 1926 GM made one of his periodic visits to
Paris, where he dined with Nancy. As he wrote to Emerald, 'we
spent a long evening together and we talked on many subjects.
You were the principal subject, naturally; and if she [Nancy] did
not feel that I would begin my life again for your sake she lacks
perception. Yet nothing precise was said and I shall see her again
before I see you.'

---

* Four family members had committed suicide, as would Hemingway
eventually.

CHAPTER 12

❥━┿━❧━○━❧━┿━❦

Love and Its Difficulties

Early in 1927 Aragon, who had been toying with the idea for some time, finally joined the Communist Party. This move brought with it internal conflicts: the simplest, because it was intellectual rather than emotional, was that writing the six-volume novel, *La Défense de l'infini*, which he had contracted to do, was against not only Surrealist principles but the views of the party he had just joined. To put it crudely, writing fiction (especially of a readable kind) was viewed as a displacement activity that should be abandoned in favour of work to bring about the revolution.

More pressing was the battle between his deep ideological convictions and the life he was now leading, dominated – ironically, in true Surrealist fashion – by his love for Nancy, a life spent largely in the cafés and *boîtes* of Paris. One of these, Le Boeuf sur le Toit, a special favourite of Nancy's, was an acknowledged bête noire of the Surrealists for whom Cocteau, the Boeuf's patron, represented all that was worst about the French literary world and was accordingly reviled by them. Knowing this, every time Aragon went there with Nancy he must have suffered a frisson of guilt.

Aragon was undoubtedly well aware that he ought to choose – indeed, should have chosen – between these two paths. But since, according to the ethics of the Surrealists, to whom he still felt closely linked, love trumped every other circumstance and excused every action, he would have felt that it was all right not to deny the passionate love he felt for Nancy. As he wrote in Les *Voyageurs de l'impériale*, he 'threw himself into this woman as into a torrent'. And, like someone tumbling into a river, he was borne along by Nancy's tumultuous life.

'To love a woman is to see her as the unique preoccupation of one's life, a preoccupation above all others,' he declared in a symposium on sex held by the Surrealists the following year, and at first, as he had written earlier, this was an entirely happy existence. Aragon was in Paris all that spring, working on his novel; Nancy was in her flat, where they often dined when entertaining. Aragon remembered Anna, the maid, bringing in *le Yorkshire pudding* and mint sauce and Nancy listening politely to the friend he had brought, talking of London, playing with her bracelets, then saying, 'Have a drink.'

Another dinner was more formal, with everyone in evening dress. Although it was enjoyable, the evening was a little ceremonious, even stilted, thought Aragon: 'It is difficult to be natural when in evening dress.' The presence of Michael Arlen, 'the toast of all London, author of the famous *Green Hat*', did not help. Aragon, who knew he had been Nancy's lover, perhaps through residual jealousy mentally dubbed him as being 'like a hairdresser' and was annoyed that he talked incessantly the whole evening.

This ended, as many of Aragon and Nancy's evenings did, at Zelli's, a smoke-filled *boîte* in the rue Fontaine that was one of Aragon's favourites – he loved the bar, so crowded that you could not even rest your elbows on it, the general glitter, the spotlights glancing off the buckets of champagne, the flower sellers, the clapping in time to the music if some couple were spectacularly good dancers, the laughter and the occasional entry of some woman so beautiful that, in his words, 'it was like a knife slicing through the room, silencing the other women as her wrap slid from her shoulders to reveal a skin so dazzling that it seemed alight'. There must have been an extra pleasure to know that his Nancy was one of these.

If it was not Zelli's, it was another *boîte*. It was the height of the Jazz Age; everyone, including Nancy, followed favourite jazz bands from club to club, drinking as they did so – sometimes this meant a Charleston danced with total abandon, sometimes it meant falling over between the tables.

But Nancy's flat, and its associations, held equal charm for him:

The last shred of daylight gave a fairylike air to the landscape, into which the house seemed to be advancing like a ship. We were above some large trees at the end of the Île; to the left one could see the city where the street lights were already gleaming and the curve of the river which encircled the Île Saint-Louis. There was Notre-Dame, so much more beautiful seen from the side of the apse than of the forecourt, and the bridges . . . the river, with a barge, a long barge with clothes drying on it. The quay, the Seine, the hooting of tugs, the sun that set over the Pantheon like a yellow dog, that was our bedroom's music.

As a couple, the impact of Nancy and Aragon's looks, chic, elegance and style was doubled, making of their affair one of those unions that did, indeed, seem meant to be, so much so that the British press announced their engagement in several newspapers, from the *Liverpool Post* to the *Glasgow Bulletin*. (The Associated Press and similar news agencies had a global news distribution system; as this included the UK, even the most provincial newspapers carried gossip and news of the personalities of the day – with the public obsessed with the lives of celebrities and those in society, this in turn meant that Nancy became a household name very quickly.)

'From Paris comes the news that Nancy Cunard . . . is soon to marry again,' ran this speculative report. 'The gentleman in the case is Mr Louis Aragon, who is described as very clever, very modern, very realistic, and in a way highbrow. He would have to be in the forefront of the newest intellectual movement to please Miss Cunard, who is one of the three or four English girls who find Montparnasse more to their taste than Mayfair, and to whom none would deny cleverness.' Within two weeks there was an indignant rebuttal from Nancy: 'Miss Nancy Cunard asks us to state that the rumour that she is engaged to Mr Louis Aragon is entirely without foundation.'

That May, the huge excitement in Paris, as everywhere else, was Charles Lindbergh's flight across the Atlantic* – it was the first non-stop solo transatlantic flight, heralding a new age in the air. There were three competitors for the prize of $25,000 but only twenty-five-year-old Lindbergh, hitherto unknown, planned to fly solo. Taking a chance on the weather, he took off in drizzle ahead of his competitors to become his country's favourite, spoken of constantly. When he landed, he achieved instant global fame for his 33.5-hour, 3,600-mile (5,800km) flight from New York City to Paris in a single-engine monoplane, *The Spirit of St Louis*.

Caught up in the excitement were his compatriots Harry and Caresse Crosby. 'Along the Seine to Saint Denis and Le Bourget to wait for Lindbergh who is reported two hundred miles off the coast of Ireland and it is dark and it is cold as we pass through the gate,' records Harry's diary for 21 May 1927. Other planes, from London and Strasbourg, landed while they waited, and searchlights scanned the sky – 'the most mammoth is the giant searchlight on the Mont Valérien at Saint Cloud and it is ten o'clock and the crowd is impatient,' continues Harry's diary. 'Suddenly unmistakeably the sound of an aeroplane (dead silence) and then to our left a white flash against the dark night and another flash (like a shark darting through water). Then nothing. No sound. Suspense. And again a sound . . . Then sharp swift in the gold glare of the searchlight a small white hawk of a plane swoops hawk-like down and across the field – C'est lui, Lindbergh. LINDBERGH! And there is pandemonium wild animals let loose and a stampede towards the plane.'

Lindbergh was mobbed in Paris, but this was nothing to his reception in the US, where for days there was only Lindbergh in the papers; he was offered wealth without stint to appear in films

---

* This was not the first transatlantic flight: these had begun with Alcock and Brown's flight from Newfoundland to Ireland in 1919, but Lindbergh was the first to fly from New York, solo.

or speak at dinners and streets and schools were renamed after him. Through it all he remained handsome, brave, modest and charming, the very model of a romantic, chivalrous hero, and the public loved him for it.

When Harry's father, a rich and conservative Boston investment broker, visited the Crosbys in Paris that month he did his best to get his son into more conventional attire, with presents of a dark suit, a dark overcoat, black shoes, black silk socks and – more to Harry's liking – a cellarful of wine and 100 black cigarettes,* as well as three dresses and a coat for Caresse. But he did not approve of the black gardenia Harry wore in his buttonhole, nor of his red-painted nails and habit of going bareheaded. (Nor, probably, if he had noticed them would he have liked the gilded claws of the Crosbys' black whippet Narcisse.)

The Crosbys were also there for the last great festivity before Paris regulars departed for the summer, their second Quat'Z'Arts Ball. For Harry, who did not care what he spent and frequently backed horses about which he knew nothing because their names reminded him of his passion, the sun, it was a chance for the kind of orgiastic revel they both loved. This time, with the previous year's success behind them, he determined that it would be even more memorable. Harry's diary for 10 June 1927 records:

> I buy ten live snakes on the Quays and take them home in a sack (this is a preparation for the 4 Arts). We go out for fard and perfume and I buy seven dead pigeons to wear as a necklace ... and afterwards to put on green paint ... It does not seem a year ago that we were doing exactly the same thing and at eight the students begin to appear (many more people than last year) and the Punch bowl is filled and the Party has begun. The room was hot and reeked with cigarette and cigar smoke, with fard and sweat and smell of underarms ... towards ten o'clock and seventy empty champagne bottles rattle upon the floor and now Gin Gin Gin.

---

* Probably the renowned Russian black cigarettes with gold tips by Balkan Sobranie.

After marching *en bande* up the Champs-Élysées they reached
their destination, this year the Salle Wagram, where, climbing up a ladder above the dancers, Harry undid his sack and
turned it upside down so that the snakes dropped down among
them:

> There were shrieks and catcalls and there was a riot. I remem-
> ber two strong young men stark naked wrestling on the floor
> for the honour of dancing with a young girl (silver paint con-
> quered purple paint) and I remember a mad student drinking
> champagne out of a skull ... [which] I had pilfered a year
> ago from the Catacombs ... and in a corner I watched two
> savages making love, beside me sitting a plump woman with
> bare breasts absorbed in the passion of giving milk to one of
> the snakes!

In the spring and summer of 1927 Paris was fuller than ever of
American tourists; some, like many of the Montparnos, drawn
over by the lure of alcohol, others because Paris and the Latin
Quarter were now well known as the habitat of everyone who
wanted to paint or write – and who knows, that young man in
shabby clothes sitting on the terrace of the Dôme and gazing into
a glass with a notebook nearby might be one of those brilliant
new writers one heard so much about? More likely, believed
Ferdinand Tuohy, a writer who had lived in Paris since 1919, the
young man was simply another tourist checking off the sights he
had seen.

The cafés were sharing in the new prosperity. The Dôme had
been refurbished, with mirrors and red plush, the Vaudeville
Brasserie, with its mirrors, mosaics, marble and elegant etched-
glass panels, was popular, while two enterprising brothers-in-law
had decided to create the largest brasserie in Paris, with one huge
space seating 450 people, decorated in Art Deco style, its thirty-
three structurally necessary columns painted by a host of artists
– in the main, pupils of Matisse and Léger – and La Coupole was
born. It had opened with a huge party the previous December
and was a success at once. Other *boîtes* simply enlarged their

premises and hired jazz bands. 'The humble little restaurant that I remembered with its floors sprinkled with sawdust had exploded into a vast gastronomic temple with brilliant lights and awnings,' lamented one habitué. 'Instead of a *plat du jour* at seventy-five centimes there was each day a different regional menu at forty francs or thereabout.'

One of the few to remain comparatively unspoilt was the Café Select, largely because of its proprietors, here described by John Glassco: 'Madame Select ... had a high colour, shrewd eyes, and a bosom like a shelf; she wore little black fingerless mittens that kept her hands warm without preventing her from counting the francs and centimes. Monsieur Select, who made the Welsh rarebits [Croques monsieur] on a little stove behind the bar, had long melancholy moustaches like Flaubert's.' It also stayed open all night.

But few of the bands of tourists who flocked into these night-spots saw the special magic of Paris – the Seine glittering under stars, the beautiful bridges with their elegant lamps, the dark, narrow streets with the glimmer of a café at the end leading off well-lit boulevards.

Tuohy was horrified by the behaviour of these compatriots, castigating them in print:

Sustained, unblushing public drunkenness among people of education can never before have obtained such momentum as it has today in Montparnasse among U.S. college youths and young and middle-aged American women. Not only do these drink almost without cessation potent 'shots' for effect but they virtually talk of nothing else but drink and the 'drunks' they were on the night before, the parties they are going on to next all shouted shrilly or stridently and with very little reticence regarding language ... the mad, insensate spinning from bar to bar which these people indulge ... they have sent prices sky-high everywhere. In studio parties, the company drinks and drinks until one after another passes out.

The arrival of these hordes made the resident colony of

Montparnos more determined than ever to escape for the summer, among them Aragon and Nancy.

In August 1927 the two went to stay at Varengeville, near Dieppe. Breton, too, was in Normandy, a few kilometres away at the Manoir d'Ango, alone and despondent because he was getting on badly with his wife Simone – who had stayed behind in Paris – and struggling with his novel *Nadja*. Aragon was working on *Traité du style* – not a book on grammar but a short treatise in which he took apart, in a style half brilliant, half nonsensical, what he thought was wrong with institutions and individuals. Fluent as always, he easily wrote a dozen pages of *Traité du style* every day. At Nancy's instigation, all three met every evening in a café in Pourville to read what they had written that day to each other.

It was a situation ripe for some kind of drama: Nancy a trifle bored with Aragon's unqualified adoration, Breton daunted by the brilliance of Aragon's work and jealous of him because of the ease with which he wrote and his luck in having a beautiful woman as his summer companion. Nor – as usual both admiring and deprecating – did Breton fail to note that Aragon had brought his collection of around 2,000 ties with him.

Aragon, for his part, was uneasily aware that 'something' was going on. He and Nancy were already beginning to quarrel, their difficulties exacerbated by a piece of typical Nancy behaviour. Although the details are hazy, it appears that she had a brief fling with Breton. As Aragon later wrote, 'in that house with its cardboard walls where Nane and I were already beginning to ... quarrel, I suddenly discovered jealousy. I can still hear André laughing at the pages of the *Traité*, without knowing that that forced gaiety of mine already hid that of Othello which I was secretly reading and re-reading in the original English.'

As for Nancy, rather as in the legend of the scorpion that stings itself to death when surrounded by fire because it cannot help itself, her self-destructive urge surfaced when she was encircled by the adoration of a lover. Sooner or later, her basic selfishness would reassert itself, never more emphatically than in matters sexual. She could not – or would not – see that physical unfaithfulness could cause pain; in her eyes, if she wished to sleep with someone – and she often did – that was reason enough to do so and if her lover at the time minded, that was his problem, not hers. The idea of not doing something, or giving something up, because it might cause pain to another was entirely foreign to her. Or, as André Thirion put it more succinctly, 'Nancy, who could be gentle, tender, loving and attentive, was a difficult and devastating companion. More than anything, she loved men.'

For Aragon, whose view of women – of *the* woman – was above all romantic, with the two of them joined in a lifelong idyll of passionate and intellectual bliss, the idea that his beloved could look elsewhere, even momentarily, was torture. The unfortunate Aragon wrote of having to keep his window wide open to the sea in order not to hear 'the sighs and the pantings of love' through the flimsy walls. Breton might have justified this episode by the habit of many in the Surrealist group of having mistresses as well as money in common – but for Aragon it meant experiencing for the first time the misery that went with loving Nancy. He had begun to realise what was completely alien to his own nature: that Nancy was sexually promiscuous, or, as she would have put it, believed in sexual freedom, taking another lover or lovers as and when she felt like it, a habit that plunged Aragon into misery and despair.

Thus Aragon found himself all alone at Dieppe on a day that was hugely important to himself and his fellow Surrealists – the day Sacco and Vanzetti were executed. These were two Italian anarchists, immigrants to the US, who were controversially convicted of murder during an armed robbery on a Massachusetts shoe company in April 1920. The verdict of first-degree murder by both jury and judge was suspected of having been influenced by anti-immigrant, anti-anarchist bias and there were a series of well-founded appeals, all denied by the Massachusetts judiciary. By 1926, the case had become one of the largest causes célèbres of the early twentieth century, with protests from Sydney to São Paulo, Tokyo to Johannesburg, with celebrated writers and artists pleading their case. But after a secret deliberation, the two were electrocuted just after midnight on 23 August 1927.* That day there were riots and destruction of property in London and Paris, where Aragon knew his fellow communists and Surrealists would have been protesting – protests he would have wished to join in – and a number of the American tourists now flooding the Paris streets were attacked by enraged French sympathisers of the unfortunate pair.

Back in Paris, the quarrels and arguments between Nancy and Aragon grew more frequent and more violent. In a city, there was more opportunity for her to indulge in a passing fancy for some man she had just met, or even seen, and disappear for a few hours; with their regular nightlife, there was also more likelihood of her getting drunk, when she would become sharp-wittedly cruel and vitriolic in contrast to her daytime self. Aragon suffered more and more distress as the differences between his life with Nancy and the path followed by the comrades were more and more apparent; slowly he was coming to a conclusion – a conclusion that to any writer would be like the sacrifice of part of their innermost being. It concerned the novel on which he had been working for so long.

His first step was to eviscerate it by taking out the centre section, which was published clandestinely the following year, in a limited edition, as a short erotic/pornographic novel entitled *Le Con d'Iréne* (*Irene's Cunt*), which details the life of a man through his adulthood to old age and in the latter half reveals his inner thoughts after he has lost his ability to speak and move due to syphilis. All his life Aragon denied writing it, at first certainly because of censorship, so that it was published under the pseudonym Albert de Routisie, although everyone in his circle knew who had written it. It is also clear from the text that much of it is about Nancy, as in this paragraph:

---

* On 23 August 1977, the fiftieth anniversary of their execution, the Governor of Massachusetts issued a proclamation that Sacco and Vanzetti had been unfairly tried and that 'any disgrace should be forever removed from their names'.

She believes without much effort that love is not different from its object, that there is nothing else to look for. She will often say this bluntly and unpleasantly. She knows how to be rude and precise. Words make her no more afraid than men do, and like them they sometimes make her happy. She never deprives herself of words even in the midst of voluptuous pleasure. They come out of her then without any effort, in all their violence. Ah, what a language she can use. She excites herself, and her lover, with a burning and ignoble vocabulary. She rolls in words like a sweat. It is quite something to love Irène.

And again:

I was madly in love with an extraordinarily beautiful woman. With a woman in whom I'd believed, as in the reality of stones. With a woman I thought loved me. I was her dog. That's my way. Then something incomprehensible occurred, something like a thought dissimulated between us, and it was the cruel time of *holidays* before I quite caught on to the peculiar turn of events, via certain glances ... I had nothing to reproach this woman for really, except that she did not love me. Even though she was so incredibly like a pearl. Physically. The lustre of a pearl.

Aragon stuffed the rest of his novel – something like 1,000 pages – into a small suitcase. When he and Nancy went on another trip to Spain in October, first to Córdoba, then to San Sebastian and on to Madrid, he took this case with him. One evening in the hotel in Madrid's Puerta del Sol where they were staying, he opened the case, pulled out the mass of paper, and flung all the pages of *La Defense de l'infini* on the fire.

It was literally a burnt sacrifice, perhaps to the principles of the Communist Party or those of Surrealism so that he could concentrate on those more fully, perhaps to Nancy herself, perhaps even as a distraction from the difficulties and pain their affair had begun to cause him. Later, he wrote of the evening in his poem 'Chant de la Puerta del Sol':

Then I tore up four years of my life
With my trembling hands. With my tightly knotted fingers
On my knees with bare feet . . .
Cesar we who are about to die by your hand salute you
Cries silenced as the cinders fly upwards
The secrets on the paper
Shrivel as the fiery mouth touches the writing.

Nancy did her best to salvage what she could from the fire, but she was not able to save much. 'Those flames,' said Aragon afterwards, 'destroyed in me all possibility of writing novels for six years.' When he wrote to his publisher, Doucet, telling him what he had done it automatically broke their contract – and Aragon no longer received the 1,000 francs a month on which he had been living. This penury would deeply affect him the following year.

Towards the end of 1927, Nancy finally found the home she had been looking for. She had always planned to put the money her father had left her into a settled property rather than a rented Parisian flat, and the summers she had spent in Normandy had given her a liking for that countryside of gently rolling fields, quiet lanes and small, ancient villages. What she bought was a small *cour Normande*, or farmhouse, that stood in about an acre but was otherwise without land, just outside the little village of La Chapelle-Réanville, about a hundred kilometres from Paris and six from the nearest town, Vernon, on the banks of the Seine.

It was, like most *cours Normandes*, a long line of buildings with a barn at each end and smaller buildings facing it around a square courtyard. In this courtyard was a four-sided well thirty metres deep, with an iron ladder leading down and an electric pump at the bottom (which constantly went wrong), so Nancy called it 'Le Puits Carré' – the square well.

Though the farmhouse itself, built of warm, honey-coloured stone, had cost little, it was so dilapidated that renovating it was expensive. The square well in the courtyard, shaded by two large lime trees, was used for cooling the white wine of which she was so fond. In the summer the branches of these trees, which swept nearly to the ground, formed a wonderful outdoor dining room in which Nancy and her guests would eat at a rough wooden table and benches; at night an electric light on a long flex from the house was hung amid the branches with their gold-tasselled flowers that gave off a sweet scent.

There were four or five bedrooms, with Nancy's at one end of the house and a sizeable sitting room at the other, which had a large window framing a Corot-like landscape. In the kitchen Nancy put some of her African heads. The dining room was painted in a dark green with red marbling and Nancy had left the original bars at the windows. Even more light was shut out by the branches of a pear tree trained espalier-fashion across the nearby outside wall. Although Nancy had adorned the dining room with many African carvings and one of her best pictures, a 1918 Chirico,* in the winter the house was so cold that everyone preferred the warm kitchen. Her collection of African bangles, now numbering over 200 – some too large to be worn, others studded with silver nails, or made of twisted gold – were immensely important to her and were hung on thick rails. She would take a selection of them with her whenever she travelled.

As soon as Nancy had managed to get the farmhouse and its outbuildings turned into a liveable dwelling, she decided that she should learn printing, chiefly so that she had the chance to promote writers she admired. Starting a small publishing firm – which was what she had in mind – was not as unusual an undertaking as it might seem today: the post-war years were the era of small presses and Paris was full of them, such as the Crosbys' Black Sun Press, William Bird's Three Mountains and Robert McAlmon's Contact Editions. These produced well-designed books in small numbers – usually between 150 and 500 – often by writers later deemed important and influential, like Ezra Pound, Ernest Hemingway, William Carlos Williams and James Joyce. Many of those who owned and ran these presses were themselves writers, so they were in the true sense self-publishers.

---

* Now in the Guggenheim Museum in Venice.

For poets, of which there seemed to be an inordinate number in Paris, they were an especial boon: in general, poetry was not in great demand in the US, whereas a well-written story could usually find an outlet.

Virginia and Leonard Woolf had always tried to dissuade Nancy from having her own press, saying, 'Your hands will never be free of printing-ink.' But once Nancy was set on a course, nothing and no one could dissuade her. A publishing house she would have.

CHAPTER 13

⊱—⊰—○—⊱—⊰

The Hours Press; Henry Crowder

The relationship between Nancy and Aragon was becoming ever more tense and difficult, in large part because of her dependence on alcohol. Aragon's friend and acolyte André Thirion, who watched his hero obsessively and therefore Nancy too, described what happened: 'Like many Englishwomen from a good social background, Nancy often drank too much. She would become nasty, aggressive and brutal, slapping men with the back of her forearm, crushing their faces with the ivory or metal that squeezed her in from her wrists to her elbows.' When she herself bore marks from these violent scenes, she hid them by attaching a thick mauve veil to one of the small cloches or turbans that she habitually wore. 'Whenever she desired someone, he had to satisfy her wishes immediately,' noted Thirion. 'It is hard to imagine the tortures that her unfaithfulness and her sudden cravings inflicted on her lovers. More and more, their affair went from bloody fighting to passionate reconciliations.'

Fortunately, the acquisition of Le Puits Carré gave both Aragon and Nancy something else to think about and a happier few months. Nancy loved her new home, she loved the country around about, and she loved having people to stay in it. Some of the Surrealists came, as did Harold Acton and John Banting from England, and of course Janet Flanner and Solita Solano. It was not long since she had sent Janet this expression of their friendship: 'I take up my pen to tell you that our tripod, triumvirate

and triplicate standeth firm, though its three legs be now strad-
dled over the very world.'

More important still (to her relationship with Aragon) was the
realisation of Nancy's ambition of owning a printing press. She
had heard that William Bird, a newspaperman from the US whom
she knew slightly, was about to sell his Three Mountains Press,
which he had run at 29, Quai d'Anjou, Île de France, since 1921
and where, in 1922, Ezra Pound had been an editor. For £300
Bird sold her his beautiful Belgian Mathieu press, almost 200
years old and painted dark green, as well as wooden furnishings,
a good deal of Caslon Old Face type and some handsome paper.
Nancy had plenty of room in the outbuildings, and the press was
set up in a small stable that had good daylight and electric light
and was only twenty-five yards from the main house. Its arrival
that April 1928 was overseen by Bill Bird, who came down to
Chapelle-Réanville to be certain that it was correctly installed.
Once the press was in place, Nancy added shelves for storage
and for the drying of the printed sheets.

Bird also found Nancy a printer, a M. Lévy, excellent at his
job but a curmudgeonly man who found it difficult to accept the
speed with which both Nancy and Aragon learnt the necessary
skills, from the setting up of type – letters had to be set up the
opposite way round for printing, with 'd's and 'b's and 'p's and
'q's especially difficult (hence minding one's 'p's and 'q's) – to
the even distribution of the thick, sticky, oil-based ink and the
locking of the formes so that the type did not move. '[M. Lévy's]
surprise was great at our learning to handle type so fast,' wrote
Nancy. 'Yet it seemed to me that anyone who likes doing this
at all must acquire the feel of it the first or certainly the second
time he brings the *composteur* or printing stick together with the
letters; a few hours are sufficient to get the feel of it all.'

Nancy had started her press, which she christened The Hours,
with the aim of printing young modern poets, not only to give
them a voice but also to reward them with a payment or royalties higher than they might expect elsewhere; it was, in a way, a
form of subsidising those in her own literary field (although she
never, in fact, used it to print her own poetry). But when GM told

her, 'I want to start your press off with a good bang,' and offered her *Perronik the Fool* – originally written as part of his *Héloïse and Abélard*, but omitted because of its length – she realised that bringing out something by so famous a writer would give helpful publicity.

The Hours was not the only significant small press then operating. Nancy's neighbours, Harry and Caresse Crosby, who had begun by having their own poetry printed and then published, largely for friends, found a master printer near their apartment. They liked his work so much that they decided to start a press, first under the name Éditions Narcisse (after their whippet), and then, in 1928, expanding it to print the work of others, changing the name to the Black Sun Press, in honour of Harry's obsession with the sun. If Caresse had seen his diary at that time, this passion might have seriously alarmed her: 'I am waiting for the real departure, the last departure into sun then there will be no more departure and hence no more freedom but who wants freedom when he is clothed in Fire.'*

Unlike Nancy, the Crosbys were not hands-on printers, confining themselves to editing, choosing typefaces, bindings and the expensive boxes and ribbons in which the books were sold. They printed much that was original and work by friends, many of whom were writers who were either just becoming known or later became famous – Hemingway, D.H. Lawrence, Hart Crane, Joyce.

None of this interfered with their life of decadent pleasure. They were now living in an expensive flat in the rue de Lille, where much of their entertaining took place in bed (where Harry also wrote) and where dinner was served on small tables set up nearby. Every evening their guests would arrive and at eight o'clock would change into embroidered robes (these were too grand to call dressing gowns) and, after caviar and champagne, were invited to bathe in the huge sunken marble bathtub in the black and white Art Deco bathroom, stepping out on to bearskin rugs and being offered perfumed oils with which to anoint themselves.

---

* Written on 26 January 1928.

There had been a last Quat'Z'Arts Ball: 'Hun costumes this year . . . one plump girl lying naked on the floor while three men color of red ochre made love to her *et comment* . . . awoke to find six of us (not counting Narcisse) in our bed,' runs Harry's diary for 29 June 1928. They took off for Venice the next day, making straight for the Lido (where Narcisse had to wear a muzzle) to scorch in the sun, as Harry put it. On 6 July his diary records, 'Tonight in Nietzche I read a significant passage "Die at the right time".' On 9 July there is an equally important entry: 'Enter the youngest Princess of the Sun.'

This was twenty-year-old Josephine Noyes Rotch, from a smart Boston family, in Europe to buy her trousseau. Dark, intense and sexy, she and Harry began an affair immediately, meeting for sex whenever possible during the eight days she was in Venice. It was Josephine who inspired Harry's next collection of poems, dedicated to her, *Transit of Venus*:

> I wish tonight I were a cat
> That I might slink
> To where you sleep demurely
> (Sleeping above the brink of dream)
> And suck your breath
> Slowly and surely
> Into death.

It was almost a warning of what would later happen.

Nancy's first commission was from Norman Douglas and was anything but poetic. Douglas wanted her to reprint an intensely boring six-page *Report on the Pumice-Stone Industry of the Lipari Islands*, which he had originally written for the Foreign Office in 1895 and which he described as 'the only meritorious action of my life' – thanks to revealing in the *Report* the exploitation of child labour and thus bringing about its cessation.

For Nancy, however, printing the *Report* was almost as good as a tutorial in her chosen craft, such were the complexities of typeface and layout. It was finally completed and most of the eighty

Nancy in her flat at 15, rue Guénégaud, Paris, 1930.

Nancy in a silver trouser suit by the couturier Paul Poiret and her father's top hat having her hand kissed by Tristan Tzara at one of Count Étienne de Beaumont's parties in 1924.

Nancy in a feathered headdress photographed by Curtis Moffat, the husband of Nancy's great friend Iris Tree.

Nancy with her artist friend John Banting, who accompanied her to New York in 1932, and flanked by the black novelist Taylor Gordon, as she calls a press conference at the Grampion Hotel.

Some of the artists, writers and performers who lived and worked in Montparnasse. They include the photographer Man Ray, Dadaist Tristan Tzara, polymathic writer Jean Cocteau, the poets Ezra Pound and Mina Loy, and the inimitable Kiki de Montparnasse.

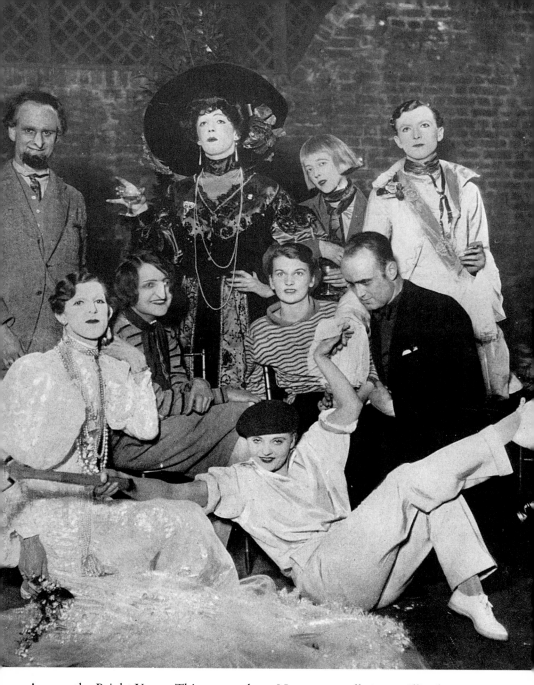

Among the Bright Young Things, to whom Nancy was, albeit unwillingly, an icon, fancy dress parties had become almost a way of life. Most of the core members of the group attended this one, held in 1927. At the back (left to right) is Richard Wyndham as sculptor Frank Dobson, Stephen Tennant as Queen Marie of Romania, Elizabeth Ponsonby as Iris Tree, and Cecil Beaton. Seated (left to right) are Brian Howard, Sacheverell Sitwell's wife Georgina as a sculptor's model, Inez Holden and Harold Acton. In front is Tallulah Bankhead as the tennis player Jean Borotra.

Kiki, who became a model at fourteen when she fled her job as a baker's apprentice to drift through the artistic underworld, until her personality and spirit of survival made her one of the best-known characters of Montparnasse café life.

Man Ray, who lived with the model Kiki, took up photography when virtually no one else was doing it and as a consequence had the field to himself.

The Dome, throughout the Twenties the favourite Montparnasse café of most of the Americans de Montparnasse.

The terrace of the American Bar the Select, on the Avenue des Champs-Élysées at the corner of the rue de Berri, in the mid-Twenties.

France's National Holiday, 14 July, was always celebrated like an open-air party, with flags and wreaths decorating shops, lanterns hanging from trees, and music and dancing in the streets – as in this photograph taken in 1930.

Iris Tree by Modigliani

Robert McAlmon, who knew everyone.

Wyndham Lewis, about whom
Ernest Hemingway said, 'I do not
think I have ever met a nastier-
looking man.'

Sylvia Beach at her desk in Shakespeare
and Company, reading the proofs of
Ulysses just before its publication in
February 1922.

Ernest Hemingway with Sylvia Beach, to whom he was devoted, in front of Shakespeare and Company, in 1928.

During the early Twenties, F. Scott Fitzgerald spent time in Paris, where Ernest Hemingway became his closest friend, much to the jealousy of Fitzgerald's wife Zelda.

Harry and Caresse Crosby at Le Bourget Airport in 1929. They had flown on the regular London—Paris service from Croydon, drinking a bottle of champagne en route, with the whippet bitch that Caresse had bought in England.

Nancy and the *New Yorker* columnist Janet Flanner, on one of Janet's visit to Nancy when she had taken a house in the English countryside.

The third member of their triumvirate, drama critic Solita Solano.

Gertrude Stein, enthroned in her favourite armchair, and her companion Alice B. Toklas. On the walls hang some of Gertrude's magnificent collection of pictures.

hand-set copies sent as a present to Douglas in June 1928. Her plan was that authors would receive one-third of the proceeds of sales of their work, after deducting the cost of production, but for GM and Douglas, because of their renown, their share was fifty per cent.

With Aragon also a natural printer, able to work out spaces, calculate pagination and design motifs using different sizes of print, working together on the press was a rare time of harmony – sometimes, when M. Lévy was telling her crossly how essential it was that most of one's apprenticeship should consist of sweeping the floor and picking up bits of type that he, the printer, had dropped, Aragon would catch her eye with a laughing glance behind M. Lévy's back.

When George Moore suggested to Nancy that she wrote a preface to *Perronik* describing her memories of him, she refused, saying, 'the learning of printing has engulfed me entirely; you cannot imagine how every hour of the day goes into it, but such is the case, dearest GM'. As Virginia Woolf had predicted, her fingers always seemed to be covered in printer's ink; to clean them she first washed them in petrol, then scrubbed with soap and water.

That April, while Aragon and Nancy were both working on the *Report* (hand-printing took considerable time), Aragon's own two new works, *Le Con d'Irene* and *Traité du style*, were published. *Irène** was printed by a specialist in such clandestine publications, René Bonnel, in an edition of 140 numbered copies. By contrast *Traité du style*, a polemic directed against what Aragon perceived as the moral, political and intellectual failures of his time and which proposed instead Surrealism to achieve a valid 'style', was brought out by the eminent house of Gallimard.

Both Nancy and Aragon visited Paris frequently – so much

---

* Only when some torn pages of this novella were found among Nancy's possessions was it possible to go on to find clear evidence that Aragon was the author. When republished several decades later, its merit was instantly acknowledged – Albert Camus thought it the finest work he had ever read relating to eroticism.

was going on there that they could not bear to miss. Aragon, who remained in the capital during the summer, was still closely tied to the Surrealists, who were in one of their states of ferment over what they saw as the misuse of their name. That June, Diaghilev was putting on his Ballets Russes at the Théâtre Sarah Bernhardt and had chosen the artist Max Ernst, a pioneer Dadaist and Surrealist, to do the décor for a Spanish court story. Already well known, Ernst was announced on the posters for the performances as 'Max Ernst, the Surrealist' (as indeed he was).

To the small band who clung around Breton and Aragon like bees around their queen this was, although not revolutionary, provocation. Ernst had linked the sacred name of Surrealism, with all it implied in the way of militant extremism, with what they saw as a reactionary White Russian organisation. Nancy, who sympathised, and who was naturally on the side of her lover and his friends, was determined to help.

So on the opening night, knowing the theatre would be filled with the smart and distinguished, Nancy took a box with several friends. As the curtain rose, down from the box fluttered hundreds of leaflets, all vigorously denouncing Ernst, while from all over the theatre came the sound of shrill whistles – then a great sign of disapproval from a French audience – and the blare of horns and trumpets. Into the pandemonium rushed the *Gardes républicaines*, and soon the Surrealists and their friends were ejected. But the management rang the curtain down and continued with the next number in the programme. Nancy had won her victory.

She returned to Chapelle-Réanville and during an intensely hot summer put in about a month's work on *Perronik*, ceasing only when M. Lévy took his summer holiday, agreeing to return in the autumn.

In August 1928 Nancy and Aragon went to Venice. Although neither of them realised it, this heralded the end of their affair. For Nancy, Venice was a natural destination: all through the Twenties, it was to Venice that the ultra-fashionable of Europe's beau monde flocked in the late summer to autumn months (the Riviera did not overtake it until the following decade). The railway network across Europe was growing and improving – even Paris trains, chaotic until the mid-Twenties, were now reliable and the *Rome Express* as well as the *Simplon Orient* now connected Paris with La Serenissima, both with luxurious sleeping cars and restaurants.

Once there, anyone from the social world in which Nancy had been brought up could be sure of meeting friends – a mere half-hour in Florian's café in St Mark's Square watching the world go by would ensure that. As for the Lido, where the smart world congregated for much of the time, in Nancy's words, it was spectacular: 'that blazing Lido strewn with society stars in glittering jewels and make-up, that brilliance of Grand-Canal barge parties, those spontaneous dawn-revels after dancing in some of the rather sinister new night-bars'. There were endless festivities. The Cole Porters, for instance, were famous for their hospitality: 'Dined with the Cole Porters. After dinner they had singers come on the [Grand] Canal under the moonlight. Wonderful moonlight. It was all too beautiful,' wrote Duff Cooper in August 1923, adding thoughtfully, 'These perfect moonlight nights in Venice are incomplete without some love affair.'

Nancy's own love affair, however, was going badly. Between them was what Aragon, still hopelessly in love with her, called 'a false situation, perfectly intolerable'. Although Nancy was much richer than Aragon, when the publisher Doucet was paying him a monthly salary to write his novel he could, if not keep up with Nancy's lifestyle, at least afford to live independently and no doubt pay for meals and drinks from time to time. Now he did not have that and, while in Paris he could always scratch a living, in Venice he knew he would be completely dependent on his mistress, something he hated, especially as Venice, with its glittering social life, was entirely different from the trips they had made to Spain or the South of France – both known for their cheapness.

So before going he decided to sell a painting by Braque – *La Baigneuse* – that on Breton's advice he had bought earlier for practically nothing. Since then, Braque's fame had increased and the painting's value had greatly appreciated; with the money from the sale he would be able to accompany Nancy on outings without loss of self-respect. But the sale negotiations, always time-consuming, dragged on and he had to leave with Nancy for Venice before the money came.

In Venice Nancy plunged into the customary round of drinks and parties, a routine of which Aragon, whose usual world was that of the cafés and bars of Paris and the company of his left-leaning fellow Surrealists, was beginning to tire. He was also by now aware of Nancy's sudden infidelities. Penniless and rather miserable, for him it was not a good start to a holiday. As he later told a biographer, 'To explain this it is necessary to speak about all sorts of things I don't like to say about the character of Nane, and of mine too . . . the parties, the Venetian society and particularly because of this man who followed her and who did not belong to their world . . . and then the liking of Nane for these odd encounters'.

The tensions between them grew worse. For Aragon the continued non-arrival of the money, which would have given him independence, made their relationship increasingly difficult. 'We went to Padua to give ourselves a change of routine – that was pure bloodiness,' wrote Nancy to Janet Flanner who was soon coming with Solita to stay. When Janet and Solita arrived they noted that the apartment was filled with rows, the packing by Aragon of his suitcase ready to depart, then a reconciliation and unpacking. Nancy was at her worst, vicious and disparaging; Aragon was wretched.

One evening, perhaps to get away from the constant friction, Nancy and her cousin Edward, a constant in her life, went out to dine and dance.

At the hotel they chose, the Luna, a group of black jazz musicians, hired for eight weeks, was playing. 'They were Afro-Americans, coloured musicians, and they played in that "out of this world" manner which, in ordinary English, would have to be translated, I suppose, by "ineffable",' recorded Nancy. 'Such Jazz and such Swing and such improvisations! And all new to me in style!' For the band, this was a prestigious engagement: the Luna, a few minutes' walk away from St Mark's Square, was one of the most fashionable and certainly one of the oldest hotels in Venice – it is recorded as having given shelter to the Knights Templar in 1118. One of the band, the pianist Henry Crowder, had determined to make the most of this opportunity, to work hard, to avoid temptation – in short, to improve his lot in life. His day began with a French lesson at the Berlitz School of Languages, with two or three hours of piano practice lateish in the afternoon, followed by dinner and then playing at the Luna.

On the day that Nancy and Edward first came to dance there, Crowder recorded, 'We were all startled to see a most peculiar and striking woman enter the ballroom, accompanied by a tall man.' It was, of course, Nancy. Edward and Nancy thought the band were so good that they came to the Luna night after night. One evening, feeling like company, they asked the banjo player, who had finished for the night, to sit down and have a drink with them. Crowder, the last to leave the bandstand, went to fetch his hat. As he passed the table where the three were sitting, Nancy asked him, 'Won't you sit down and have a drink?' He accepted and sat with the other three. So began what would be the most important love affair of Nancy's life (and the fifth of my title).

Crowder was a good-looking man of mixed Native American and African blood, born in Georgia in 1895, the youngest of the twelve children of a tanner. He had played the piano since childhood; 'it just came natural'. But he had also learnt to read scores, however difficult. His was a churchgoing family and he had acquired much of his musical skill singing in church and playing the piano for the YMCA, although he first earned a musical living as a pianist in Washington brothels (he was married to a seamstress who worked for Eleanor Roosevelt at the White House). Gradually, through hard work and moving around, he moved up in the world and eventually, with his band, the Alabamians, came to Europe.

A few days after they had met over that first drink, Nancy made her move, telephoning Crowder while he was having supper with the band to ask him to join her for dinner. When he told her he was already eating, she said it did not matter and she would send a gondola immediately.

As the black gondola she had sent to fetch him glided noiselessly over the dark waters, Crowder, unable to speak a word of Italian or to recognise his surroundings, wondered what lay in store. He was ushered into an elegant apartment where dinner was served; after it, Nancy said she had some things to show him that might interest him. She took him into her bedroom, where she brought out some of her bracelets and beads, often standing close to him.

Crowder, hesitant at making a false move yet wondering if this closeness was deliberate, was suddenly aware that he was immensely attracted to her: 'My heart was thumping at a terrific pace. I could feel my blood excitedly racing to my head.' When they said goodbye, she looked at him meaningfully and he tried to kiss her but she leaned her head away. Feeling he had made a blunder, he turned away, then Nancy suddenly kissed him full on the lips. He went back to the hotel and played his stint on the piano in a daze.

A day or two later there was one of her restless departures. When she and Crowder were having drinks together, she told him she had to go to Florence to see Norman Douglas.

In Florence that October, she stayed in Douglas's apartment at 14, Lungarno delle Grazie, overlooking the Arno, full of artefacts – a great yellow-marble tortoise that Douglas had dug up in his garden near Baia, bowls, plaques, statuettes, a lapis-lazuli dagger handle from Persia, rare stones and fossils. It was here, too, that Nancy learnt much about the business side of publishing, which Douglas had down to a fine art by publishing his own books in expensive private editions that sold well. Douglas did everything except the actual printing, starting early in the morning with a busy day built around the long lunches and dinners he so enjoyed – collecting bundles of mail from Thomas Cook, meetings with the printer, accounts and the packing and despatch of books ordered.

One book he had published that year was one about which he did not appear to have told Nancy, possibly fearing that she might be horrified – despite her behaviour, she was if anything puritan in her spoken words. This was a small volume entitled

Some Limericks, of which he wrote, 'I may be abused on the ground that the pieces are coarse, obscene, and so forth. Why, so they are,' and which became one of the most pirated books of all time. What made it so successful was the juxtaposition of filthy limerick and erudite comment from Douglas, affecting to be a literary critic:

> There was a young student of John's
> Who wanted to bugger the swans.
> But the loyal hall-porter
> Said: 'Pray take my daughter!
> The birds are reserved for the dons.

'The family of the *Anatidae* seems to be favoured of mankind,' wrote Douglas in his pose as an academic, 'and this much may be said in extenuation of the young man's proclivities that the swan is a comely bird. Not for nothing was it chosen by the Father of the Gods on a certain memorable occasion. If Zeus had transformed himself into a duck, Leda would hardly have succumbed to his charms.'

While Nancy was in Florence, she and Crowder kept in touch by telegram; when she returned and Crowder saw her again, he suddenly realised that 'I was infatuated beyond all reason'. All his plans and good resolutions faded away in the heat of this passion. 'I love you as I have never loved anyone,' he wrote. Nancy would go round to the band's hotel and watch them playing their endless card games. She gave them all Venetian glass rings – Crowder got a wonderful green one lined with gold. And when she decided to give a masked ball, she asked them to play.

Masks, and thus masked balls, were very much part of the history of Venice. There was a strong Venetian tradition of dressing up, often for Carnival, costumes that almost always involved a mask. In the days when it was a republic and a centre of trade, such (full-face) masks were originally designed to conceal a person's identity: someone who wished to remain anonymous when making a deal could do so; a citizen could answer one of the state's officials frankly and without fear of retribution. They quickly became the symbols of Carnival, enablers of decadent behaviour without damage to reputation. Some were stylised: the Plague Doctor with its long, sinister beak, who presided over the Black Death, Pulcinella's gold-trimmed white mask and women's black-velvet *moretta* masks, held to the wearer's face by biting on a button at mouth level and considered weapons of seduction. Above all, masks were fashionable.

Nancy's ball was both fashionable and decadent – theatre designer Oliver Messel with silver eyelashes, an old nobleman dressed as a mandarin, another fantastic figure rushing about frantically because he had mislaid his little jewelled box that held cocaine. Her elderly gondolier was solicited by one of her female guests ('I could have understood if it had been my nephew,' he said to Nancy afterwards). The party ended in a downpour of rain; Nancy asked Henry to stay behind, and they watched the other three Alabamians leave at six in the morning in bright sunlight with their pick-ups. That night she and Henry became lovers. As they parted after a late breakfast, Crowder realised that 'I was infatuated with a white woman. Somehow I felt this woman had something I had never discovered in any other person ... I ... allowed myself to be held by an invisible power she seemed to possess.'

For Aragon, Nancy's new affair was literally almost a death blow. Nancy's sudden passion for Henry hit him where he was most vulnerable – his fear of being abandoned, induced by his childhood, his passionate desire to be wholly loved, the feeling of humiliation when the woman whom you thought loved you prefers another, as well, of course, as intense sexual jealousy. His anguish was such that suicide seemed the only way out. Having studied medicine, he knew the necessary pills to buy and found them at a nearby pharmacy.

Next, he rented a room in a hotel overlooking the Riva degli Schiavoni (the waterfront promenade along St Mark's Basin), where he swallowed the pills. He owed his life to an English friend who, worried by his absence, scoured the city to find out where he might be and managed to reach him in time. Several days later, Aragon decided to try again and went back to the same pharmacy, but this time the pharmacist, either alerted to what had happened or, alarmed by his appearance, guessing what he wanted the pills for, refused to sell to him, saying that the sale of this product was now forbidden.

There was only one alternative: to leave and go back to Paris. This time Nancy could not persuade Aragon to unpack, and he left for Paris at the beginning of October. Ironically, just before his departure the promised cheque from the sale of his painting arrived, so that he now had all the money he would have needed for the life in Venice that he was about to renounce. On the return journey to Paris, he stopped off in Milan where he went to La Scala to hear Verdi's *Otello*, with its central theme of jealousy, six times.

One evening André Thirion arrived back at the rue du Château to find a huge blown-up photograph of Nancy by Man Ray, her arms covered with African bracelets, pasted up on the wall, a suitcase covered with travel stickers in his room and a collection of cravats and ties hanging from a rail. He realised that Aragon must have come back from Venice, learnt almost immediately of the rupture, and saw its effects. His friend Georges Sadoul,* also one of the Surrealist group, described Aragon as being 'distraught, desperate, haunted by the idea of suicide', moving miserably from furnished room to furnished room. Thirion, however, grasped at once that, above all, Aragon did not want to be alone, and as he and Sadoul had just taken over the lease of the rue du Château house, they took him to live there, along with the actor Marcel Duhamel, the poet Jacques Prévert and the painter Yves Tanguy. Fortunately (though that is perhaps the wrong word), two of the others were also heartbroken and the three of them compared, commiserated and tried to console each other, in a bond described by Thirion as 'a camaraderie of the wounded'.

*

---

* A journalist and film critic, he later became known for the first scholarly, worldwide study of the cinema.

When the band's contract ended during the first week of October, at around the time Aragon left Venice, they departed for Paris. Against their advice, and that of Nancy's cousin Victor, Crowder, persuaded to do so by Nancy, stayed behind in Venice for another ten days. Aragon might have been cheered had he known that Crowder, within weeks of beginning his affair with Nancy, was already experiencing the same pangs when she went off for the night with a young Italian nobleman who was also pursuing her. Not for the last time, Crowder swore that he would tear himself away: 'But I never did. There was that same indefinable attraction, that same pulling force, that same something so intriguing and interesting that I could not shake myself loose.' He was soon to learn that to Nancy the idea of physical faithfulness meant nothing. At the same time, it was clear that she was anxious to further his career and that she could do a lot for him.

Today it is difficult to realise quite how shocking the sight of a black man on obviously intimate terms with a white woman then was to most European eyes, especially when emphasised by the contrast between Nancy's gleaming blondeness and Crowder's dark skin. Both of them began to feel they were being watched – not just 'ordinary' stares but something more sinister, on behalf of Mussolini's fascist Italy. It was time to leave, especially as the weather was changing: 'The cold is on a par with that of regrattier mornings, on a larger scale, that's all. 5 stone walls and floors, instead of 3,' wrote Nancy to Janet. 'Out of doors is agony too – the gondola (taken on for the sake of friendship with Angelo the gondolier and last year's etc) increases this quite unbearably.'

On the train to Paris, Nancy began to tell Crowder about what she called her 'difficulties' with Aragon, winding up by saying she was frightened that he would be at the station when they arrived and would make a scene, so much so that she insisted they went straight to a small hotel in Montmartre, rather than her more usual haunt of Montparnasse where Aragon, if not at the station, would certainly be.

Montparnasse itself was steadily changing. Thanks to the

tourists,* the cafés were still expanding and putting up their prices, the current most popular one being the Trois et As, because Jimmie Charters had moved there. Then, too, a number of those who had given the *quartier* its special flavour were beginning to depart, some because they had simply got older and thought it time to go home, some because, like Hemingway, they had suddenly become successful and their lives had changed – the previous year, his parting from Hadley now irrevocable, Hemingway had married Pauline Pfeiffer. When she became pregnant, they decided that their baby should be born in the US, where Hemingway's career now seemed set fair.

Nancy herself was now based in Normandy, although Paris was still the centre of much of her life. The Crosbys too had departed. In late 1928, they bought for $220 in gold a twenty-year lease on a medieval mill outside Paris in Ermenonville, abandoned as a mill probably because the millstream had dwindled to a trickle. Le Moulin du Soleil, as they christened it, consisted of three old stone buildings, with a single bathroom but no electricity or telephone. Gradually the Crosbys converted it, turning the old washrooms and cellars into a large kitchen, with the ground floor of the central tower as a dining room, where guests sat on logs cut from the neighbouring woods. They added a small swimming pool and flattened a piece of land on which to play donkey polo. Here they would entertain constantly, announcing special guests with a shot from an old brass marine cannon and using a whitewashed wall near the stairs as a visitors' book, with future signatures from D.H. Lawrence to Douglas Fairbanks.

Other Montparnos had slid down the ladder. One was Harold Stearns, now more dilapidated and alcoholic than ever but still clinging to his job of racing commentator by his fingernails. To raise money for drinks, he would approach a sympathetic-looking acquaintance and tell him how, a few days ago, a horse had fallen in a steeplechase and broken its leg but he, Harold Stearns, had prevented it from being shot, had got the vet to set

---

* In one year alone, 250,000 American tourists arrived. Hardly any of them could speak French.

its leg and was now caring for it, but the cost of the vet, the oats, the hay, etc., was so prohibitive that he had to take up a collection every evening. This mythical horse, and the kinder hearts of Montparnasse, usually kept him in liquid refreshment.

Aragon, in Paris, was doing his best to break free of Nancy's spell. That autumn, rich from the money from the sale of his Braque, he flung himself into a round of drinking, bars, sleepless nights and brief liaisons. But nothing seemed to do any good: he was still anguished, and he certainly had not broken with Nancy. Although he knew she had become the mistress of Henry Crowder and that, perhaps to prove she had lost nothing of her independence, she had already engaged in other 'adventures', he was unable to free himself from her.

She, for her part, still summoned Aragon whenever the fancy took her – perhaps because these brief infidelities did not touch upon her love for him and her wish to keep him near her. Thirion, watching all this, recorded, 'Nane, with tenderness and a snake-like power, fascinated her victims for a long time, preventing them from regaining their liberty from her. She loved seeing her former lovers. In reality, she took life in all its complexity and could not see why she should stop loving Aragon just because she wanted to sleep with Henry Crowder.'

Aragon wrote, seduced any woman who would let him and gave parties at the rue du Château; these usually began around midnight and were fuelled largely by the white wine that most people drank. Often he declaimed his own poetry at these gatherings. He decorated the downstairs toilets sacrilegiously, with the contents of a parcel sent to him by some of the Château's inmates who had gone to the country – the Surrealists took a great and childish pleasure in minor but unpleasant actions against organised religion, especially if these shocked people.

In one country church, records Thirion, they stole the Bible from which the priest had to read the gospel before Mass so that he would be left floundering; in another, to fill in a couple of hours between trains, they filled the collection box with pebbles, stole all the ornaments on the altar including the crucifix, opened the tabernacle and took the bowl in which the Communion wafers were kept, and concluded by peeing into the holy water basins. After this, they bought paper and string, wrapped up what they had stolen and posted the parcel to the rue du Château, addressing it to Aragon, who attached the artefacts to the lavatory chains. Often the guests who used these toilets were so horrified or terrified that they left at once.

In spite of all he had been through, Aragon remained fascinated by Nancy. He still went on seeing her; for him it was a love that went so deep he could not break it off in a few days. If she called, he went. Almost every week Aragon would spend a day or two in Chapelle-Réanville, 'and of course', recorded Thirion, 'he would come back in pieces'. But nothing, even the anguish of these days, seemed to dislodge Nancy from Aragon's mind.

CHAPTER 14

><del>·₊·<del>·O·<del>·₊·<del>

Elsa and the Power of Will

The last few months of 1928 and the beginning of 1929 saw a complex dance of relationships, with Nancy and Aragon, still linked, the central poles.

For Nancy, the most obvious was with Henry Crowder. After one of the Alabamians had got into trouble, the band had broken up, and it was agreed by both Nancy and Henry that it was best Henry should go to her house in the country at Chapelle-Réanville. Nancy got hold of a piano, they had long walks among the rolling hills of the nearby countryside and Henry enjoyed reading the books in her excellent library. It was a happy time, Nancy was at her best; one of his letters tells her that she is 'the sweetest woman I have ever known', regretting that 'my command of words is entirely too inadequate to permit my ever telling you what a divine person you are'.

With the long summer over, the Hours Press was busy. GM's letters, tender and affectionate as ever, hinged mainly on the subject of finding Nancy something of his to publish. 'Dearest Nancy, I have neglected you shamefully, but there was no help for it,' he wrote on 14 June 1928. 'When I was ill I had no inclination to write to anybody ... My affection for you is, as of course you know, unchanged, never doubt it. My first thought on landing in France will be to see your dear face, and next day, I hope, I shall see you, not with the eyes of the imagination but with my corporal eyes, working at your press'. He went on to discuss finding something for her to print. A week later, he thanked her for her 'letter in French, and very pretty French too. I should answer it in French if I had anybody to whom I might dictate. It isn't so much I can't spell French as that I cannot spell. *Perronik* went to you at once . . . it is in your hands at the present moment, maybe you are setting it . . . Please do write.'

Nancy and the printer were indeed hard at work on *Perronik*, joined sometimes by Aragon, still in thrall. Henry Crowder went back to Paris, where he got a job playing in the Plantation Club, a chic *boîte* with a restaurant with walls covered in pinkish velvet and tables with red and white check tablecloths and a modernistic design of blue and silver around the dance-floor walls – in a nod to the club's name there was a picture of a Mississippi steamboat in an alcove.

As winter drew in, Nancy complained that the house was freezing; although the printing room was warm the chief problem was the sudden electricity cuts, when in mid-printing the room would be plunged into darkness because, say, a branch had fallen on the only powerline. Sometimes cuts lasted for up to three days, but more generally it was a question of hours or even minutes. But work continued on *Perronik* although GM, who would have liked to see the printing process, wrote to Nancy lamenting that he was not fit enough to leave Ebury Street – in September he had written to her talking of coming to 'your lovely house, which I long to see almost as much as I long to see you. I shall not be happy until I am there, walking round the little domain with you and hearing about the pointing. But when will this be, Nancy?'

*Perronik the Fool** was completed just before Christmas 1928, the 200 hand-set and signed copies (the relevant pages had been sent to GM for signature while the work was still in process) bound in blue stamped with gold lettering. As GM told Emerald, he was extremely pleased with it: 'The edition is printed on beautiful rag paper, the finest I have ever seen.' It sold extremely well.

Despite having put down roots in the country, Nancy had lost none of her restlessness. She was often away – in England, in

---

* *Perronik the Fool* was a story told by Héloïse to her small son Astrolabe, in the hope that it would help him regain the French he had lost during his years in Brittany.

Paris – and Crowder would write to her. 'I know that I love you as I have never loved anyone,' said one letter, written a few weeks after they met. 'Whatever the outcome of this romance of ours, you may know now that mine is a love that though deep, strong and passionate is withal highly protective of you, and intensely sympathetic.'

In Paris, Nancy saw much of a new friend and admirer, the tall, red-haired Richard Aldington. Shortly after she had met Crowder Nancy had gone to a party given by Ezra Pound (every summer his wife Dorothy went to England to see her son, being brought up by his grandmother, and Pound moved to the Venice apartment of his paramour Olga Rudge). Nancy had long given up her pursuit of Pound, but they maintained a strong and loving friendship.

The morning after the party she was woken by Aldington, one of Pound's oldest friends, who came into her room saying, 'I've come instead of Ezra.' Knowing her reputation as a woman who would take a man into her bed on a spur-of-the-moment fancy, he pounced on her almost straight away. He was out of luck: she rejected him ('Oh, no, no! Not this!'), perhaps put off by his generally slovenly look and filthy trousers and how, as she told a friend, 'he held his hand over his balls'.

Nevertheless, they became friends. Aldington, then thirty-six, erudite, clever and good-looking, was one of the most literary men around, writing endless reviews, articles and essays as well as being an editor, biographer, novelist and poet – Pound had helped him get his poems published both in England and America. With Pound, he had been one of the three original Imagists – the third was the poet H.D. (Hilda Doolittle), whom Aldington had married in 1913. When Aldington met Nancy, he was well into the novel for which he would become known, *Death of a Hero*, which expressed his disgust at war.

During the 1914 war, the Aldington marriage had begun to disintegrate. The Aldingtons were then living at 44 Mecklenburgh Square, where there was a tangle of relationships with D.H., Frieda Lawrence and others; these were further complicated when a beautiful young woman called Dorothy (Arabella)

Yorke moved into a room upstairs. H.D., six years older than Aldington, had begun to find his sexual demands tiresome, and he turned to Arabella. In the spring of 1927 Aldington, who for some time had wanted to leave England, moved to Paris with Arabella, published more poetry, did much literary journalism and began the translations (of Italian and Old French) that were to become a lifelong work.

On a visit to the island of Port-Cros with Arabella, the Lawrences and Brigit Patmore, an old friend ten years older than himself, with whom he had had a brief affair when he was eighteen, he fell passionately in love with Brigit, who was unhappily married to a philandering husband, and Arabella departed.

Despite his passion for Brigit, Aldington was uncontrollably fascinated by Nancy, so much so that Ezra Pound sent him this warning verse:

Behold what perils do environ
The man who meddles with a siren.

Aldington took little notice of this advice; when Nancy and Aldington both returned to Paris in the autumn, they met again one weekend in November and Aldington began to hover around her. In part this may have been a subterfuge designed to conceal his relationship with Brigit, who did not want their liaison known as her own life was complicated enough. All the same, the numerous letters full of news of Nancy must have worried Brigit slightly. One written on 3 December 1928 ran:

Well, I went out and posted the pencil note to you about Nancy . . . I felt a bit annoyed with Nancy for bolting off at once, but then thought she was justified, since I hadn't made love to her. However, at 10.30 just as I was finishing a page, & thinking of bed, comes a tap at the door, & enter Nancy literally clothed in cloth of gold . . . She insisted that I get into evening clothes & come to Montmartre. I didn't particularly want to go, since I'd been up since 7.30, & was tired. However, out we went, sat in a café and talked for an hour, and agreed to be good friends &

not lovers . . . well that important point settled, we went off to Montmartre chattering vigorously, we taxied to Montmartre & went to a most amusing n---- cabaret [Plantation Club]. (Between ourselves, I deduce that Nancy has now passed to the culte des nègres & is no longer interested in poor white trash.)

It was an eventful evening. Both Nancy's cousins, Victor and Edward, were there, also Aragon, and they were joined by Henry Crowder after his shift at the piano. While Nancy and a friend danced with the two Cunards, Aldington watched and talked to Henry or Aragon. His letter continued:

I like Aragon very much. He has a very beautiful & sensitive face, and a charming manner. But he is jealous as a million devils, & made a frightful scene with Nancy at about 3 a.m. apropos a girl whom he said Nancy had taken away from him, and also apropos the "Henry". Nancy was furious, & they went and had a row in the street, & then came back & rowed over supper like husband and wife . . .

We all four gazed at our plates and said nothing. Then Nancy jumped up and & took Louis away in a taxi, saying she was going back to Chapelle-Réanville at once; but whispered to us to stay, & returned in half an hour! The others then left & Nancy & I went back to the dance room & discussed the unfortunate Louis until 4.30. I tried to persuade her to make it up, but she wouldn't, & I left her to Henry at 4.30 & returned home. I didn't drink much – 1 sherry cobbler and 1/2 bottle of white wine, but O Lord! These scenes of midnight dissipation are not for me! I woke at 10.30 and felt very nasty. After this, if I go again, I shall ask Nancy to let me leave early. Getting to bed at 5 a.m. is not for old gentlemen like me.

Aldington was also one of the friends invited to stay at Chapelle-Réanville, from which he wrote reassuringly to Brigit:

Darling, I find I like Nancy very much but I'm not in the least little particle in love with her. We kiss each other on meeting and parting but it is almost perfunctory . . . What Nancy is going to do about the Press, I don't know. I hope it doesn't collapse too soon. She began with a long thing of George Moore's and is bored with it. And the hand-press *is* a bore. I set up a couple of lines of type & helped pull off a few sheets of G.M. – & it takes ages. Also, Nancy has only just begun to realise what publishing means – i.e. sending out circulars, correspondence, filing letters, acknowledging cheques, designing ads, keeping daybook, Press accounts & authors' accounts, despatching parcels . . . & &. She is horrified – &, I can see, wants someone to do it for her. I can see that she wants *me* to do it, but after the *Egoist* & the *Criterion* [two small magazines on which he worked] I have had enough of that sort of thing.

What Nancy did do was suggest to Henry, as his contract with the Plantation was now ending, that he move down to Chapelle-Réanville to help her, something that he was happy to do on condition that his stay was treated as a job – that he worked full-time and received a regular salary. He arrived shortly before Christmas, and what with packing and despatching books, painting the outside of the house and other odd jobs, and practising on the piano, the days passed quickly.

The Hours Press was now in full swing. After *Perronik* came *Saint George at Silene*, a four-page poem by an earlier adorer of Nancy, Álvaro Guevara. They had kept in touch, and now that he was no longer desperately in love with her they had become friends – Nancy was much better at friendships than at love – so that he was able to watch, probably with fellow feeling and a certain amount of wry amusement, Aragon suffering as he had ten years earlier. The little book, for which Guevara had designed the cover, was published in January 1929 and favourably reviewed by Pound in the *Dial*. Together Nancy and the wretched Aragon printed Aragon's translation into French of Lewis Carroll's *The Hunting of the Snark*. Soon after learning to print, Aragon had decided on this new project, the first French version of the *Snark*, to be printed, of course, by the new press.

Although Carroll had died many years before, the Surrealists had long felt he was one of their own: his nonsense verse, into which they read everything they wished of the surreal and the subconscious, seemed the forerunner of their own attitudes and view of life. Aragon himself was convinced that the poem he was translating was a subversive political protest against the rigid structures of Victorian England and, despite Nancy's belief that his English was not up to it, went ahead:

Ils le traquèrent avec des gobelets ils le traquèrent avec soin
Ils le poursuivirent avec des fourches et de l'espoir
Ils menacèrent sa vie avec une action de chemin de fer
Ils le charmèrent avec des sourires et du savon.

(They sought it with thimbles, they sought it with care;
They pursued it with forks and hope;
They threatened its life with a railway-share;
They charmed it with smiles and soap.)

The Hours' success was quickly picked up by the English press. 'Miss Nancy Cunard, that popular and enterprising daughter of the lovely blonde Lady Emerald Cunard, founded an entirely new branch of society "shop keeping" when she started her own private printing press in France,' wrote one gossip columnist* in February 1929. 'Money-making is not her chief aim. She is undertaking to print and publish a number of stories and poems of rising young modern authors who cannot afford to pay for production themselves. Miss Nancy is a great friend of the Sitwells, and at one time was a regular contributor to a magazine (of course "highbrow") they used to run.'

Aragon also published (in Paris) the poem into which he had poured out his feelings of rage and misery when he learnt of what he saw as Nancy's betrayal of him. This was 'Poème à crier dans les ruines'. He gave Nancy a copy, but there is no record as to what she thought of it:

---

* 'A Man about Town', by Jack Londoner.

Let's spit the two of us let's spit
On what we loved
On what we loved the two of us
... I remember your shoulder
I remember your elbow your linen your footprints
... I remember your look which scorched
... I remember so many things
So many evenings rooms walks rages
So many stops in worthless places
Where in spite of everything the spirit of mystery rose up
Like the cry of a blind child in a remote train depot

So I am speaking to the past Go ahead and laugh
At the sound of my words if you feel that way
... The last word of love imagine that
And the last kiss and the last
Nonchalance
And the last step No kidding it's comic
Thinking simply of the last night
Ah everything takes on this abominable meaning
I meant the last moment
The last goodbye the last gasp
Last look
Horror horror horror
For years now horror

Yes let's spit
On what we loved together
Let's spit on love
On our unmade beds
On our silence and on our mumbled words
On the stars even if they are
Your eyes
On the sun even if it is
Your teeth
On eternity even if it is
Your mouth

And on our love
Even if it is
Your love
Yes let's spit

Yet Aragon was still vainly trying to free himself from the hold Nancy had over him. As his friend Thirion put it, he was 'in a vicious circle, going to the woman he loved but with whom he now knows that nothing will ever be real or lastingly possible and turning to other women he does not love but in whose arms he gives himself the illusion of being able to do without the first one'. What Aragon knew with certainty was that to return to Nancy, to admit that he still wanted her, would have been to deliberately enter hell. Ironically, he had accurately summed up her destructive pose in *La Defénse de l'infini*: '[She] has entrusted her fate to the unknown, rather than settle for security, which has boundaries ... apart from her talent, her only asset is her faith in a future linked to a ferocious independence.'

As all his friends knew, he was not at heart a philanderer but a man who wanted one faithful woman to love. He needed, both he and they thought, someone else to replace Nancy. Soon after arriving back in Paris, two possible contenders had appeared. The first likely candidate was Lena, a lithe young Viennese dancer, much sought after by the young men of the *quartier*. Then, in the first week of November, he had met Elsa Triolet, thirty-two, small, red-haired, full-bosomed, separated from her husband and, once she had set eyes on Aragon, utterly determined to become his woman. This was soon her only goal; something she would pursue by every means within her power.

First, Elsa had to organise a meeting with him. On 6 November 1928 she succeeded in this by persuading a young Russian writer who she knew was acquainted with Aragon to accompany her to La Coupole, the bar where she had heard Aragon would be that evening. Here her Russian friend would make the contact and, if the meeting seemed to be going well, make some excuse and leave Elsa with Aragon.

Her ploy was successful. The pair were soon left on their own, and at the end of the evening Aragon accompanied Elsa to her room in the Hôtel Istria and spent the night with her. For Elsa, this was a major step forward; for Aragon, it was simply another night with another woman. Then, at one of the numerous parties at the rue du Château to which she was now invited, Elsa followed Aragon up to the gallery above the main room and out of curiosity pulled aside a curtain and saw behind it a chaise longue. Never one to miss an opportunity, she then took Aragon by the hand and pulled him on to it. Thirion, who had seen them disappear, kept guard as they made love.

Aragon was now between three women: Nancy, Lena and the purposeful Elsa. Knowing there was no hope with Nancy, he decided that the beautiful Lena would be the one for him and began steadily to court her. One evening when he had a date to meet Lena at the Jungle bar at 11.00 p.m., he asked Thirion to go there and tell her he might be a bit late and keep her company while she waited. But at 11.00 it was Elsa who walked in, saw Thirion and immediately sat down opposite him. 'Where is Louis?' she demanded of him, saying that she had not seen Aragon for ten days. 'I can't get hold of him . . . He asked me not to come around. I'm very unhappy because I love him.'

Thirion decided to be frank with her. 'Don't you think you ought to work out why he hasn't seen you for several days? You know I like you, Elsa, so I don't want you to get on the wrong track. For Aragon it's just a fling . . . He finds you beautiful, intelligent, desirable, but he doesn't love you, he's never loved you. You've profited from his confusion, the break with Nancy Cunard.'

Elsa burst into tears and at that moment Aragon and Lena, clearly delighting in each other's company, walked in together. Where another woman might have at once confessed herself beaten and crept away, Elsa seized the moment to stake her claim. 'It was short and awful,' said Thirion. Elsa, telling Aragon that he had to choose between them, cried out, 'I'm the one you love! I'm your mistress!' Lena, only nineteen, was struck dumb and Aragon did as any man faced with the two women with whom he was sleeping would have done: he bolted.

Elsa, realising that her best chance of guiding events her way lay with the young and impressionable Lena, despatched Thirion after Aragon to the rue du Château to 'make sure he doesn't do anything stupid'. There Thirion found him sitting in front of the portrait of Nancy, drinking. At first furious with Thirion for discussing his private feelings with Elsa, he soon simmered down, and the two were in the midst of talking about what had happened when in walked Lena and Elsa, now apparently the best of friends.

Elsa told him that, as he seemed incapable of making up his mind about them, they had taken matters into their own hands and she had succeeded in convincing Lena not only that she, Elsa, loved Aragon the most (which was true) but that Aragon loved her more than Lena. Her force and conviction had carried such weight with the younger woman that Lena, who had other irons in the fire, including a lover in Germany whose daily telegrams she kept in her hatbox, felt she had little choice but to yield gracefully.

There only remained Nancy. As Elsa realised, thanks to Nancy's grip on Aragon's heart and imagination, she was a much more dangerous rival. A mere glimpse of Nancy put all other women out of Aragon's head as when, one evening when he was in a *boîte* with Elsa, Nancy came up to their table, greeted him as if they were merely friends and was asked to dance by Aragon. Once holding Nancy in his arms, nothing else existed for him and he abandoned his new mistress to spend the night with her predecessor.

Nothing daunted, Elsa continued her campaign, pursuing Aragon until finally she managed to persuade him to allow her to move in with him at the rue du Château (the flat he had rented was still being made habitable); once installed, she knew her influence would increase. Yet it was not until several months later that she was able to write in her diary that she had managed to get rid of all Aragon's other women – except Nancy.

Meanwhile, the Hours Press was busy. The next serious work was printing 200 copies of Aldington's poem *The Eaten Heart*.

This, to be bound in green marbled paper with gilt lettering, involved a disturbing incident. As Nancy and Henry Crowder were driving to the binder's workshop Henry, at the wheel, ran into a car occupied by three Frenchmen, one of whom wrote asking for payment for the damage to his car. Knowing that this was covered by insurance, Nancy contacted the insurers and she and Henry set off for a planned visit to London.

It was Henry's first visit there and he was a little apprehensive. He already knew that in England attitudes to anyone of colour were quite different from those in France – even on the train journey from Folkestone to London a man left his seat in the dining car when he saw Henry come in with Nancy. In London, hotel after hotel refused them (it was Derby week, so the Tower was full). 'Nancy for the first time was facing the fact that colour prejudice did exist in England,' wrote Henry. At last they found a Bloomsbury hotel that took them in without question. Otherwise it was a happy trip; Henry went sightseeing and enjoyed meeting Nancy's friends, while Nancy – 'treating it like a dose of medicine,' said Henry – went to see Emerald almost every day for lunch, tea or dinner.

Yet although Nancy did not hide her romance with Henry Crowder, she took care to see that her mother and Henry did not meet, and to leave Emerald ostensibly unknowing of the situation. But the fact that both of them knew and saw many of the same people, all of whom would have thought the Nancy/Henry relationship highly unusual and would have been likely to comment on it, makes it probable that at some level Emerald would have been aware of it. Perhaps, moving in a society where the convention was that much – such as her own love for Sir Thomas Beecham – remained unspoken knowledge, Emerald had decided that what she did not see should remain both unseen and unspoken of.

There was one near miss, when Emerald turned up unannounced at the house of a man who was a close friend of both herself and Nancy. Fortunately, her car was spotted from the window by the host as it drew up outside his house. 'Utter confusion reigned for a moment,' wrote Henry later. He saved the situation by saying he would go upstairs, where he remained until Emerald left a few minutes later, taking Nancy with her (Nancy soon returned and the lunch party went merrily on).

Among the friends of Nancy whom Henry met was Wyn Henderson, a jolly, red-haired woman so sizeable that Nancy nicknamed her 'the double goldfish', when not describing her as 'a fat, very fat, rollicking redhead'. Wyn had had a lot to do with hand-printing and early in 1929 had founded the Aquila Press,* which planned to publish Nancy's *Poems (Two) 1925*. It was a useful encounter, as Wyn would soon come to Nancy's aid.

When Nancy and Henry returned to France, there was a nasty shock awaiting them. While he was away, Henry had been summoned to court; the letter had not been forwarded to him and because of his non-appearance he had been sentenced to a month in prison for contempt of court and a fine of 10,000 francs. Both of them hastened to tell the court why Henry had not attended, and to their relief it was agreed that the case would be heard again in the autumn.

At the beginning of the summer Nancy, for once, gave an interview, though in the form of questions and answers. It was to the *Little Review*, possibly the most well-known of all the small literary magazines of the Twenties, largely for its publication (until banned) of Joyce's *Ulysses*. Nancy was one of around fifty writers, poets, artists and publishers, such as T.S. Eliot, Picasso and Gertrude Stein, asked to respond to the same questionnaire to mark this, the magazine's last issue. Many refused, citing the extreme banality of the questions, but Nancy was one of those who responded. To the question 'What would you like to be?' she answered, 'Indifferent to criticism, egocentric, concentrated, private, indisputably right and yet always loved by others.' It was a pretty fair summing-up.

Other answers she gave declared that she wanted perpetual change, what she most disliked in herself was a feeling of incapacity, but what she appreciated in herself was 'a feeling of latent

---

* It did not survive the Depression, which began a few months later with the Wall Street Crash of October 1929.

resistance'. Many of those in her circle, faced with her practice of doing exactly what she wanted regardless of anybody else's wishes or claims, would have known what she meant by that. Henry certainly did, writing, 'I had discovered that she was a very selfish person. Her likes and desires came before everything . . . as soon as anything ceased to give her personal pleasure she was finished with it.' Yet, like previous lovers, he remained hypnotised by her.

There is also an echo of her in 'A Great English Lady', an article by the French novelist Roger Vailland (who himself used a pseudonym for this piece), as one who had 'left England because she felt herself watched and could not without scandal give free rein to her sensuality. She speaks with horror of her country. She is tall, thin, angular.'

Nancy and Henry spent the summer travelling around the south-west of France. They visited caves and châteaux, Nancy wrote and Henry studied French. It was, he said, 'a hectic summer'. They returned to face the court appearance, only to find that the lawyer they had employed had failed to turn up. In the event, Henry escaped a prison sentence but had to pay a fine and the insurance company paid the costs of the accident.

That summer they printed *Mes souvenirs*, by the poet Arthur Symons, and Norman Douglas's *One Day*, with a signed edition of 200 handsomely bound in scarlet leather, priced at three guineas and almost entirely sold out before publication. Nancy was delighted to find that in the eight months of the Hours Press's existence she had doubled her capital – certainly something very satisfying for any publisher. The Hours Press was becoming well and favourably known in England, everything it had produced had sold well, Douglas's advice not to allow booksellers more than a ten per cent discount had saved money, and those same booksellers had been prompt in their payments. All in all, Nancy had much to be pleased about.

But there was something in Nancy that would not accept life as it was when going well, as when she spurned Aragon while still loving him. Now it was Henry Crowder's turn. He had, at Nancy's persuasion, left the band; now penniless, he was dependent on her financially for everything from daily living to money for a cup of coffee. When they travelled Nancy naturally paid, but in Paris her resentment at this forced dependence grew. One day at lunch with two friends she needled him again and again about getting something to do. Fed up, Henry replied, 'By heaven, I will!' left the table and went straight to the owner of the Bateau Ivre, a bar near the Panthéon, who employed him immediately at a good salary to play and sing every night.

He would finish around 2.00 a.m., go straight home and fall into bed. One night, around 4.00 a.m., he was woken by a loud knocking at his bedroom door. It was Nancy and Eugene McCown, both blind drunk. Nancy insisted on a hot bath, Eugene made a pass at him, and finally he found himself sandwiched between the two of them in bed. 'They were both so drunk, however,' he wrote, 'that they went straight to sleep,' and he was able to creep out and sleep elsewhere for the rest of the night. Next day Nancy did not even allude to this bizarre episode.

CHAPTER 15

><++>·O·<+>·<

Friendships – and the Crash

Successful as the Hours was, Nancy was finding difficulties in
running a press in the heart of the Normandy countryside. There
were the constant electricity cuts, if a piece of type got lost or
worn out it meant a visit to Paris for a replacement, and business
dealings by mail took longer and were often less satisfactory
than if dealt with by personal visits. Above all, the prospect of
another cold winter spent largely on her own – Henry was working in Paris and visits from Aragon, now that Elsa's influence was
increasing, were becoming rarer – was unappealing. The answer,
thought Nancy, was to move the press to Paris, something she
did towards the end of 1929.

Through Georges Sadoul, close friend of both Aragon and
André Thirion, she found the right place, a small shop with a large
back room that had just become vacant, at 15, rue Guénégaud, a
narrow side street on the Left Bank near the Seine. The rent was
reasonable and Nancy took it at once. She had the floor of the
front room, once the shop, covered in large black and white linoleum squares, added a leopard-skin divan and, as the office table,
a beautiful Buhl writing desk that had belonged to Sir Bache.
On the walls she hung a few modern paintings, mainly by Miró,
with sculptures from Africa, New Guinea and the South Seas on
grey-painted shelves, along with Brazilian tribal headdresses of
parrot feathers and bright African beading. The faithful Mathieu
press was in the room at the back and there was now a second
press.

Harold Acton described the effect. Referring to a postcard in her pencilled handwriting in which she talks about 'hysterical shop stuff', he said that indeed the shop did have an hysterical atmosphere, as the printing press only seemed to work in fits and starts and everything else seemed to have lost control. In a typical flight of fancy he went on to talk of the fetishes from Easter Island and the Congo talking among the freshly printed poems. 'What are we doing here?' he imagined them asking. 'Let's run away . . .' Their appearance, he thought, was disruptive to conversation and distracted one's thoughts, so alien did they seem that one almost expected them to march out of the door into the street, shouting slogans in a belligerent procession.

Monsieur Lévy had now gone, certainly to Nancy's relief and one suspects to his also; instead, she was joined by a nice young printer who worked a solid eight hours a day. She was also lucky in that Sadoul, who had just found himself unemployed, needed a job at that moment. The blond Sadoul, stocky and tough – he could walk thirty miles a day – was a great addition. Fascinated by books and a great reader, he did much of the necessary clerking, packing and posting, which often involved the shifting of a heavy weight.

Soon, the little shop became a port of call for Nancy's friends. Officially it closed for business at 5 p.m., and at first it was then when they would often drop in for a drink and a chat, perhaps to move later to the wine shop next door where a glass of wine could be had for as little as 4d. The Café de Flore and Les Deux Magots were also nearby, as was the Galerie Surréaliste in the rue Jacques Callot; this had become the mecca of avant-gardisme, with works by Picasso, Picabia, Miró, Dalí, Klee and Man Ray, along with sculptures and carvings of primitive peoples and pre-Columbian art. As time passed, some would not wait until closing time but simply arrive at any moment of the day to drink and gossip. If these interruptions became too numerous, Nancy would lock the door of the shop, but this was often fruitless as many of them knew of the side entrance. Fortunately, nothing stopped the printer at the back.

Through her Surrealist friends, Nancy printed a couple of

erotic books written and illustrated by Surrealist authors and painters. When a man came in and asked if she had any French books for his waiting room, saying that this was 'in rather special taste', she offered him Aragon's translation of *The Hunting of the Snark* which he crossly refusef. Afterwards the printer, working in the back room, told her that the seeming customer was a detective hoping to trap her into selling him pornography, for which he would then arrest her, but that she had innocently foiled him.

The Crosbys' Black Sun Press was also enjoying success. Harry Crosby's first book of 1929 was *Mad Queen*, a collection of essays, rants and poems, of which the longest was 'Assassin', a transmuted version of his own experiences in Constantinople earlier in the year, when hashish and opium followed by a few bottles of champagne had affected him with a sort of madness for a time:

I crash out through the
Window, naked, widespread
Upon a
Heliosaurus
   I uproot an obelisk and plunge
   It into the ink-pot of the
   Black Sea
   I write the word
       SUN...

Another sentence runs 'I the Assassin chosen by the Mad Queen I the Murderer of the World shall in my fury murder myself'. His twin obsessions, with the sun and death, were growing daily. In another poem, 'Sun Death', he listed famous suicides – Diogenes, Socrates, Brutus, Cato, Dido, Cleopatra, Modigliani and Van Gogh. The previous Christmas Harry had received a telegram from Josephine that excited him so much he wrote that he wished to become a necromancer, that he *was* a prophet of the sun. Robert McAlmon, visiting the mill, drinking, watching

Harry take opium and guests riot in the main room, listening to the wild talk, thought it was all 'too damned depressing. It's so depressing I can't even get drunk . . . they aren't people. God knows what they've done with their realities.'

Harry had also been studying *Ulysses*, having bought a first edition for $100 the year before. He was determined to meet Joyce and finally, on 4 March 1929, was taken to Joyce's apartment off the rue de Grenelle. Both Crosbys were anxious to have a portion of *Work in Progress* (eventually *Finnegans Wake*) for their Black Sun Press. Joyce, who approved of what they had already done, agreed to give them something.

A month later, a contract drawn up by Sylvia Beach (who had Joyce's power of attorney) agreed on a payment of $2,000 for 600 copies, 100 of them signed, of a book containing three fragments already published by *Transition*. For Harry, working with Joyce was extraordinarily exciting, despite Joyce's habit of endless corrections to his MS – his sight had so deteriorated that now he needed an enormous light bulb and a magnifying glass to make these.

In the summer, Harry spent hours sunbathing naked on top of the mill tower. There was a swimming pool, fed by the mill-stream; ten bedrooms, each of a different colour, had been made out of the original hayloft, and Harry had a menagerie – two racehorses, cockatoos, a ferret, a cheetah, ducks, carrier pigeons, a python and four 'polo' donkeys. The sitting room, lit by candles, had soft-covered benches where guests could sit or lie and zebra-skin rugs on the floor. Salvador Dalí, a frequent visitor, noted that there was always a huge quantity of champagne cooling in corners.

There were wild parties and famous guests. Harry wrote in his journal:

Mobs for luncheon – poets and painters and pederasts and divorcées and Christ knows who and there was a great signing of names on the wall at the foot of the stairs and a firing off of the cannon and bottle after bottle of red wine and Kay Boyle made fun of Hart Crane and he was angry and flung *The*

American Caravan into the fire because it contained a story of Kay Boyle's (he forgot it had a poem of his in it) and there was a tempest of drinking and polo *harra burra* on the donkeys and an uproar and a confusion so that it was difficult to do my work.

Both Crosbys had affairs, though with one difference: Caresse with one man at a time while Harry was always involved with several women at once, each of them believing that she was the only one who *really* understood him.

Harry's behaviour got wilder and wilder, taking opium pills, branding himself with hot coals, drinking a couple of bottles of champagne at a time and picking up girls at the races so that Caresse, who felt she could no longer understand him, spent much of that summer in tears. Robert McAlmon, one of the many visitors, thought Harry 'rather a spoiled and pretentious rich boy playing with fire, refusing to believe that it would burn him'. It was a life that seemed an upward spiral of excess, the only question being: with what would it culminate?

The affair with Josephine had continued – the Crosbys had visited the US the previous winter – punctuated with cables, telegrams and letters, most from Josephine and often semi-frantic as she sought to arrange trysts. When she married Albert Smith Bigelow on 21 June 1929, there was silence – but only for two months. In August, Josephine contacted Harry again as her husband had become a first-year graduate student of architecture at Harvard, with study that would safely take up much of his time.

Harry had also become fascinated by aeroplanes and flying, a passion begun by seeing Lindbergh's arrival, after which he had often flown over to Croydon and back – on 24 January 1929 his diary had recorded, 'At eight o'clock exactly on the dot we took off, the twin exhausts spouting their feathers of red flame. Altitude 1000 feet. Air speed 90 miles an hour . . . and there is a peasant ploughing a narrow field . . . who stops and looks up at us his face the size of a white pinpoint.' On the return journey from Croydon airport by its regular service Harry and Caresse, who had met him in Croydon, brought back a whippet bitch they had christened Clytoris and drank a bottle of champagne.

Nancy and Henry were still together, although when Henry discovered that she was having an affair with another black man he decided it would be a good time to return to America. By working, he had saved enough money and he thought it would give him a good chance to clear his mind and think things through. When he told Nancy, she begged him to come down to Chapelle-Réanville and talk to her before making arrangements. As he had to collect some of his things from the house there, he agreed. When Nancy came, they had a long discussion, and although he told her he had definitely made up his mind to return to the US for a visit, 'in the end, the same pulling force, the same indescribable attraction I had first discovered in Venice, triumphed. I dropped my plan to go to America.' He went back to work and their affair continued as before.

That autumn, Nancy also became friends with André Thirion, through a rather unusual introduction – he was far too poor to frequent the clubs and bars she went to every night. His father, disgusted that, as he saw it, his son was wasting his time over the planning of an unlikely communist revolution, had cut his monthly allowance. Often Thirion only had money for a bowl of tea and two slices of bread and butter all day, and when he went to the Café Cyrano for the daily Surrealist meetings he would order the cheapest drink, a bock, and make excuses not to join the others for dinner. Sometimes Aragon and one or two others would sense what was wrong and take him out. This privation eventually made him so ill that when the day came for him to be called up* he was in hospital. Most of the time he wore a black suit, made over from a tuxedo his parents had bought him when he was sixteen for his cousin's wedding, over threadbare shirts; in the winter he added a beige sweater, a shabby black double-breasted overcoat and a workman's cap.

---

* In 1928 compulsory conscription at age twenty was dropped from eighteen months to one year.

More importantly to him at the time, he could not afford to date girls – unless one succumbed at once, he was out of luck. Although he was in love with a young, unhappily married Bulgarian girl called Katia, he had not seen her for over two years and so was always delighted if he could find a bed partner for the night. 'Isn't true fidelity the fidelity of the heart?' he asked himself, fortunately finding that according to his Marxian principles this reasoning was sound, so that other distractions could be indulged in with a clear conscience.

One evening, wandering about Montparnasse with Georges Sadoul, they met a couple of girls whose 'beat' was the Stock Exchange, busiest for them between one and five in the afternoon. With nowhere to sleep – the girls were being turned out of their hotel because the proprietor had guessed what they were up to – they offered to move into the rue du Château, do the cooking, clean the place and share the boys' beds, using what they earned in the afternoons to pay expenses. 'It was funny and sad enough to make us cry,' said Thirion.

But cry they did not; instead they made the pragmatic arrangement that the girls would make the beds, wash the dishes and clean the place but not belong to anyone exclusively. Then they would go off on what Thirion described as their 'serious duties'. 'When they got back they would prepare a soup and wait for us in their most suggestive negligées. We would then all eat together and entertain our friends,' recalled Thirion. 'Next, they would share our beds according to whatever arrangements we agreed upon.'

At first it worked like a charm. The soup was delicious, the house had never had so many visitors and the girls kept everyone's glasses filled with the usual white wine. But Thirion's girl, Jackie, kept refusing to have sex with him, often on the most trivial of pretexts. One day he gave her an ultimatum, offering her the choice between surrender to him or exile to the downstairs room. Jackie began to cry: 'I feel like it, too, but I can't. It's for your sake that I don't want to have sex.' Thirion was too young and naïve to guess why, Jackie gave in, and soon he found he had gonorrhea. Three days later, so did Sadoul. At the

Café Cyrano, their troubles provoked much ribald laughter.

Then began the boring and arduous business of the only known treatment at that time, douching the infected parts with potassium permanganate. All was going well until one morning Thirion woke up with one testicle the size of an orange, after which he had to lie in bed with the offending part raised on a small board, smearing himself day and night with a cream prescribed by the doctor. What made this bearable was the kindness of Elsa Triolet, who would come every evening with food – butter, fruit cake, ham – sit on the side of his bed and tell him all the gossip. She would also post his letters and send him other visitors.

After a while he felt much better. One December night, with still a few more days in bed, he heard someone struggling with the latch then entering the large room below, switching on the lights, then walking unsteadily up the stairs. A drunk woman dressed in a black fur with bracelets up one arm stepped into the room. 'Hello,' she said. 'I'm Nancy Cunard. You've never seen me but we've often spoken on the telephone. You're André Thirion.'

Thirion stammered out a few words of excuse for not getting up, to which Nancy replied, 'I know. I know you've been sick. I'm worn out. I'm going to stay here.' She took off her clothes and, wearing nothing but a black silk slip, crept into his bed. 'Good night,' she said. 'You can put out the light and go to sleep if you're tired.'

Thirion found it difficult to sleep, and while the invitation was clear he felt he could not accept it as he did not know if he was fully cured yet: 'So my relationship with Nancy was established on a basis of loving friendship – which was much better anyway.' They maintained this friendship, a genre at which Nancy excelled; 'her kindness was marvellous,' said Thirion, who often repaid her solicitude by fishing her drunk out of some nightclub and setting her on her way home. Sometimes she would take the penniless young man to dinner or a *boîte*; to hide his threadbare clothes she gave him a beautiful black cape similar to the one she had given Aragon.

Only once, during a visit to Chapelle-Réanville, was their *amitié amoureuse* almost changed to something more passionate when, as Thirion rather ambiguously put it, 'Play-acting, I found myself in the hostess's bed. We were rather content with one another, yet we never really made love. And we never tried it again.'

As the Twenties wore on, Montparnasse and the lives of the Montparnos were changing. There was still dancing in the streets and squares on Bastille Night, with branches of the trees hung with lanterns and music from a violin and an old piano set out in the street. But the Hemingways had already left, in the autumn of 1929 Aragon's flame, the dancer Lena, was killed driving her Bugatti, which skidded and burst into flames, Solita Solano's relationship with Janet Flanner suffered a severe blow when Solita started an affair with another woman, and Robert McAlmon, whose *entrechats* on those dancing nights had been higher than anybody's, left for New York via Mexico City because 'what Paris once offered it no longer does'.

Soon the *quartier* would reverberate to a shock more dramatic than disenchantment or a failed relationship. All through the Twenties, American share prices had risen and the stock market offered the potential for making huge amounts of money – it was the new gold rush. People bought and bought, borrowing, buying on credit or spending all their savings. It seemed as though prosperity was limitless and would go on for ever. The average earning per share rose by 400 per cent between 1923 and 1929, and anyone who wondered if this phenomenal growth was sustainable was labelled a doom-monger.

When the bubble burst, panic selling began. In Wall Street shares rapidly dropped in value. On Black Tuesday, 29 October 1929, the Dow Jones fell like a stone, 16 million shares were sold at a fraction of their price and the collapse of the economy was complete. Banks closed, so savers lost all their money, farming was devastated and businesses went bankrupt. Apart from the loss of tourism, the effect of the Depression began to rage through Europe: banks failed, poverty took hold and in England there was massive unemployment and the poor suffered appallingly; most of the rich survived, often by selling land or jewellery – Maud Cunard sold some of her emerald and diamond jewellery and had paste replicas made, so good that they deceived everyone.

France was not really hit until several years later; even in October 1931 *Le Figaro* was saying smugly, 'For our part let us rejoice in our timid yet prosperous economy as opposed to the presumptuousness and decadent economy of the Anglo-Saxon races.' But now that the value of the dollar had dropped vis-à-vis the franc, many of the Americans living in Paris, often dependent on funds from home, found that their only option was to return to the US, the country they had fled in disillusionment and with the determination to have a good time after the ever-present threat of death in the war years. (Often, though, the thought of death remained, especially death by suicide after youth had passed – Scott Fitzgerald used to tell his editor that he wanted to die at twenty-nine.) Overnight, many of the American writers vanished from the Select, their favoured café because it was open twenty-four hours.

Although death was a central theme in the poetry and journals of Harry Crosby, he was not one of those forced back by short-age of money – his return trip to the US in November 1929 was planned both to visit his parents and to see the Harvard–Yale football game (he was a Harvard alumnus). His family was one of the richest in New England and all through his years in Paris he had spent well over his annual trust fund income of $12,000, from time to time soliciting more from his father. During 1929 he had made several such requests, twice asking his father to sell $4,000 worth of stock 'to make up for past extravagances in New York', and in mid-July requesting a further $10,000 sale of stock, as 'we have decided to live a mad and extravagant life'. Harry's only reference to the Crash was his diary entry for Black Tuesday: 'The worst one in the history of the U.S. SRVC [Harry's father] must be at his most nervous. I am glad I am not in Boston.'

The Crosbys set off on the RMS *Mauretania* on 20 November. Soon after they arrived, Harry met his lover, Josephine Rotch Bigelow, whose husband was away busy with his studies. The pair went to Detroit – the sort of city where they felt no one would know them – registering at an expensive hotel as Mr and Mrs Harry Crane. For four days they stayed in their room, making love, smoking opium and ordering room service, returning to New York on 7 December, with Josephine saying she was going back to Boston and her husband.

But Josephine did not go back to Boston. Instead she sent Harry a telegram reading 'I love you I love you I love you' and went to stay with one of her bridesmaids in New York. The next day, Harry wrote in his notebook, 'One is not in love unless one desires to die with one's beloved' – that morning, he had twice asked Caresse to jump with him from the twenty-seventh floor of their hotel, the Savoy-Plaza. Not surprisingly, she had refused to do so.

On 9 December, Josephine sent a thirty-six-line poem to Harry. It talked of the things they loved: orchids, caviar, champagne, the colour black, and that together they worshipped the sun as a god. The last line of the poem read 'Death is *our* marriage'.

The next day, Harry, Caresse, Harry's mother and his friend the poet Hart Crane were to meet for dinner before going to the theatre to see the hit Broadway play *Berkeley Square*. A few days later, Harry and Caresse were due to return to France on the *Berengaria*.

Uncharacteristically, Harry failed to appear at the restaurant; although the Crosbys had an open marriage, Harry was punctilious about not causing Caresse any worry. So she telephoned a friend of his, Stanley Mortimer, whose studio she knew Harry sometimes used for trysts. Just as they were leaving the restaurant Mortimer, who had left his studio at 4.15 p.m. and since been at his mother's apartment, rang back to say he had gone back to it but had been unable to get in as the door seemed to have been locked from the inside and no one had answered his knock – he wondered if perhaps Harry was asleep.

Crane took the Crosby women to the theatre and told the box office that there might be an important message for him. It came during the first act, a telephone call from Mortimer, who had asked the manager of the building to open the ninth-floor studio with his pass key. Unable to do so, the manager had ordered the door to be broken down. The first thing they saw were the dead bodies of Harry and Josephine lying on the bed.

What became clear after forensic examination was that Josephine, who had a .25-calibre bullet hole in her left temple, had died about two hours before Harry, who had a matching bullet hole in his right temple and was still clutching his Belgian automatic pistol in his right hand. There was no suicide note or other clue, so that Josephine's husband became convinced that Harry had murdered his wife in a jealous rage because he could not have her as his own while others believed that it was a suicide pact. The coroner gave an open verdict.

The New York papers were filled with accounts of the tragedy, the *Daily Mirror* calling it 'an erotic epic of twisted lives, illicit love and hearts in exile' as they filled pages with every detail – Harry's toenails were painted red, he had a Christian cross tattooed on the sole of one foot and a symbol of the sun on the other – while the papers in Boston, where all of the parties came from patrician families for whom discretion was a given, handled it with what could be called social distancing: 'Man and Girl Dead by Pistol: Suicide Pact Evident in New York Tragedy'.

But perhaps the best summing-up was in Harry's writings, many of which concerned the theme of death as violent, quick and liberating, and his hope, one day, to commit suicide by flying higher and higher, to the sun, until he crashed. His theme was always the sun as life-giver and destroyer, fiery, destructive and cleansing. Yet in one sense his death could also be viewed as a metaphor for the end of the decade, those febrile years that saw Paris, rather than the sun, at the centre of hopes, ideas, imagination, spinning ever faster until it finally burnt out.

>─┤─‹›─○─‹›─┤─‹

CHAPTER 16

Publishing Success and the Beckett Poem

Once back in Paris, Nancy's approach was becoming more organised, though her personal style could probably best be described as businesslike chaos. 'The clock did not exist for her:
in town she dashed in and out of taxis clutching an attaché-case
crammed with letters, manifestos, estimates, circulars and her
latest African bangle, and she was always several hours late for
any appointment,' wrote Harold Acton, one of her frequent visitors, who also commented on her increasing thinness: 'A snack
now and then, but seldom a regular meal, she looked famished
and quenched her hunger with harsh white wine and gusty talk.'
    She was certainly thinner, but just as elegant. Her friend John
Banting, now living in Paris and strongly drawn towards the
Surrealists, was consequently seeing more of Nancy. Always, he
recalled, she was at the cutting edge of the latest style. One of
her favourite ensembles in 1930 was a hip-length leather jacket
divided diagonally, one side black the other yellow. The matching black-leather skirt was crisp and short. As for the hat that
everyone wore in those days, this was a close-fitting black and
yellow 'crash helmet', and her habitual ivory bracelets, one of
them a four-inch cuff. She could, said Banting, 'take a chain store
dress, remove the trimmings, change the fit (she was an expert
seamstress), or soak it to remove the "make up" or glue found in
such fabrics, or shrink it to nearer her size' and the result would
look like couture.
    Early in 1930, Nancy printed a handsome circular, setting

out her plans for the year and the books she would be printing, among them poems by Laura Riding, Robert Graves, and two of her lovers of some years back, John Rodker and Ezra Pound. In her circular Nancy wrote, 'All the poetry will be hand-set and most of these volumes will be printed on a Hand Press over a hundred years old . . . Lithographic, typographic, photographic paper covers on boards by contemporary artists. Each copy signed by the author.'

There was a promising response, and not only in Paris. In England the *Observer* commented, 'Miss Nancy Cunard's Hours Press announces a number of new poems mainly by the modernists. All of them from this house are sure to be agreeably turned out in a large plain format.' The *Nation* called it an interesting experiment in printing and publishing, and *Everyman* said it was 'one of the most interesting of the newer small presses . . . Miss Cunard has for some months past been issuing exquisite limited editions of modern writers and she has the good sense which the English private publisher so often lacks to issue her wares at a price which the ordinary book collector can well afford.'

It looked as though Nancy had at last found a secure and continuing purpose to her life. The incessant restlessness that was so much a part of her was still there, but now the frenetic dashing about was seemingly channelled into one main task, maintaining the existence and success of the Hours Press. Yet at heart Nancy was, if not a revolutionary, certainly a natural rebel. She had begun by rejecting the values and aesthetics of her mother and the society she had grown up in, and in any amorous relationship there certainly came a point when she rebelled against the idea of fidelity. Friendship was the only form of commitment she seemed able to tolerate, for although the love affair foundered she usually managed to keep the man as a friend, for whom she could not do enough.

With André Thirion, for instance, her advice and efforts were central to his rescue of his beloved Katia from Bulgaria, something Nancy had been urging on him for some time. 'We'll review everything together because I'm more experienced at travelling than you are,' she said. She told him not to worry about money, she would help him if he needed it, and she added that if he got stuck in Bulgaria she would come and get him out.

She gave him letters of introduction to the ambassador and to others she knew in Bulgaria; she stressed it was essential that he was seen with the 'right' people, to allay any suspicions. She told him to buy decent clothes and fix himself up with journalistic credentials. Thirion's preparation consisted of selling his paintings – for rather less than they were worth – having a beautiful new navy-blue suit made, buying shirts, socks and ties and, through a friend met at La Coupole, fixing himself up with journalistic credentials. Through a series of twists and turns, he was able to extricate the willing Katia in the spring of 1930, bringing her back to Paris, where they married later that year, on 30 September. For this, Nancy always had his immense gratitude.

Helping Thirion had been worthwhile, exciting and a battle against the repressive regime of Bulgaria. What really stirred Nancy's inner fire, though, was anything that she saw as a flagrant injustice. 'Her life's purpose was to use her universal anger for the moral evolution of mankind,' said her friend Solita Solano. Perhaps one reason for her zeal in campaigning was that she sensed, albeit dimly, that for once she was not leading an irredeemably selfish life. And, as yet, the Hours Press had provided nothing to rebel against.

She was seeing a lot of Richard Aldington, whose semi-autobiographical novel *Death of a Hero* had been published the previous year to great acclaim – one reviewer called it 'the best war novel of the epoch'. Nancy would summon Aldington, or call in at his hotel, demanding that he come out and keep her company until Henry Crowder had finished his stint at the Plantation, then that he join them both, perhaps with other friends, for further carousing and, of course, drinking – she herself was drinking more and more. For his part, Aldington found her so compelling that he could never say no, even though he usually wound up exhausted on some nightclub seat.

'Yesterday I met Nancy in a squalid little bar near the Opera.

Nancy was dead drunk, of course, but even so I managed to take her as far as La Plantation,' runs one of his letters. 'How does Nancy do it? I've no idea. But I do like Henry. I think Nancy is right to love him – I like the fact that he is mysteriously sensible, composed. He's not good looking, like Louis (whom Nancy torments disgracefully), but he has the stability, the Blacks' feeling for life that we Whites are in the process of losing.'

Aldington, though passionately in love with Brigit Patmore, was to some extent bewitched by Nancy, allured not only by her glamorous looks but also by her buccaneering attitude to sex – never did she hesitate to go straight for what she wanted, though how intimate she and Aldington became is for conjecture. For Brigit Patmore, however, ten years older than her lover and stuck in England, Nancy's friendship with Aldington was a matter of concern. Letters like 'Nancy has been at Chapelle-Réanville . . . [she] returns today and I lunch with her on Saturday. She is a lovely creature, and I think grows more beautiful,' can hardly have been reassuring.

'My mother feared Nancy's capacity to dominate and devour her lovers,' said Derek Patmore, Brigit's son. 'For Nancy, with her masculine brain and physical attractions, was a huntress and demanded the complete surrender of the loved one.' Nor did Derek think there was any doubt that Nancy was attracted by Aldington. 'She published his poem *The Eaten Heart* in the Hours Press,' said Derek, 'and both my mother and Richard spent weekends at her house at Réanville outside Paris.'

The most successful of the books printed in 1930 was *Ten Poems More*, by Robert Graves, which sold out immediately on publication in May, so that Nancy was able to send Graves £80 in royalties. Yet although the Hours Press was doing so well, Nancy was disappointed in one respect: one of her aims had been to give a voice to younger, more avant-garde writers not yet known, but those on her list for 1930 were already well established. When, at one of their meetings in the spring, Aldington said to her, 'Why not offer a prize for the best poem on a certain subject?' she jumped at the idea. In that way, continued Aldington, new talent might emerge – and such a competition would make the Hours even better known. 'A poem on what subject?' said Nancy. Aldington suggested that the subject should be time and they agreed on a length of up to one hundred lines.

Quickly, Nancy printed an announcement in red ink on a small square card that read, 'Nancy Cunard, Hours Press, in collaboration with Richard Aldington, offers £10 for the best poem up to 100 lines, in english or american [sic] on TIME (for or against). Entries up to June 15, 1930'. It was sent out to all the literary reviews she knew of. It was, she realised, quite a small prize – but then, it could be won by only four perfect lines.

There was an enthusiastic response of almost one hundred entries. Nancy and Aldington took them down to Chapelle-Réanville to judge, first by reading each poem aloud to each other, then by studying them again individually. None, they thought, was much good. With three or four days left before the closing date for entries, they returned to the rue Guénégaud, to which all entries had to be addressed.

Then, in Nancy's words, 'a miracle there was'. After closing time on the last date an entry had been slipped under the door, where Nancy found it the next morning. Across its folder was written the title, *Whoroscope*, and under it the name of the poem's author, Samuel Beckett, a name that meant nothing to either Nancy or Aldington – unsurprisingly, as Beckett had then never been published. Immediately, both of them realised that here was the winner, a remarkable work written by someone clearly very intellectual and highly educated.

They summoned Beckett, who arrived quickly. He turned out to be a tall, thin, fair young man of twenty-four who had been living in Paris for two years and working as a part-time assistant to James Joyce on his *Work in Progress*, looking up data for him; both Nancy and Aldington thought they saw a look of Joyce in Beckett's appearance. Beckett told them that he had known nothing of the competition until the previous afternoon, upon which he had written the first half of the poem before dinner – 'salad and Chambertin at the Cochon de Lait' – then gone back to the École Normale Supérieure, where he held the post of *Lecteur d'Anglais*, to finish it. 'About three in the morning it was done,' he said, 'and I walked down to the rue Guénégaud and put it in your box.'

Even on the first feverish read-through the strength and originality of the ninety-eight-line poem struck both Nancy and Aldington, although it was so modernist that they realised that its references would be meaningless to ordinary readers unless by some strange chance they were fully conversant with the omelette preferences of the philosopher René Descartes.* This difficulty might be overcome, they felt, by explanatory notes. Nancy's printing of his poem would be the first time Beckett was published. It came out in an edition of 300, with a dull scarlet cover, and sold well.

Around the same time, Nancy first met James Joyce, although it would be more correct to say that she was approached by James Joyce demanding – there is no other word – that she do him a favour. One day, when she was lying ill in bed in her room in the Hôtel Crystal in the rue Saint-Benoît with an abscess in her throat, there was a knock at her door and in came Joyce, fumbling his way along via the furniture. 'I am James Joyce,' he said, 'and I have come to talk to you about something it seems to me it is your duty to accomplish.'

This turned out to be an introduction, through Nancy's mother Lady Cunard, to Sir Thomas Beecham. Both were in Paris at the time and so was Joyce's countryman, the singer John O'Sullivan, whom Joyce thought to have 'the greatest human voice I have ever heard', compared with which, he proclaimed, John McCormack's† was 'insignificant'. He told Nancy that O'Sullivan should be heard at once by Beecham and engaged to sing grand opera in England. Through her mother, Nancy was to organise this meeting.

In vain did Nancy protest that she had little influence with her

---

* Descartes only liked omelettes made with eggs that were between eight and ten days old.
† Probably the most renowned tenor of his day, who sang both opera and more popular songs – he was the first to record the First World War song 'It's a Long Way to Tipperary'.

mother and that a direct appeal by Joyce, whom Lady Cunard had already befriended and for whom she had tried to raise money, would have much more effect. Joyce refused to believe her and insisted that she speak to her mother about the importance of Beecham hearing O'Sullivan. Nancy felt she had no option but to do this.

A few days later, Joyce came to the Hours Press in the rue Guénégaud towards evening. Nancy and her friends greeted him and invited him to have a drink with them in the nearby bistro, which he refused. Nancy told him she had passed on his message to her mother, who had said she would tell Beecham, but knew no more, while reiterating that it would have much more effect if it came directly from someone as distinguished as Joyce. Her remarks were brushed aside. O'Sullivan *must* be engaged for grand opera. Could Nancy not realise the urgency of this? If she had already tried to achieve the Beecham interview, she should now try much harder. It was her *duty*. Eventually he left. Nancy learnt later that while Beecham did listen to O'Sullivan, he was not engaged. There was no further contact with Joyce.

That July Nancy paid a briefish visit to London, where as usual she saw her mother, with their last meeting on 21 July before Nancy returned to Paris, leaving GM complaining to Emerald (on 17 August), 'Nancy left London without coming to bid me goodbye, which was unkind.' He would have been even more upset had he known that Nancy would shortly be cutting her mother out of her life completely and that the two would never see each other again.

By August 1930 Nancy could not wait to leave Paris, but there was so much work at the Hours Press that she found it impossible. When she heard that the Aquila Press, managed by Wyn Henderson, whom she had earlier met, was closing down, she quickly offered Wyn the job of managing the Hours (later, the competent Wyn would manage Peggy Guggenheim's museum). She also took on a young printer, John Sibthorp, who had worked for Wyn at the Aquila.

This left Nancy free to go with Henry Crowder to south-west

France, where Henry planned to set several poems to music, for a book to be called *Henry-Music*. Nancy gave Wyn Henderson £300 to cover the costs of publishing a short story by Richard Aldington, and three volumes of poetry by Brian Howard, Harold Acton and Bob Brown. Wyn was also to print a catalogue of the Hours Press publications.

Nancy and Henry left in August, motoring south very fast in the small dark-blue car with scarlet leather seats that Nancy had given Henry. They intended to find somewhere really quiet where both could work, Nancy on her poetry, which she had had to neglect because of the Hours Press, Henry at his music for the proposed book of music and songs. Having almost reached the Pyrenees and finding nothing to their liking, they drove back slowly, finally settling in the village of Creysse, by the Dordogne.

This would be one of their happiest times together, living in two rooms that cost £1 a month 'like peasants', drawing drinking water from the village fountain and cooking by candlelight. Harold Acton talked of them 'eating at an inn which was always ringing with succulent patois ... with the Dordogne rushing below over the abandoned wash-boards'. To the villagers, who scarcely ever saw an outsider, the appearance of this tall, handsome, well-dressed black man, who spoke little French, and Nancy, thin, white-skinned and golden-blonde, who spoke French like a Frenchwoman, was so mystifying that one market day a man exclaimed on seeing them, '*Té! Ils ne sont pas de la même couleur!*'

They were very soon able to hire a small upright piano from the nearby town of Martel. It arrived on a farm cart drawn by two oxen and was hoisted up the stone stairs into the cottage. Henry began to compose at once, and Nancy wrote outdoors. Gradually, the local people began to view them as '*des intellectuels étrangers*'.

At first Henry had jibbed, out of modesty, at writing a book, but finally agreed to do so if words that inspired him could be found. Nancy wrote what she described as 'a sort of battle hymn', called 'Equatorial Way', her vision of the Negro bidding a fierce farewell to the United States and setting off for the continent that should be his, Africa. She also wrote 'Blues', for Henry to sing (later he often sang it in the Boeuf sur le Toit and the other nightclubs where he would play). One verse ran:

> Each capital's not more than one café
> Wherein you lose, wherein you love
> Yourself in what you have and have had,
> Why worry choose, why worry choose?

Her friends Harold Acton, Richard Aldington, Samuel Beckett and Walter Lowenfels all told Henry to choose whatever of their poems he wanted. Beckett's offering was rather typically entitled 'From the Only Poet to a Shining Whore', which contained the verse

> Puttanina mia!
> You hid them happy in the high flax,
> Pale before the fords
> Of Jordan, and the dry red waters,
> And you lowered a pledge
> Of scarlet hemp.

Henry settled down to work at once, all day and on into the hot, velvet darkness, for as late as they thought would not be disagreeable to their neighbours. The notes of music were accompanied only by the sparks from the fire under a copper cauldron in which an old village woman spent all day washing heavy piles of linen.

The work was done in about four weeks, the final result a collection of six pieces. Then came the question of the cover, for which Nancy engaged Man Ray; his elegant black and white photomontage featured Henry's portrait full-face with Nancy's arms, covered wrist to elbow in her thinnest ivory bracelets, resting on his shoulders. Only 100 copies, all signed by Henry, were printed.

It was here, too, that Nancy made a momentous decision. She

would compose an anthology of African-American history, art and politics, an idea that would develop into the central cause of her life.

While Nancy was away on holiday, Wyn Henderson chose the bindings for the two editions of Aldington's *Last Straws*, a story about three English army officers who meet in a Paris nightclub and discuss the war that they have been through; at the end, one of them returns to England and shoots his wife's lover and himself. It was to be published early the following year. However, advance sales were so good, thanks no doubt to the success of *Death of a Hero*, that Wyn decided to send Aldington a cheque for advance royalties.

This had an unexpected and unfortunate sequel. Aldington sent back the cheque with an angry letter to Nancy saying that he had given the story to *her* to publish and not the manager of the Hours. 'But the royalties are from the *Press*,' responded Nancy, only to receive another furious letter, so that a full-blown epistolary row ensued. When Nancy told all of this to Norman Douglas, who had come to Paris for a month to see her, he seemed unsurprised, merely remarking, 'Why *do* authors have such difficulties with each other? I'm sure *grocers d*on't behave that way among themselves.'

Douglas's avuncular, seen-it-all persona, with definite views on everything, was now so well developed that around this time his younger friends began to refer to him as 'Uncle Norman'. None of these views was stronger than his attitude to meals, which meant a lot to him – apart from seeing Nancy, one of his reasons for coming to Paris was to sample as much of its food as possible. 'He looked forward to his next meal with a ravenous appetite,' said Harold Acton, whereas Nancy, said Douglas disapprovingly, 'has the appetite of a dyspeptic butterfly'. In addition, she was always late, while Douglas was punctual. Acton and Douglas would knock on the door of her room in the Hôtel Crystal to collect her to find what looked like a party going on, with the room cloudy with cigarette smoke and books scattered all over the bed. 'This is no place for us,' Norman would say, 'let's hop it.'

Once settled in a restaurant, said Acton, Uncle Norman would attune his mind to the bill of fare, studying it like an operatic score, weighing Chateaubriand steak against tournedos Rossini, *pots de crème* against cream cheese.

Although Douglas largely disapproved of Nancy's hangers-on he did, however, agree to accompany her to see André Breton, a meeting recorded by Acton: 'After one horrified look at the Dali dominating Breton's room – an intricately demoniac picture of William Tell in his underwear with a vivid phallus protruding, and such details as the carcass of a donkey on a piano with a horse galloping over it – Uncle Norman said sharply "I can't stay here. That picture will spoil my dinner. See you later. I must get some fresh air at once." He had come to Paris to enjoy Nancy's company but there were limits.'

It was not surprising that Nancy took Douglas to visit Breton, as her links with the Surrealists were still strong. She would pass messages to Aragon through Thirion and Sadoul, and she was still strongly sympathetic to the movement and its left-leaning culture. That autumn, their numbers were augmented by the arrival of a number of young recruits. 'A group of young vagabonds heaved into view,' wrote Thirion. One of them was a boy of only seventeen, Raymond Michelet, the son of a police chief in Clermont-Ferrand, who had run away from home and come to Paris.

Later in the year Michelet's father, who had failed to recall his son by either pleading or scolding, came to Paris to remove him physically. His first step was to have the house in the rue du Château surrounded by police. The Surrealists, however, were determined to save their protégé, sending Michelet to hide in Sadoul's room upstairs, while Thirion managed to fob off Michelet *père* by saying that the reason why an eighteen-year-old boy (as Michelet was by then) had not returned home was almost certainly a girlfriend, and the pair could likely be found in or around the boulevard Saint-Michel.

As it was highly likely that Michelet's father would return to the house when he could not find his son in the streets, it was decided that Michelet must be properly hidden. Sadoul took him down to Nancy's house in Chapelle-Réanville where Nancy, discovering that he knew little about sex ('he seems a little bashful,' she told Henry), wasted no time in educating him. Or, in Thirion's words, 'Nancy gobbled down that fresh body in no time.'

Nancy soon became even more diverted from the business of the Hours Press by a major Surrealist event – or rather, creation, commissioned by the Vicomte de Noailles.

The Vicomte and Vicomtesse de Noailles were a couple at the heart of upper-crust Parisian society; in addition, Marie-Laure de Noailles, whose nephew was the Director of the Museum of Modern Art in New York, was a noted patron of the arts and artists, including of course the Surrealists – in her circle were Jean Cocteau, Salvador Dalí, Man Ray and Luis Buñuel. Early in their marriage, the de Noailles had begun to collect works by Max Ernst, Man Ray, Francis Picabia, Giorgio de Chirico and Yves Tanguy; these artists, along with composers such as Poulenc and Georges Auric and many Surrealist writers, became their favourite guests.

In the living room of their palatial house in the Place des États-Uni, solid-looking chairs and sofas were covered in white linen, black leather, or white fake fur and the walls hung with large panels of square parchment, which made a neutral background for their art collection, in which a Dalí hung between two Goyas. Having installed Paris's first private screening room in their house, the de Noailles became interested in avant-garde cinema, and Charles began to finance a film each year as a birthday present for Marie-Laure. In 1930, he gave the iconoclastic filmmaker Luis Buñuel 260,000 francs to shoot a Surrealist film, to be called *l'Age d'Or*, in collaboration with Dalí.

It proved to be a satirical comedy mocking everything from the more absurd aspects of modern life to bourgeois sexual hypocrisy and the values of the Catholic Church. It consisted largely of a series of vignettes depicting scorpions, a couple making love in the mud while a religious ceremony is going on, a horse-drawn cart filled with rowdy men drinking from large bottles passing through the elegant company in the ballroom, a small boy being shot and killed for a minor prank, and a woman fellating the toe of a marble statue. When it received an exhibition permit from the Board of Censors, *L'Age d'Or* had its premiere presentation at Studio 28, Paris, in October 1930, where its extraordinary and often obscene content created a sensation. The de Noailles ('les Charles', as they were known) had invited a group of their smart friends to the premiere, half of whom were so scandalised that they walked out. *Le tout Paris* was split in half, and Charles was suspended from the Jockey Club.

On 3 December – presumably after word of its content and outrageousness had spread – there were angry scenes at Studio 28, provoked by the right-wing Ligue des Patriotes (League of Patriots). The Patriotes interrupted the showing by throwing ink at the cinema screen and assaulting viewers who opposed them. They then went to the lobby and destroyed art works by Dalí, Miró, Man Ray, Tanguy and others.

The Board of Censors took a swift decision to re-review the film and a week later the Prefect of Police of Paris banned it from further public exhibition, confiscating as many copies of it as could be found. A contemporary right-wing Spanish newspaper published a condemnation of both Buñuel and Dalí and the film, describing its content as 'the most repulsive corruption of our age . . . the new poison which judaism, masonry, and rabid, revolutionary sectarianism want to use in order to corrupt the people'.

The de Noailles were so shattered by the reaction of their friends and others that they withdrew *L'Age d'Or* from commercial distribution and public exhibition for more than forty years (although, thanks to Marie-Laure's brother, it was privately exhibited at MOMA three years later*). Nancy, predictably, thought it wonderful and, knowing there was still another copy of the film somewhere, immediately began planning a campaign for a private showing in London.

It was at this point that Yvonne Kapp (usually known as

---

* On 15 November 1979, the film had its legal US premiere at the <u>Roxie Cinema</u> in San Francisco.

Bimbo), who had seen Nancy with Aragon five years earlier and whom she now met through Wyn Henderson, entered Nancy's life – or, as Yvonne later wrote, 'For a few months I was caught in the searchlight of Nancy Cunard's dazzling and alarming personality . . . once drawn into Nancy's magnetic field, I found myself shuttling between London and Paris as part of her entourage.' Once again, the faithful Henry had been pushed to one side. By now he had realised that she had taken other black lovers, almost under his very nose and often only for a night or two.

At Nancy's bidding, Yvonne wrote the notes for her planned showing of *l'Age d'Or*, and spent night after night in smoky, dimly lit *boîtes* to the sound of loud jazz while Nancy transacted some bit of business – as she no longer had a base in Paris, she would put up in one of the seedy hotels where, often, the rooms did not even have a table on which to write. Sometimes, usually when very drunk, she would write out a cheque to some person or cause she thought deserving, often on an piece of toilet paper.*

Yvonne was bisexual, and it is probable she had a lesbian relationship with Nancy. Henry Crowder recorded that while waiting for the secret copy of *l'Age d'Or* to arrive, Nancy told him the evening before the planned showing that she was going to spend that night with Bimbo. Perhaps just as conclusively, only an intimate would have seen Nancy's brutality and even physical violence when drunk when she would often use her bracelets as weapons, striking someone across the face with an upright arm; more often it was verbal cruelty which, said Yvonne, knew no bounds: 'I have sat by, appalled but too craven to protest, while she humiliated some harmless old queen or insulted the waiter with whom she had been to bed the night before . . . some of her worst excesses . . . were reserved for her good-natured, patient lover, the black pianist Henry Crowder.'

Such behaviour was too much for Yvonne: what helped free her from Nancy's dominant personality was the cruelty Nancy so

---

* At the time, as long as bank details, account details, signature and amount to be transferred were present, anything could be used as a cheque, provided that the 'anything' was not in itself illegal.

often displayed to those weaker than herself: 'I came to hate and dread the surge of her unpredictable aggression.' Gradually she withdrew from Nancy's orbit; even so, Nancy's effect had been so powerful and so destabilising, throwing many of Yvonne's previous beliefs into chaos, that it took her some years to recover her own internal equilibrium. The legacy of her time in Nancy's orbit was a lasting dislike of the half-drunk.

Then came a development that served to focus the anger that increasingly seethed beneath Nancy's glittering surface. Just before Christmas 1930, Emerald Cunard gave one of her large luncheon parties, to which she had asked Margot Asquith – now Margot, Lady Oxford and Asquith – widow of the former Prime Minister, Emerald's own former 'landlady' and in some sense rival hostess. Margot, all her life known for her outrageous frankness, walked into Emerald's drawing room and asked loudly, 'What is it now, Maud? Drink, drugs or n——s?'

It was a remark impossible to pass off, so shocking that it reverberated around London society, especially as Emerald rang up all her friends to find out if it was true. As Nancy wrote later, 'No one could fail to wish he had been at the lunch to see the effects of Lady Oxford's entry.' It had forced Emerald to face what was to her the unthinkable: that her daughter was actually living with a black man. Nancy had never hidden the relationship, and plenty of the friends she had in common with her mother knew about it but hitherto it had not, so to speak, been put in the public domain. This meant that although Emerald could allow herself to realise vaguely that her daughter was 'helping a black man study music', she need know nothing else, so much so that when one reporter asked her, 'Have you met Miss Cunard's friend, the Negro musician Henry Crowder?' she replied, 'Do you mean to say my daughter actually *knows* a Negro?'

Just before Nancy and Henry were due to depart for London there came a telegram from Sir Thomas Beecham. 'Seriously advise you not to leave Paris for London until you receive my letter tomorrow,' it read. Nancy, spoiling for a fight, insisted that they left for London immediately (the letter did not reach her until she had returned to Paris). Together she and Henry arrived at the Tower, where they were staying, but soon they were asked to leave: detectives had called round, as had the police – causing poor Mr Stulik, who said he had received an anonymous note threatening him with imprisonment, to exclaim, 'Ve vill all be killt!' Nancy was furious that the Stuliks wanted them to go, but also worried: her mother knew so many eminent people that was it possible she could cause Henry to be deported? She was assured by the lawyer she consulted that anyone of any nationality could come into England provided they had not committed an offence against the state.

Now, Nancy had all the justification she needed for an open vendetta against her mother.

CHAPTER 17

> ──◆──○──◆──

The Break with Emerald

Back in Paris, Nancy wrote a long letter to her 'first friend', GM, telling him why she had not seen him in London, 'though the desire to do so was strong'. She went on to remind him that when she had earlier asked him, 'Do you have friends of colour?' he had replied, 'No, I think none, but the subject has never come my way. You see, I've never known anyone of colour, not even an Indian. I have met neither a brown man, nor yet a black man. I think the best I could manage would be a yellow man.'

Her letter then brought up the crucial point: 'I did not tell you that I have known and closely loved a black man for over two years.' Explaining that she did not feel able to argue with her mother about this, she concluded by expressing her admiration for coloured people and saying, 'If you want to write to me, would you do so here, at the Press?'

What Nancy wanted was unequivocal support from the man she had known and loved all her life and whose moral judgements she respected. GM had always stood up for her during her childhood, his earliest, forward-thinking works had challenged the ethos of the day and he had never hesitated to offer an opinion contrary to the prevailing attitude if he felt like it. She expected an answer to her letter, but the ambiguity of the phrase '*If* [author's italics] you want to write to me . . .' left GM a loophole.

For the seventy-nine-year-old Moore, Nancy's letter must have presented a horrible dilemma. For almost forty years Emerald had been the fulcrum of his life, the woman he had never ceased to love, the woman about whom he had written in *Héloïse and Abélard*, 'He who has enjoyed divinity turns aside from merely mortal woman,' and from her childhood on he had also loved Nancy deeply. Until this moment, he had managed to make himself believe that, give or take a little bickering, all was well between the two – had not Nancy been to see her mother every time she returned to London and always visited Emerald when she came over to Paris? Had he not been able to write to Nancy, only a few days before the fatal lunch, 'I spent yesterday with your mother and we had some heavenly talks about you. We both love you'?

Now each of them was furious with the other, and he was asked to take sides. Instead, he took refuge in silence (according to Nancy, he did not answer her letter). It was perhaps the only thing he could do, but it did not serve him well with Nancy.

January 1931 was a busy month for Nancy, who wrote to Brian Howard, whose poems she was publishing, telling him that her mother had found out about her liaison with Henry. Brian, an old friend, who had also been published in the Sitwell anthology *Wheels*, was a key member of the Bright Young Things and model for several characters in the novels of Evelyn Waugh. He was, perhaps, best known for his involvement in the Bruno Hat hoax of the previous year – a spoof exhibition of paintings said to be by the unknown German 'artist' Bruno Hat but actually done by Brian. When Brian, who adored Nancy, heard her news, he instantly asked her to stay. In his journal he wrote, 'If only she can come here with Eddie [Gathorne-Hardy]. I want no one else but Eddie and she. The only PERFECT people.'

January also saw the showing of *l'Age d'Or*, to the screening of which Nancy had invited both friends and those she thought would be interested and influential. This too was highly upsetting for Emerald, who was frightened that Nancy would be prosecuted for showing a film that was both blasphemous and obscene. She certainly could have been, but in the event the screening passed off quietly, with none of the public raging seen in France.

Brian's poems – the only book of poetry he ever wrote – were published in an edition of 150, each copy signed by the author. The cover was by their mutual friend John Banting – Nancy thought it the best cover the Hours Press had ever produced. The author's copy which Nancy gave Brian had a handwritten dedication from her that read:

> For Brian Howard
> (Heart and Brain
> get them together)
> With the love and delight
> Of the publisher of these first poems
> Nancy Cunard

In return, Brian inscribed a copy for Nancy as follows:

> For Nancy Cunard
> Hours Press
> 1931 – Paris*

Meanwhile, the row with Aldington, whose book *Last Straws* came out at the same time in an edition of 500, was rumbling on. Nor was his temper improved when *Last Straws*, although it sold well, did not go down too happily with reviewers. 'The conversation of three drunken men in a night club is hardly worth recording and the end is pure melodrama,' said one.

'That stupid Nancy sent more propaganda about her silly communist film [*L'Age d'Or*] to Norman & Pino† and me,' he recorded from Florence. 'Norman has written to her, on behalf of us all, to say she must *not* send any more to Italy, because it might get people into trouble. Still not a word from her about my story and not a penny of money. Ah! *Les sales riches!* How foully

---

* Ten years later he added the words, 'With all the love there ever was, all the love there ever will be. B. London, Sept 27, 1942'.
† Pino Orioli, Florentine bookseller best known for privately publishing the unexpurgated first edition of D.H. Lawrence's *Lady Chatterley's Lover*, was the close companion of Norman Douglas.

dishonest. She goes and spends on n——s and saphs the money she owes me. To hell with her. I'm finished as far as she is concerned. When I get my cheque from her – *fini, nais fini*. Rotten little beast.' The following month he went as far as complaining about her to the Authors' Society (a complaint that came to nothing). The rumpus only finally calmed down when Nancy sent him a royalty cheque personally signed by her.

What concerned Nancy much more was a letter from Emerald saying that she had had to cut Nancy's allowance by twenty-five per cent as her own income had dropped. Nancy believed this was vindictiveness at discovering the affair with Henry and wrote to Ezra Pound saying that she had been disinherited. A much more probable reason for this diminution was that much of American-born Emerald's fortune was in US shares, badly affected by the Crash of the previous autumn. In fact, Nancy continued to be subsidised by her mother's money for the rest of her life, nor did Emerald stop sending her wonderful clothes, though now Nancy refused to wear them and gave most of them away.

Nancy and Henry arrived to stay with Brian at the beginning of February 1931, Nancy in a brown hat with a black veil and long fur boots, Henry in Sir Bache's sable coat and a Homburg hat with a rolled brim. Even on the train en route, Nancy had made another conquest, an attractive English newspaper correspondent called Roy Randall who lived in Vienna and whom, though Henry did not realise it at the time, she intended to see again.

The only place Brian had been able to find for them to stay was in the house of the local priest, whose possible reaction worried him. 'The priest is tremendously severe and *I* can hear him praying all day and all night from *my* bedroom, so considering their room will be next to his I simply cannot imagine what will happen.' He was right to worry. It proved to be an appalling visit and, for Brian, psychologically exhausting, largely thanks to Nancy's nightly drunkenness which often culminated in anger – once, regardless of the sub-zero temperature outside, she broke every piece of glass in the double-glazed windows of her room with her shoe.

Almost the moment they arrived, Nancy plunged straight into the details of the breach with Emerald, the detectives her mother had set on them and the consequent difficulties. In his diary Brian wrote:

> She talked so much, seemed unable to stop. The whispery, staccato, disjointed voice goes on and on. A kind of sober drunkenness. Drinking is now fatal to her. Particularly cognac. She has the most marvellous face. The best woman face of our time. That extraordinary, wavering perched walk. Thinness – other people are thinner, of course – reaches a sort of thing-in-itself in her. She is the only woman I know who can be *really impassioned about ideas almost continuously*. She is anything but 'right' of course. And her bickering with impassive, infinitely patient, stupid Henry is very rasping to me. She is in an extremely nervous condition now, of course.

Brian found himself increasingly worried by Nancy's mental state: 'She is rather terrifying. She is as if permanently drugged without being – which is frightening. I think she is a little in love with me [Brian was openly homosexual] – talking all the time of doing things together, "come to Réanville – come away etc". Divine of her, but she has gone over the *edge*, somehow. Alternating between extreme solicitude and sudden unprovoked ugly coldnesses.'

The next day, 8 February, he went even further:

> I find myself unable to face putting down all I feel, plus overtones about Nancy. A) She is ill. Drink plus never drawing any line. Henry says she drinks far too much and she obviously does. Those awful snarling little yelps of self-assertion. B) Before lunch today she came into my room when I was finishing dressing, lay on the bed, pulled me down beside her and did a lot of hair smoothing and kissing, and 'comforting'. Not sexily but with sex near *enough*. She is definitely in love-ish, put it like that. It simply makes me freeze . . . I sometimes shiver at the sight of that small, inefficiently eager mouth. Soft,

tiny, narrow, bright, puckered, dangerous, with hard teeth so *near* behind it. I AM IN FOR A PLAGUE OF WOMEN. Oh, Christ, if only she wouldn't smooth my hair. It makes me feel bald and ill.

At the same time, he was conscious of her beauty, 'Her *divine* appearance ... The best appearance in the world', her affection, concern and desire to help him: 'Her superiority to all other women, and *most* men, in *many* ways. If only she was (i) *well*, (ii) I felt she would never require anything much given *emotionally*. I *could* give, *have* given, and I think *do* give, a lot in this way. *But I can't be kissed and mauled.*'

Nancy and Henry left on 14 February, wrapped in their furs and with a bottle of white wine and another of liqueur sticking out of the rugs on the sledge taking them down to the station. They did not go back to Paris but to Vienna, to stay with Roy Randall, with whom Nancy had kept in touch by telegram. One evening, they were all three having drinks after a Strauss concert when, Randall having left the room for a moment, Nancy quickly said to Henry, 'I want to be alone with our host for a while.' She only returned to the room she was sharing with Henry at daybreak. The same thing happened the following night. Two days later they returned to Paris, Henry wondering why he was still attached to Nancy and deciding that he would soon return to America.

Some time after Nancy and Henry's visit Brian, perhaps in an attempt to sort out the jumble of feelings their stay had caused him, wrote a long letter to his mother. It illuminates the ghastliness of their stay so successfully that it is worth quoting at length:*

Now, mother, there is one thing I want you to realise. And that is that I adore and admire Nancy and always will. She has the kind of integrity, spiritual purity and devotion to ideas that is

---

* Quoted by Marie-Jaqueline Lancaster in her book *Brian Howard: Portrait of a Failure.*

unique. Nothing can deter her or make her dishonest. She is a marvellous woman, and if she were younger and less ill and attracted me, I'd marry her. I almost believe.

But really her advent here, and Henry, was simply volcanic. She is *ill*, which I didn't realise. Her mother and Beecham having her hounded by detectives and the fact she is hiding a young surréaliste in her house near Paris who is running away from his father, who is a *chef de police* – these things have made her almost distraught. She also had incipient sinus, awful catarrh, and a bad throat. Also it was too cold for her, she couldn't ski, and she was uncomfortable in the annexe (there was no room here). Well, she was all right in the daytime but at night she simply drank. Added to this, she fell quite insanely in love with me. Letters and telegrams, they never stop, even now. Well, it was AWFUL. There were fights, with poor dear coal-black Henry being so good and patient, D. [Brian's boyfriend] being irritated and Nancy threatening to go every minute and then crying in my arms all night, having smashed all her windows with rage because I couldn't come to Vienna.

Now, mother, you must make an effort to understand. Nancy, for instance, has *never* taken drugs. She is *devoted* to her art and to poor dear Henry. She drinks a *lot*, normally, but never like that. I KNOW her. She is a fine, noble creature. You cannot know how her nerves have been wrecked, fighting her mother because her lover happens to have a black face. She is ILL, now. That's why she flies to drink. Anyhow, it was BEDLAM. And it all devolved on me. Complaints from other visitors, rows over bills – all had to be smoothed over by me . . . Do you know that Henry was the first negro who had ever come here? They touched his face to see if it would come off.

Brian's letter went on to say that he saw Nancy about twice a week and that once he had taken Alannah Harper to meet Nancy in her flat. It was a visit that made a deep impression on Alannah, who later wrote, 'She lay on a tiger skin rug, her arms encased in huge African ivory bracelets, with a necklace made from equally large lumps of ivory. Her great green eyes were quite the most fascinating I had seen. Brian said in a loud voice: "Nancy is the only type of woman a man like me could fall in love with, in fact I was, my dears, and reciprocated too."'

Back in Paris, where she stayed mostly in the Hôtel Crystal, Nancy heard various stories from friends of her mother's attitude to her liaison with Henry that only served to fuel her sense of outrage, as did the long letter written to her by Sir Thomas Beecham, its underlying agenda an attempt to smooth things over. Emerald had told him that she was going to cut Nancy out of her will; Beecham had responded that he was sure she was far too fond of her daughter to do so. 'Thereupon she appeared to soften somewhat,' he wrote. He went on to list what Emerald felt were her grievances against Nancy: that Nancy had never loved her, that she associated with 'undesirable' people and led a scandalous life, all of which reflected badly on her, Emerald.

From Emerald's point of view all this was, of course, true; if Nancy had had a more forgiving nature, she might have remembered her mother's support and enthusiasm for her poetry, her introductions to many who became Nancy's friends, that it was her mother who had tried to prevent her from plunging into a disastrous marriage, let alone the financial generosity that allowed Nancy to live exactly as she pleased . . . and so on. But compromise was not a word in Nancy's vocabulary.

Harold Acton also wrote to her, telling her that GM was ill and 'so pained' that he was no longer going to leave her his Manets. Nancy's response to this was to write instantly to GM to find out if this were true. He wrote back on 27 February to say, 'Dearest Nancy, I have made no change in my will, always affectionately yours . . .'

Their next contact was not so happy. Nancy had planned to publish a short piece by GM called 'The Talking Pine' that he had told her about when they once breakfasted together in Ebury Street, in an edition of 500, each to be signed by GM. It was very slight – a mere four pages of folklorish tales of the sea and ships – but was printed on beautiful paper. All it lacked was GM's signature to go on sale. To Nancy's surprise, Moore refused this, saying the piece was not worth its ten-shillings price and he was not selling his signature. Nancy was furious at what she regarded as a broken promise and may also have believed that he was punishing her for what her mother saw as her intransigence. It is also possible that Moore, now eighty and in poor health, may have felt that the effort of signing 500 copies was not one he wished to make.

Whatever the reason, for Nancy it heralded the end where the Hours Press was concerned, although its last publication turned out to be a pleasant surprise for her: Wyn Henderson had managed to negotiate the publishing of Havelock Ellis's forty-page *The Revaluation of Obscenity*, with its message denouncing all forms of censorship. Nancy was delighted at this coup. Havelock Ellis, famous for his studies of human sexuality, had completed this short book only a few months earlier, and Wyn and the printer John Sibthorp sometimes worked on it most of the night, walking back to their rooms in the Hôtel Crystal through narrow, dark streets, with rats leaping out of the dustbins as they passed, black against the snowy February cobbles.

Nancy, however, had become so busy working on *Negro* that she wanted no more to do with the Hours Press. Debts of almost 3,000 francs had accumulated – for which Nancy held Wyn Henderson responsible – and, as Nancy wrote to a friend, 'This is too much to pay for the freedom I had wanted, idiot that I was.' They parted on bad terms: Wyn, who felt she had been misunderstood and wanted to keep the press open, wrote to Nancy to say so, to receive the answer: 'Do you really think I ever want to have anything [to do] with publishing again? You must be crazy! I despise the whole thing and am disgusted. Thoroughly and permanently . . . Damn all business!'

In late March or early April 1931, Nancy's decision to compile an anthology by and about *les noirs* was given added stimulus by a case, now widely considered a miscarriage of justice, that aroused strong feelings everywhere: the conviction of nine African-American teenagers, aged from thirteen to twenty, who had been falsely accused in Alabama of raping two white women on a train. The nine were known as the Scottsboro Boys, as the first, rushed trial was held in Scottsboro, Alabama. All but the thirteen-year-old had been tried and sentenced to death even though there was medical evidence to suggest that they had not committed the crime. They had been tried by an all-white jury (black Americans in Alabama had been disenfranchised since the late nineteenth century and were likewise not allowed on juries).*

Nancy sprang into action, circulating an appeal to raise money for the defence of the Scottsboro Boys, outlining a brief history of the case, emphasising that the trial had been farcical and that an appeal for a second trial had, after immense effort, been won.

She concluded, 'If you are against the lynching and terrorisation of the most oppressed race in the world, if you have any innate sense of justice, sign this protest and contribute towards the defence funds.' Among the leading writers and intellectuals who replied were Gide, Aragon, Breton, Beckett, Sinclair Lewis, Janet Flanner and Ezra and Dorothy Pound. At the bottom of his reply Pound had written, 'I not only protest but if this sort of judicial sanction of murder and frame-up continues, I should be disposed to advocate direct action. We have had enough criminals in high office already. A state even a state sanely founded cannot indefinitely continue if it condones and sanctions legal murder of innocent men.' The various cases went on for years; it was not until 1946 that all the accused had been released or escaped.

By now Henry's patience with Nancy was wearing thin. They had been together for several years, with her supporting him, but the promises of a rosy future she had made to him and on which

---

* The convictions were so controversial that there was trial after retrial through the years. The women turned out to be prostitutes, one of whom admitted she had lied on oath and fabricated the rape. On 21 November 2013, the Alabama Board of Pardons and Paroles granted posthumous pardons to Weems, Wright and Patterson, the only Scottsboro Boys who had neither had their convictions overturned nor received a pardon.

he had banked had not materialised. She had frequently treated him abominably, sometimes striking him – the flat of her arms, loaded with ivory bracelets, could deliver a heavy blow. When Janet Flanner once asked him about some bruises on his face, he replied, 'Just braceletwork, Miss Janet.' More than that, she had taken other lovers under his nose, many of them black – to Nancy, the darker their skins, the better; she often said to Henry she wished he was darker-skinned.

At thirty-five, her promiscuity was such that she was widely thought of as a nymphomaniac. Raymond Michelet described her as being unable to bear prolonged solitude, which terrified her:

> Thus it happened, that she would pick up along the way the first person who came to hand, even if of all her friends he was the least likely to share her life, until she sent him away – and in what manner, with what arrogance – a few days later, or even the next day.
>
> Nancy pursued her sexual needs as she pursued her emotional needs. She had many black lovers, nearly all musicians, some of whom she loved passionately, but whom she left, or who left her, scorched by the flame she kept burning within herself.

For Henry, the situation had become too much. The last straw seems to have been the escapade with the attractive stranger, Randall, on the return journey from Obergurgl. The solution, he thought, would be to return to the US: 'I was thoroughly disgusted and wanted to leave at the earliest possible chance.' When the subject had come up before, Nancy had always talked him out of it. This time, when he made it clear he was determined to go, she bought him a return ticket; and at the station, when she saw him off, she made him swear to come back.

Once back in his homeland, Henry hoped to clear up matters with his wife and decide his future. The former question was soon settled. His wife, who had heard about Nancy, began to question him, to which he responded frankly. He in turn told her that she had never replied to any of his letters. His wife, having told him that he was not the sort of husband he ought to be, made it quickly apparent that they would never live together again. This major problem solved, Henry, now a 'free' man, away both from the spell Nancy seemed to cast over him and the fraught atmosphere she so often created, found himself relaxing and enjoying his visit.

While Henry was away, Nancy, wishing to concentrate undisturbed on the making of *Negro*, had decided to move away from Paris and its distractions for a few months. To those who had lived through the Twenties, the changes in the capital were unpleasant. All through the decade the number of tourists, particularly from America, had increased,* and they had also become much less welcome. Many of them had the attitude that Paris was a sort of glamorous sideshow, put on for their benefit, so they felt that loud voices discussing what they were looking at, breakages in hotel rooms, sometimes unpaid bills, were all part and parcel of what those entertaining them should put up with. Parisians, who now often found that they could not get a table at 'their' café or restaurant and that when they did its prices had gone up, found all this intensely irritating.

There were also aspects of the cultural conflict that caused trouble, notably the attitude of some of the white Americans to those of colour. Paris, always infinitely more tolerant, was warmly enthusiastic about everything to do with African or African-American culture – the artworks, the music, the dances, the entertainers. Nobody, in Parisian eyes, could play jazz like the musicians from New Orleans or dance the Charleston like Josephine Baker. Yet some of the tourists, especially those from the South, would demand that bars and restaurants stop serving black patrons or employing black entertainers, demands that were firmly rebuffed, at one point by decree.

There was, too, less money around, so that much of what Paris

---

* In the late Twenties Paris was home to 40,000 expatriates, with 400,000 tourists annually – up from 100,000 in the summer of 1921.

was known for had begun to disappear. By the spring of 1931 the Depression, which had barely affected France at the time of the Wall Street Crash, or indeed the following year – thanks in large part to the national habit of hoarding gold – was just beginning to bite. Some of the larger apartments were emptying as their formerly rich owners went home or retired to the countryside to retrench, and many of the luxury trades for which Paris was famous began to feel the pinch. The American market for the books printed by the little presses of Paris disappeared, so that many had to shut down. Communism took firmer hold, sweeping most of the Surrealists into its embrace, although it was not until the following spring that the magazine *Advocate of Peace* reported that 'Semistarvation is frequent . . . Long queues of men and women wait near the old gates of Paris for free soup.' Nancy herself had long parted with cook, chauffeur and housemaid and, in Paris, lived in cheap hotels.

That April she rented a house near Cagnes, taking her young lover, Raymond Michelet, with her. At the same time, she wrote a circular for the work that was to dominate her mind, her emotions and her life for the next three years: the anthology she planned to produce in support of black people. 'The new book on COLOUR here described,' she wrote, 'comprises what is Negro and descended from Negro. It will be published as soon as enough material is collected.' She went on to give an outline of what its contents would hold – these included poems and articles by French, English and African writers, citings of injustices, political and social commentary – and requests for contributions. Soon, letters and documents would pour into the Cagnes villa.

It was here, under the warm sun of Provence, that for Nancy the sixteen years between herself and Michelet seemed to fall away and she fell in love with him, treating him with all the sweetness and kindness of which she was capable. To keep Michelet amused while she was at work, she sent for Georges Sadoul. To all intents and purposes, thought both men, Nancy had finally broken with Henry Crowder. Every day Sadoul, Michelet and Nancy would lunch or dine on the terrace of a small restaurant near the fifteenth-century Château Grimaldi,* with a wonderful view over Vence and the mountains of Provence. In this romantic setting it was by talking to Nancy through these starlit evenings that Sadoul learnt of the struggle black people had in the US. Others of their Surrealist friends – including André Thirion – also came to stay; there was fun, laughter, gaiety.

Yet despite the happy atmosphere, aspects of Nancy's character confounded Michelet – her sudden rages, her insecurities. She seemed, he thought, to be running from something, never stopping to reflect, never looking back, burning everything behind her – the things she had loved, the people whom she could have loved. What was she fleeing, he wondered? He also noticed how much she drank, later writing that she could be drunk for hours, without ceasing to be lucid, 'on the edge of tipping into unreason yet somehow always keeping her balance'.

Henry Crowder, in pursuance of his plan to leave Nancy for good, had decided to use his return ticket to France, travel to Paris and there tell her of his decision and say goodbye. He wrote to her that he was coming back and arrived in Paris in mid-May 1931, only to find she was not there but had left money for him to travel to Toulon, where she said she would meet him. Feeling that after their years together he at least owed her that, he set off for Toulon, where he and Nancy spent the night in a hotel before going on to Cagnes. He had naturally imagined he would be staying with her, but she told him that as she was living with Michelet in a villa he, Henry, must get a room in a nearby hotel. Unsurprisingly, Henry did not find this as funny as did the nineteen-year-old Michelet.

When Henry then asked Nancy what her plans were for the summer, she told him she intended to go into the mountains with Michelet – he could go to Italy and practise his music there. Even for the complaisant Henry this was too much. 'Nothing doing,' he answered, 'I shall go back to Paris.' Once there, he found he had been invited to a party in London and decided that after

---

* From 1966 the Picasso Museum.

going to it he would cut loose from Nancy for good and return to America: 'I wanted to say goodbye to the whole affair.'

Nancy, one of whose habits was to goad her lovers to the extreme then lure them back, now wrote a long letter to Henry. To his huge surprise, she said she wanted to accompany him to New York. Knowing the apartheid that existed there, he was aghast. 'Imagine, a negro man sailing into New York in the company of a wealthy white woman!' he wrote in his memoir. 'I couldn't. To make matters worse, Nancy was the kind who would want to go everywhere and see everything. Had she been willing to go [to places] alone that would have been alright but I knew she would want me to go with her.'

Henry knew as well as anyone that if Nancy had made up her mind to do something she would do it. Arguing was futile. Then, thinking of it again, he wondered if the trip would change her and if, perhaps, they might build something together again. They sailed on a German boat early in July 1931. From Henry's point of view, the trip would turn out to hold some of the worst days of his life.

CHAPTER 18

>─┤◆>─○─<◆┤─<

Black Man, White Ladyship

Knowing of the intense feelings that the sight of a black man with a white woman would arouse in white Manhattan, Henry Crowder was determined from the moment he and Nancy set foot on board the ship that when they reached New York they would stay in Harlem. 'As we docked my fears of what might happen rose to a frenzy almost,' he wrote. 'I thought of myself, a poor Georgia black man, going through the United States Customs with a reputedly wealthy English white woman. I shuddered. But we got through without any trouble.'

After two nights in a Harlem hotel where bedbugs were rampant, they settled in the Grampion (an apartment hotel near 119th Street formerly for whites but turned over to what were called 'Race Guests' in 1927). Henry was in a constant state of dread – dread lest his wife should hear that he was in New York with Nancy and cause trouble, dread that being seen with her would provoke white men to pick a fight with him and he would be beaten up, dread that, somehow, their presence together would cause misfortune. Nancy, fearless and, anyway, white, could not see the problem; again and again she would urge him to come with her to, say, an ice-cream parlour, where he knew he would not be allowed to sit down at a table or be served at the counter, and, when he refused, be angry that he was not standing up for himself.

For Henry, the best part of their three-week visit was the weekend spent with the William Carlos Williamses at their home in Rutherford, New Jersey. Williams, the man who so idolised Nancy that he kept a photograph of her on his desk, also acted as her poste restante while she was in New York. This brief interlude, however, did not stop the constant altercations between Nancy and Henry, with Nancy accusing Henry of cowardice, Henry explaining that what she wanted was impossible and unhappily wishing he had never agreed to the visit. She wanted challenges and confrontation; he wanted peace. He was, as he repeatedly told her, no activist.

He did, however, manage to introduce her to the editor and staff of the African-American magazine *The Crisis*.* One of the *Crisis* team took Nancy round Harlem, but the colour barrier was too strong for any of the black Americans to communicate readily with her. However, she did meet some who agreed to contribute to her anthology.

This project had become by now almost a *raison d'être*. Where others thought of black music as entertainment, Nancy's longtime interest in black culture and artefacts had expanded into a socio-political credo, the central plank of which was the cessation of injustices against the black man and his restoration to his rightful place in the world – one of equality and worthy of respect. She made copious notes for her anthology, worked in the Harlem Public Library, went to public meetings, noticed all the Harlem beauty salons offering treatments for the whitening of the skin and danced the night away in Harlem's celebrated Savoy Ballroom, of which she said, 'Until you have seen dancing in Harlem, you can't imagine the extraordinary brilliance of black dancers. And I am not talking of professionals but of the boys and girls from the street.' Nancy herself learnt the Lindy Hop, which, when the girls' short skirts swirled, she described as 'a hurricane sweeping over the dance floor'.

She commented that white people in New York seemed dull and unreal beside their black neighbours: 'And the whites know it. That's why they come to Harlem – through curiosity, jealousy,

---

* Her pamphlet *Black Man and White Ladyship* was published in it in September 1931.

FIVE LOVE AFFAIRS AND A FRIENDSHIP

perhaps not even knowing why.' She was enthralled by the vigour of the black children as they tumbled out of school, she went to a black evangelist service where she found 'an extraordinary rhythm' in the raised arms and swaying bodies, and she saw the effects of the Depression in the poverty around her.

None of this, however, stopped the incessant rows with Henry, quarrels exacerbated by the imbibing of huge quantities of 'moonshine'* by both of them. Nor was Henry's temper improved by Nancy's constant fretting about her young lover, Raymond Michelet. Eventually, Henry snapped. 'Why don't you go back to France and your Raymond?' he demanded. 'I will,' responded Nancy instantly. Henry booked them passages on a German boat and – both dead drunk – they embarked. Nancy spent much of the time in her cabin, sending telegrams to Michelet, who was waiting near Cherbourg, but she found time to agree with Henry – who was planning to go to London for singing lessons – that on his return to France they would go on a tour of Germany together. The trip duly took place, but without Michelet, who found himself unexpectedly and abruptly sidelined.

Nancy and Henry travelled over much of Germany, Henry driving them in the car she had given him. Meeting Brian Howard, with Eddy Gathorne-Hardy, in Munich, they went to many gay clubs – almost all Nancy's greatest friends were gay or lesbian. On the whole the visit was successful, until Nancy suddenly decided she wanted to go back to Michelet, which would have meant leaving Henry in Germany with the car and no money. After another of their violent quarrels, Henry persuaded her to continue their journey.

As Nancy wanted to keep both her lovers, once she and Henry were back in Paris she planned to install Michelet in a village near Chapelle-Réanville while Henry, she said, was to stay in the Réanville farmhouse itself, driving up to Paris for the lessons and company he wanted, and she would divide her week between them. It can be seen as another example of her solipsistic view

---

* High-proof distilled spirits, illegal during Prohibition.

of life: that she could not see that for someone like Michelet, a mere twenty years old, life in Paris with his many Surrealist friends was infinitely preferable to days on his own in a remote Normandy village waiting for a mistress who might or might not turn up.

When Henry heard the plan, he realised its flaws at once. 'It would never do,' he said, and told Nancy that he was going to leave her and return to America (for the third time that year). Hearing this, Nancy told him she intended to visit the US again in 1932 and they agreed to meet in New York in the spring. Again, Nancy hated Henry's going and there were tears in her eyes when he left. Although Henry, too, was affected, he was determined that this time it really would be the end: 'I was through and I intended for my subsequent conduct to prove this parting would be the final one.' He did, however, have a constant reminder of Nancy in the elegant little French car she had given him, which he was taking with him.

When Henry set foot on the boat taking him to America, he vowed that he had said goodbye both to Nancy and to Europe for the last time: 'For me, the affair was finished. I could have stayed in France, yes, but as I saw it nothing could be gained by my doing so.' The voyage itself was pleasant, with his talents at piano-playing and singing much in demand. After a night in Harlem with friends, he drove the 175 miles to Washington, the car attracting much interest along the way.

Once in Washington, the attention drawn by his car became troublesome rather than pleasing. Unfamiliar with the make, police constantly stopped Henry to demand his authorisation for driving it, only to be puzzled by the sheaf of French documentation he carried. Eventually, he decided it was more trouble than it was worth, put it in a garage, left it there, and concentrated on work. He contacted fellow musicians, joined the Musicians' Union and spent much time at piano practice. He also found that his relationship with Nancy, now a public figure, caused him to be unpleasantly well known: 'My appearance in public always caused a murmur of whisperings.' To his surprise, he received no offers of work. In his autobiography he claims that most of the social elite – i.e., his potential employers – were aware of his links to Nancy and did not want to offend her mother.

Like most of the Montparnos, Nancy left Paris during the summer tourist season. She and Michelet settled at the Hôtel de Mer in the former fishing village of Le Mourillon, near Toulon. Here she worked at compiling her anthology all through the rest of the summer and autumn, with Michelet by her side. Still in the throes of his first real love, he asked nothing better than to be with this glamorous older woman, to watch her, to follow her – 'you had to follow. Anyone who didn't ceased to be her friend' – and to sleep with her.

For Nancy, sex had become almost as important as alcohol, a pattern set early. Even during her convalescence after the bout of Spanish flu that nearly killed her, and despite a chaperoning friend there were lovers. 'The tenor in the night club goes to Marie and offers her 500,000 francs to let him take me away,' she recorded in April 1919.

After her hysterectomy at twenty-four, an age which most would consider tragically early, there was no barrier to life as a free-living femme fatale, able to take a lover on the spur of the moment, as the fancy took her. For although contraception was available, there was no pill, so that any method used required preparation; thus spontaneous or unexpected sex could easily result in an unwanted pregnancy – and in days when an illegitimate birth often meant social ostracism or shame for both mother and child, this was something to be avoided at all costs. Early abortions took care of these for the sophisticated and well-off; for others, the only really safe contraceptive was a firm No. It is possible that freedom from the fear of this stigma, as well as an instinct not to bewail her misfortune in being condemned to be childless, had caused Nancy to make the fullest use of the sexual freedom she had been granted – indeed, she often flaunted this liberation.

At the same time, sex per se was often a disappointment. I can do no better here than quote her biographer, Anne Chisholm, who had interviews with Raymond Michelet, the only one of her lovers to talk about the sexual side of such a relationship: 'Michelet says she found orgasm difficult but not impossible. Other men and women who were close to Nancy have said that, in their view, she was not someone of real sexual warmth and that she was probably technically frigid most of the time. Michelet has said that oral sex seemed abhorrent to Nancy, that she perhaps found it humiliating or disgusting.'

What seems to emerge from the picture is that love and sex were thought of by Nancy as two separate strands – that sex was, in a way, an itch to be scratched. This, combined with her total independence and personal selfishness, may have accounted for her habit of sleeping with anyone she chose even while engaged in a love affair.

But that summer and autumn she and Michelet were happy, both busy and caught up in a cause in which both believed (Michelet later wrote a thirty-nine-page pamphlet entitled *African Empires and Civilisation*, which was translated by Nancy's cousin Edward). Nancy cast her net wide, sending out letters to friends and anyone she thought might be a possible collaborator, from some of the black people she had met in Paris and London to journalists, writers, academics and names she had picked out of the black press; money did not come into the equation as all of them, she assumed, would contribute free. She collated offerings, edited, compiled, sorted and typed. The dossiers, answers, files, lists of possible contributors and a few of their offerings grew. She also wrote a short article for *The Crisis* that described her mother's attitude to black people as well as her own experiences of colour prejudice since meeting Henry (whom she identified by name).

For Nancy the compiling of the book was now a passion, the commitment to a cause that she had always wanted, a fight to right an injustice into which she could throw her whole heart and soul. At last, it seemed, her life's purpose was clear, putting to use the integrity, courage and fiery spirit that lay under the elegant exterior, and which those close to her had always sensed.

One of the first answers was from Norman Douglas:

I can tell you nothing more about the natives in those parts than what you know yourself, namely that the Masai is a fine fellow who plasters his hair and body with mutton-fat and brown ochre, eats a whole sheep at a sitting (if he can get it), and is bored to death just now because the English discourage him from indulging in his old amusements of cattle-raiding and fighting. I think I sent you the photo of the Masai girl loaded with bangles. These are made out of the telegraph and telephone wires, of which they cut down a mile or two and then manufacture into such ornaments to the disgust, obviously, of the British postal authorities.

But first, still fizzing with anger against her mother, wishing that the reasons for this should be known and, no doubt, fired up by the injustices of the Scottsboro trials earlier that year, she launched into a polemic, an eleven-page pamphlet entitled *Black Man and White Ladyship: An Anniversary*. It was in large part a diatribe against her mother and all her mother stood for in Nancy's eyes, with Sir Thomas Beecham and even George Moore also figuring pejoratively, followed by her feelings of outrage against racial discrimination, and why.

It began by setting out the reason why she was writing it:

An anniversary is coming . . . By anniversary I am not, indeed, referring to Christmas, but to the calendar moment of last year when the Colour Question first presented me personally with its CLASH or SHOCK aspect.

I have a Negro friend, a very close friend (and a great many other Negro friends in France, England and America). Nothing extraordinary in that. I also have a mother – whom we will at once call Her Ladyship. We are extremely different but I had remained on fairly good (fairly distant) terms with her for a number of years. The English Channel and a good deal of determination on my part made this possible. I sedulously avoid her social circle both in France and in England.

Nancy continued by describing the lunch party at which Margot

Asquith hurled her 'bomb', and what Beecham had said in his letter:

> in which he pointed out that, as the only one qualified to advise, it would, at that juncture, be a grave mistake to come to England with a gentleman of American-African extraction whose career, he believed, it was my desire to advance, as, while friendships between races were viewed with tolerance on the continent, by some, it was . . . in other words it was a very different pair of shoes in England especially as viewed by the Popular Press.
>
> . . . And what has happened since this little dust-up of December last, 1930? We have not met, I trust we shall never meet again.

The vicious, mocking assault on Emerald continued, depicting her as vain, snobbish, interested only in gossip, a bad business-woman and unable to come to terms with anything in the modern world. Emerald's angry and fearful reaction to the fact of her daughter having a black lover meant that, for Nancy, it was impossible to acknowledge that there was anything good about her mother, from her gift for friendship to her kindness, financial and otherwise, to young people and her genuine love of music and French and English literature. That, far from ignoring or disapproving of new and unorthodox trends in the arts, Emerald it was who had introduced Nancy to many of the modernists who had later become her friends, from the Sitwells and the painter 'Chile' Guevara to Ezra Pound.

The last part of the pamphlet, devoted to Africans and the wrongs they had suffered, reads much better, perhaps because it is based on fact rather than opinion. It begins with a horrific, gut-wrenching description of the slave trade:

> From 1819 to after the middle of the nineteenth century hundreds of thousands of Negroes, men, women and children, were sold, stolen and torn out of Africa. They were herded into boats at one time specially built for their transport. The trade

prospered; more profits were made at it, and more quickly, than at any other trade in history. Its apex, in number of slaves shipped from Africa to the New World, was the last two decades of the 18th and first two of the 19th centuries – about the time there was most agitation for its abolition. An estimate puts the figure at over 1,000,000 slaves a year. On the special boats the slaves were manacled to each other two by two and to the ship itself; a space of 6 ft by 1 ft 4 was allotted each on deck for the many weeks of the voyage.

At night they were stuffed into the hold. Many would be found dead in the morning. Those that looked for death from starvation were forcibly fed – many hanged themselves, leapt overboard, died of the flux and despair. They were made to jump up and down in their irons after eating; this was called 'dancing' to obtain exercise. They were flogged, tortured and maimed. After three or four such passages the slave ships had to be abandoned – having become unusable from filth. The stench of them spread some four miles out at sea. Once landed the slaves were sold by auction. Everyone knows how things went for them then until 1863. 244 years of slavery in America.

She concluded by detailing the numerous lynchings, 'an average of six a month'.

The conversation with George Moore was given verbatim, concluding with his remark, 'the best I could do is a yellow man'. 'Thus Mr Moore – after a whole long life of "free" thought, "free" writing, anti-bigotry of all kinds, with his engrossment in human nature, after the *injustice* of the Boer War, as he says himself, had driven him out of England. There is no consistency; there *is* race or colour prejudice.'

Black Man and White Ladyship was published in Toulon in the late summer of 1931, while Nancy and Michelet were staying there, and Nancy immediately sent copies to all of her mother's friends – and enemies – that she could think of, as well as to many of her own friends and to newspapers she thought might be interested. What she wanted was not only to state her own case but to wound her mother as deeply as possible.

The fallout was intense. Brian Howard was, predictably, sympathetic, writing to his mother:

I was only thinking last night, as I was reading the pamphlet that Nancy has written about her mother and Beecham, etc. and which she is sending out broadcast, how different and lucky you and I were – and how the same pamphlet is sent out, but invisibly, by *most* children about their parents.

You've no idea what it's like. Her mother behaved with the utmost folly and narrow-mindedness and has, of course, brought it upon herself . . . Her mother has been 'asking for it' from Nancy, by behaving *vilely* to her and her friends, for years. I am having you sent a copy. Her Ladyship: 'Now what's this I hear about *fairies* – what do men *mean* by such things? I don'*t understand*. What does it *mean*?' The homosexuals present grin. ETC. You'll see. I think it is going to create an explosion such as has never been known and will very likely be her end 'socially'.

One effect, which Nancy did not foresee, was that many in her mother's circle saw Emerald as the victim of an aggressive daughter who led a scandalous life. It is also possible that some would have seen Nancy's abuse of her mother, followed directly by her horrific descriptions of the slave trade, as implying that Emerald's fortune would have descended to her through slave-owners, especially as Emerald herself had always been somewhat reticent and evasive about her origins (in fact, her alleged father – her mother's husband – had been a San Francisco businessman, while her putative father, her mother's lover, had made a fortune in silver during the California Gold Rush, and her so-called guardian had become immensely wealthy through property*). It is highly unlikely, though, that Nancy would have either seen or meant it this way: one of her most attractive traits was her truthfulness, and to her, her mother's attitude would have been all that mattered.

---

* See a previous book, *The Husband Hunters*, by the author.

Those of Nancy's generation defended her, saying that among their contemporaries black people were liked. But many of Nancy's own friends were also part of her mother's circle – Emerald had always mixed generations with abandon – and, though they might have sympathised with Nancy and understood and perhaps admired her stand, they also liked Emerald, who had been good to many of them, and they disliked this intemperate attack on a woman whose only fault, as they saw it, was to be of her time and age.

Harold Acton, fond of both mother and daughter,* was one such, writing to Nancy to say that he had dined with her mother and 'there is a distinct cloud between us' – when she had asked him about Henry Crowder he had replied that he knew and liked him: 'She then asked me not to speak of this to anyone.' Acton concluded by saying, 'It is a difference of generation and the rigidity of mondaine prejudice. Her L. [Ladyship] has always been, for me, the magnificent exception.'

As for Emerald, already worried by Nancy's promiscuity and dependence on alcohol, concerned for her daughter's well-being, she now saw Nancy as having crossed one social line too many. Although she must have remained angry and upset for months, she behaved with dignity and restraint, merely saying, 'One can always forgive someone who is ill.' Fortunately, she had what could almost be called two surrogate daughters, both, like her own renegade child, dazzling blondes. One was the beautiful Lady Diana Cooper (as Diana Manners had become), whom Emerald had known since she was a child, and a great friend of Nancy's in their debutante days. The other was a newcomer, the twenty-one-year-old Diana Guinness (née Mitford), a beauty whose impact on London society when she arrived as the wife of the immensely rich and charming Bryan Guinness was so impressive that Emerald had already designated her as her successor as a social queen.

Others too thought Nancy had behaved badly. A letter attached

---

* Diana Guinness (later Mosley) always claimed he was the only person who succeeded in remaining friends with both Emerald and Nancy.

to the British Library's copy of *Black Man and White Ladyship*, thanking the addressee for sending it to him, talks of 'this regrettable publication'.* Henry Crowder, the unwitting cause of Nancy's final rupture with her mother, strongly disapproved: 'I could never understand how anyone could feel as she did toward her own mother.'

For Nancy, the main benefit was that she had now irrevocably broken with her mother, her background and much of her past. As to any further damage to her reputation, this did not concern her in the least. Nor did Brian Howard's forecast that Emerald's career as a hostess was over come true: it remained unaffected. And Nancy continued to receive money from her mother, although she now allowed most of it to pile up in the bank.

---

* The letter is addressed to 'My dear John' (possibly John Banting), but the initials at the bottom are indecipherable and there is no address at the top to aid identification.

CHAPTER 19

⊱─◈─○─◈─⊰

New York

In the spring of 1932 Henry Crowder, in Washington, received a letter from Nancy saying that she was coming to New York, where they had agreed to meet in Harlem and then go to islands in the West Indies. They had often talked about this, and the letter arrived at exactly the moment that Henry had become deeply dispirited by the lack of employment after all his hard work and planning.

All the same, he knew of the negative publicity her arrival would cause – which, if they met as planned, would also rebound on him – so wrote to tell her this, and to advise her against coming to the US at that moment. His letter drew a furious response. She did not need any advice about coming to America, stormed Nancy, she would do exactly as she wanted. She added for good measure, presumably because they had earlier spoken of going on the West Indies tour together, that Henry was a traitor and a rotter. Henry's reply was short and to the point – a single sentence: 'My, what a temper you must have been in when you wrote that letter.'

Nancy set off for New York via London. Here she met John Banting, since his arrival in Paris one of her on-off lovers and a close friend. She was, of course, full of her project and her campaign to fight for justice and equality for black people, a principle with which Banting was in total agreement. Fired by her enthusiasm, he agreed to accompany her to the US where, in late April, they installed themselves in the Grampion Hotel. They

286

began to look up friends, to see the sights, to go to nightclubs; all seemed quiet, but suddenly the press storm broke.

That March, the twenty-month-old son of America's national hero, the aviator Charles Lindbergh, had been abducted from his cot in a room on the upper floor of the Lindbergh house in New Jersey. The baby's disappearance was a complete mystery and for weeks had been headline news. But as no clues or developments in the crime had appeared since the kidnapping, the story had finally died down and the press was ready for a new sensation. This would be Nancy and her doings.

On 2 May 1932 the *New York Daily Mirror*'s front page blazed with the headline 'CUNARD heiress found in HARLEM!' and a story inside, chiefly implying that she had come over to the US in search of the famous black singer Paul Robeson – the implication, of course, being that she wanted him as her lover. Even the elevator operator was bribed to say she shared communicating rooms with Paul Robeson. Reporters rented rooms opposite and took photographs of anyone going in and out.

Other New York tabloids (the *New York American*, the *Daily News*) picked up the story, again for their front pages, on her arrival in Harlem, and her residence at the traditionally black-only Grampion. Nancy's celebrity status ensured that all the stories were distributed nationally by the wire news agencies and appeared on at least one cinema newsreel, so that news of her doings appeared everywhere.

It was the signal for what Nancy called 'a spate of frantic, unsigned and threatening letters' from anonymous private individuals as well as from bodies like the Ku Klux Klan:

'You for your nerve should be burned alive at a stake.'
'Repair for ransoming 25,000 dollars will be demanding for kidnaping, H-B kidaping inc.'
'Miss Nancy Cunard, take this as a solemn warning, your number is up.'
'Miss Cunard you are making a lousy hoor of yourself association with niggers can't you get a white man to satisfy you I have always heard that a negro has a large prick so I

suppose you like large ones is that why you are taking the part of these 9 niggers [the Scottsboro Boys].'

(To modern eyes, it seems odd that even the most extreme, vicious or obscene used the polite prefix 'Miss'.)

There were lies and libels; she wished they could have been dealt with by an English court, which went solely by evidence. None, thought Nancy, was 'written by a literate being'. She wrote a furious rebuttal of the Robeson story, demanding that it be published (it wasn't), though a similar denial by Robeson was.

Nancy, never anything but courageous, decided the only thing to do was, as it were, to take the war into the enemy's camp. Accordingly, flanked by John Banting and a black novelist called Taylor Gordon, she immediately called a press conference, greeting the assembled reporters with a typed statement to be handed out. She straight away declared that she was not the Hon. Nancy or Lady Cunard but plain Miss Cunard, that she had travelled over third-class on a German line and she hotly denied the sexual slander.

She went on to tell them that she had broken with her mother over a friend who was 'a gentleman of colour'. She continued that the purpose of her visit was to work on the huge anthology she was making on the 'Negro race', and she was in Harlem 'because you should be close to the subject you are studying'. She concluded by talking of the Scottsboro Boys case and asking for money for their appeal by way of an apology for the inaccurate slurs the press who were facing her had printed. To aid the appeal, she herself had sold the crested gold cigarette case given her during her debutante years by the Prince of Wales.

She described what had happened in a letter to the black poet and novelist 'Claude' (Festus Claudius) McKay: 'Well, the Grampion was all quiet and OK for two weeks and then the "news" burst out . . . in case you haven't by now heard the splendour of those lies, the press proclaimed that I had followed my coloured lover, Robeson, over to USA and that I lodged in a negro hotel to be near him . . . the truth of this is that I had met him just once – about the way we met – and you know how much meeting there was in <u>that</u>, years ago in Paris. I suspected a mistake in the identity of the woman and sure enough, it is now public news that Mrs R is divorcing R and citing Lady E. Mountbatten as correspondent.'

Nancy had approached McKay to contribute to her anthology; he had been a central figure in the Harlem Renaissance, an important literary movement of the Twenties – his novel *Home to Harlem* (published in 1928) was a best-seller that won the Harmon Gold Award for Literature. She had eventually tracked him down to where he was then living, in Tangier and, as evidence of her bona fides, had sent him a copy of the article she had written for *The Crisis*. Mckay's answer, in which he gratefully acknowledged receiving the article she had sent and also accepted her invitation to write something for the anthology, told Nancy, 'I feel very excited about your book, of course, because I think from your attitude and angle of approach, if I surmise rightly, you will produce a fresh and artistically stimulating contribution.'

Nancy replied by asking him what subject he would choose for his article, and if she could have it by the following Easter: 'It should not be longer than about 2,500 words, as there is so much to get in, and not fiction, everything else but fiction, viz: personal experience, travel, historical, criticism, etc. Indeed, a descriptive piece by you of Maroc . . . ? But you will know best.' Thus began an exchange of thirty-six letters that lasted over thirteen months (much of their correspondence taken up with Nancy's efforts to find a London publisher for McKay's novel *Banana Bottom*). Together with the number of other potential contributors she was soliciting – answering their queries, requesting photographs, suggesting subjects and so forth – it is clear her correspondence at that time was hugely time-consuming.

To carry on with her work and escape the constant wearisome interruptions of telephone calls or visits from reporters, Nancy accepted the invitation of a sympathetic white friend to spend a month on a secluded farm belonging to a friend of his, staying there until the end of May. Then it was time, she felt, to set off for the West Indies. She had not seen Henry Crowder since her arrival: telegrams to arrange a visit in Washington had arrived too late, and although she had sent him the money for a ticket to New York, he had spent the money and stayed in Washington. His real reason was reluctance to be involved in Nancy's notoriety; she for her part was understandably annoyed at his non-appearance while still accepting the money. Unused to not having a man by her side, she took with her a married black Bostonian named A.A. Colebrooke, ostensibly as secretary/bodyguard. Such was the press of reporters when she was leaving that it was reported that 'her dark-complexioned companion had to hold a sports coat in front of her face' to prevent her being photographed.

McKay, who had sent Nancy press cuttings, had also given her introductions to leading personalities in the literary world of Jamaica, from which, on 17 July, she wrote him a long letter as to an old friend:

Am now in Jamaica. I cannot tell you how remiss I feel about not having written to you before. You have been so very good with interest, sympathy, letters and so on . . . I left NY with a Negro friend met there this year. As we stepped on the Orizaba to Cuba some representatives dashed out and began their usual scrimmage. We refused to tell them anything, and to let them photograph us. It is amusing therefore to see what happens when one does not give an interview. Either way things are turned into the crassest form of lie, snobbery, insult, etc etc. These dogs got busy while we were on the sea, with the result that on arrival in Havana (a pestilential place anyway) a perfect army of reporters came out on the tender, armed with cameras. Continuing our line of 'nothing to say' (and indeed why should one have to waste time with the vultures gassing about the rottenness of America etc when they're going to fabricate their own crap?) We had a whole gang of them . . . the whole thing went on for about three hours, to the accompaniment of touts and following taxis, and agents waiting at the station, at the post, on the sea-front, to see where we would go. On top of this the authorities had almost tried to prevent us from landing and were bloody rude. What was it all about, one wonders? Some of them said a report had come from the USA that we had run away to get married. Well, we had to get out of the town to avoid all this incredible pursuit. So *now* I have sampled both means of 'dealing with the press,' having given them a mouthful in NY in May, and having tried to avoid them ... So it was very pleasant arriving here on a freighter from Santiago yesterday.

She concluded by saying, 'And now, <u>please</u> tell me how you are getting on with the article for the book ... I am terrified at the time it takes to get in the material promised, and finally the date set for the last things to come in must be December at very latest. I hope that your article will reach me in Paris very soon now. I am longing to read it.'

After the success of the Jamaican visit Nancy returned to New York, where John Banting had remained. Together they decided to return to the Grampion Hotel and most of the rest of their stay was devoted to enjoyment, visiting bars, nightclubs and dance halls, dancing the Charleston, the shimmy and the latest craze, tap-dancing, which had started in the streets.

They left for France on 11 August 1932, Nancy by now anxious to return. In Paris was Michelet, still in love with her and still enthralled by the projected book. Together they went to what was becoming one of Nancy's favourite parts of France, the Dordogne, living simply and working hard. They stayed in Carennac, a medieval village of creamy-stone houses with brown-tiled roofs in the lushly green Dordogne valley, their temporary home the Renaissance castle that had once belonged to the writer and archbishop François Fénelon. When not working, they explored much of the beautiful surrounding countryside with its villages such as Castelnaj, Loubressac, Padirac, Souillac. The days were full: material was pouring in; Nancy was writing, editing and translating; other contributors needed prodding letters before anything came. One of these was McKay, to whom she sent a gentle reminder from Carennac, but without result.

Once back in France, Nancy had not tried to contact Henry, perhaps because she was angry at his defection, perhaps because she was too busy to think of anything but *Negro*. For Henry, however, life in Washington was going badly. Unemployed, with no money, he had slid into a downward spiral, spending most of his days in search of a drink. 'I was very despondent,' he wrote of those terrible months. 'I lost energy and ambition. I even reached the stage where moonshine whisky was more important to me than food. I did not care whether I lived or died.'

Suddenly, out of the blue, came a lifeline, in the shape of a cable from Carennac. It was from Nancy. 'Where are you?' it asked. 'Very worried must have news.' She had thoughtfully prepaid an answer so that Henry was able to reply, and in the correspondence which followed throughout the next few months he told her of his straits. With her usual generosity, Nancy sent him some money.

In the autumn of 1932 Nancy and Michelet returned to Paris. She had tried in vain to sell Le Puits Carré but had been unable to find a buyer, and in preparation for such a sale she had had almost all the farmhouse's furniture removed and stored in the rue Guénégaud shop, which from then on was shut. With no real other option, thanks to the mountain of documents that accompanied them, Nancy and Michelet installed themselves in the near-empty Le Puits Carré to complete the work on *Negro*. In Paris, Nancy's cousins Edward and Victor helped with translations, joined by Samuel Beckett, with whom Nancy had kept up a warm if sporadic friendship. The work Beckett did turned out to be his most extensive publication at over 63,000 words.*

For Nancy and Michelet at Chapelle-Réanville, it was a harsh existence, with only the bare minimum of furniture and constant hard work. 'For three months we camped there working late each night, so much so going to bed in the early morning we often started our day as the winter night began to fall,' said Michelet.

One disappointment was the acrimonious withdrawal of McKay, who had finally completed his article, and the ending of an epistolary friendship in a bitter dispute – the cause, as so

---

* It was later published as a separate book, *Beckett in Black and Red: The Translations for Nancy Cunard's Negro*, edited by Alan Warren Friedman, in 2000.

often with many who wrote on a lofty plane, being money. The first part of his letter shows his unprofessional dislike of editing while the rest states his central complaint: lack of payment. In December 1932 he wrote:

My dear Nancy Cunard,

This your latest letter irritates me no end in manner and matter and I most emphatically refuse permission for my article to be mutilated and quoted from before published in its entirely, I am astounded that you, yourself an artist, should calmly announce that you're abbreviating and quoting from a writer's work before first consulting him about it. That doesn't seem to square with the rules of the writing game and my commercial publishers have never yet attempted to take any liberties with my work without first obtaining my authorisation.

. . . The point is this: writing is my means of livelihood. I wrote the article for payment. You are not paying for articles, you say. Well, the very obvious way out is to <u>leave my article altogether out of your anthology</u>. I have not the slightest wish now to appear in your anthology and I hope you will respect that wish.

He concluded by offering to return the books she had sent him.

Nancy rebutted his charges politely but vigorously (in a letter from Puits Carré dated 16 January 1933):

I am indeed sorry you wrote the article under a false impression . . .

Now, you do not mention what I was anxious to know – whether or no I did (or did not) say in the beginning that collaborations to this anthology were ALL voluntary, and that it was quite impossible to envisage any payment. I should really like to know this, as I cannot remember. But what I do very distinctly remember is having said again and again: NOT more than 3,000 words, less if you like. But you sent me over 8,000 words. I know how irritating it certainly must be to feel that you have done this work for nothing, and I should <u>like</u> you to believe that I did not try to get you to write under false pretence . . . I can only repeat that had I thought you expected payment I would have <u>immediately</u> told you this was impossible.

As to my 'exigence'. No, that is quite untrue. I asked you in <u>December 1931</u>, from near Toulon, if you would care to collaborate. So that is some time ago!

Another article that was withdrawn was one of Raymond Michelet's. Nancy had suggested that he write on the African ivory bracelets that she loved so much. Anne Chisholm described what happened: 'Michelet did some research and came back to her with a piece that included discussion of the erotic significance of the ivories. He gave as an example the fact that when the bracelets were worn regularly and the ivory became warm from contact with the wearer's body, they gave a smell very close to that of semen. This was too much for Nancy and, as Michelet refused to omit the passage, the article was never used.' Nancy, despite her behaviour, often exhibited a curious streak of prudishness, of which this may have been an example; on the other hand, she might have simply felt that it was too close to home.

The beginning of 1933 opened sadly. On 21 January, George Moore, Nancy's 'first friend', died after a long illness. The last time Nancy had seen him was in early December 1930, when he had been in relatively good health; he fell ill shortly afterwards. Although their last contact was one of disagreement, their life-long bond was unbroken and (as Anne Chisholm makes clear) she always spoke of him with the greatest affection; as she wrote in her memoir of him, she continued to 'talk' to hm in her mind. Most of the letters he had written to Nancy were destroyed by German soldiers or French peasants during the Second World War, when her house at Chapelle-Réanville in Normandy was sacked.

He left Nancy his Manets, but the bulk of his £80,000 estate went to Maud. Although she did not see much of him in his last years, flashing in and out of Ebury Street like a glittering dragon-fly, and often leaving a purple orchid in a pot, his devotion to her never faltered. 'Dearest and best of women, life would be a dreary thing without you,' he wrote a few months before he died. 'Come to see me soon.' In his book *Héloïse and Abélard* was the passage, 'My death, which cannot be far away now, only affects me in this much, that I shall not see Malberge any more; and not seeing her, I am indifferent to all things after death as I am during life, indifferent to all things but Malberge.' As he had explained to Emerald, Malberge represented M for Maud while he, George, was G for Gaucelm d'Arembert.

His ashes were taken from London to Ireland, in an urn that his brother Maurice, still running the family estate, had had copied from one dating from the Irish Bronze Age. It was rowed out to Castle Island on Lough Carra and buried, with a cairn built on top.

Finally, by the beginning of 1933, *Negro* was finished.

'It was necessary to make this book – and I think in this manner,' began Nancy's foreword. 'An Anthology of some 150 voices of both races – for the recording of the struggles and persecutions and the revolts against them of the Negro peoples . . . The reader finds first in this panorama the full violence of the oppression of the 14 million Negroes in *America* and the upsurge of their demands for mere justice, that is to say their full and equal rights alongside of their white fellow-citizens.' There then followed a horrifying statistic: 'At no other time in the history of America have there been so many lynchings* as in the past 2 years, so many "legal" murders, police killings and persecutions of coloured people.'

(It is worth noting that by 2019 not much had changed. A research team led by Frank Edwards of the School of Criminal Justice at Rutgers University published a report on the risk

---

* Since 1900, both the House of Representatives and the Senate sought to pass a federal anti-lynching bill but were invariably blocked. It was not until February 2020 that such a federal bill was passed.

of being killed by 'police use-of-force' in the US by age, race/
ethnicity and sex. They reported that African-American men
and women, American Indian/Alaska-Native men and women
and Latino men faced a higher lifetime risk of being killed by
police than do their white peers, while Latino women and Asian/
Pacific Islander men and women faced a lower such risk than
did their white peers. The most noteworthy statistic was that
black men faced about a one in 1,000 chance of being killed
by police over their life course, with risk peaking between the
ages of twenty and thirty-five for all groups. 'For young men of
colour,' concluded the report, 'police use-of-force is among the
leading causes of death.')

Negro's span was wide, covering literature, education, social
conditions, poetry, art, sculpture, black music and many personal
experiences – 'Flashes from a Georgia Chain Gang', Nancy on
the colour bar in Europe, 'Pushkin and Peter the Great's Negro'
by Harold Acton, and John Banting on the African-American
dancing which had so impressed him on his visit with Nancy, in
particular of the wonders of one particular Harlem dance hall,
but 'I do not give its name or the "ofays" [see below] will start
flocking in, the prices go up, the dancing down and an Italian
gangster take it over as a "speak"'.

Nancy wrote of the Harlem she knew:

> When I first saw it, at 7th Avenue, I thought of the Mile End
> Road – same long vista, same kind of little low houses with,
> at first sight, many indeterminate things out on the pavement
> in front of them, same amount of blowing dust, papers, litter
> . . . these avenues, so grand in New York proper, are in Harlem
> very different. They are old, rattled some of them, by the El on
> its iron heights, rattled, some of them, underneath, by the Sub
> in its thundering groove.
>
> Why is it called Harlem, and why is it the so-called capital
> of the Negro world?

She went on to describe how it was Dutch in origin, white until
1900 after which, gradually deteriorating, it became colonised

by the city's poorest inhabitants – the black ones. There were race barriers on all sides, she said – even in the centre of Harlem there was a hotel where blacks were not allowed to stay – and 'it depends on chance whether you meet them or no. Some Negro friends will not go into a certain drug-store with you for an ice-cream soda at 108th (where Harlem is supposed to begin, but where it is still largely "white" . . .) Just across the Harlem River some white gentlemen flashing by in a car take it into their heads to bawl "Can't you get yourself a white man?"' Both of these were memories of what happened with Henry.

Ofay came from a section on African-American slang and meant 'a white person'. Other words and phrases were *Arnchy*, one who puts on airs; *Astorperious*, grand; *Boody*, 'a lighthearted term for what Momma does her loving with'; *Brash*, boastful; *Bring mud*, to disappoint; *Catch air*, get out!; *Go choke*, stop talking nonsense; *Dickty*, smart, swell, highbrow; *Dogs*, the feet; '*Dogs is barkin*', my feet are hurting; *Eight-ball*, a very black man.

Before his departure for America Nancy had got Henry Crowder to write two pieces. They contrasted sharply. One was about his first trip to Europe with his band, on an English boat, which after several months led to his meeting Nancy in Venice: 'the English crew was very nice and courteous, the food excellent and everyone friendly', and each member of his band collected around 2,000 francs in tips by entertaining those in first class. In Venice, he recalled, they were stared at because of their colour but with no signs of discrimination.

The English, he said, certainly *have* colour prejudice and to a marked degree – most of the larger hotels draw the line as to Negroes, and there are certain restaurants and even public houses that refuse to serve black people: 'But the English people I met were as sensible about the question of color as I could want anyone to be, I was received as a guest at all sorts of parties, went about everywhere with my English friends and in fact was wined and dined to the point of suffusion.' He added, 'I recall the amazement of some of my English and French friends when I described conditions as to the Negro in America. They could hardly believe what is commonly known to any fifteen-year-old Negro lad.' In 'Hitting Back' Crowder described some of the insults, indignities and fights he had to put up with in America, often having to pick up iron or wooden bars or heavy rocks to defend himself with.

There was a generous tribute to Michelet who, after both his labours and the conditions in which he had worked, all for love of Nancy, certainly deserved it: 'My thanks and appreciation are particularly due to my chief collaborator, Raymond Michelet, who worked with me during the two years of collecting and editing this Anthology.'

For the present writer, perhaps the most effective contribution in the entire massive work is the short poem by the black American novelist, poet and playwright Langston Hughes, then well known as a leader of the Harlem Renaissance. It was called 'I Too':

I, too, sing America.
I am the darker brother.
They send me to eat in the kitchen
When company comes;
But I laugh,
And eat well,
And grow strong.
Tomorrow
I'll sit at the table
When company comes,
Nobody'll dare
Say to me
'Eat in the kitchen'
Then.
Besides, they'll see how beautiful I am
And be ashamed –
I, too, am America.

CHAPTER 20

><+>··O·<+>·<

Partings

To achieve the publication of *Negro* Nancy had to go to London to seek a publisher prepared to take on this mammoth task. She set off in the spring of 1933, first settling in a small hotel in Bloomsbury and later renting a studio flat. Her search for a publisher was not helped by her insistence that the book should be exactly as she wanted it; any suggestion of possible reshaping, or indeed editing, was turned down flat. She had been a printer, she knew what was what and, above all, it was *her* project – and it would stay that way. To counter suggestions by various of the publishers she spoke to that it would not sell, she told them that it would create great publicity – a perfectly logical premise, since she had always been in the news – and insisted that it must be accompanied by considerable advertising (paid for, naturally, by the publisher).

She had begun her search for a publisher through personal contacts. The first she approached was Rupert Hart-Davis, the son of her old friend Sybil with whom she had once shared a house, and who was now an editor at Jonathan Cape. This came to nothing, as when Cape himself tried to explain to Nancy how, with editing and restructuring, the book's massive bulk and chaotic layout could brought under control, she simply said to him, 'But you don't understand, Mr Cape – this *is* the format.' Cape turned it down, as did Gollancz.

Nancy's eventual saviour was a young man called Edgell Rickword, whom she had met a couple of years earlier. Rickword, two years younger than Nancy, was slight, fair-haired, bespectacled and shy, with a soft voice and quiet manner. He was a war poet (he had won a Military Cross in the 1914–18 war), writer and literary editor, and would soon become one of the leading intellectuals of the Communist Party, an ideology with which Nancy was in total sympathy (without ever becoming a Party member) – *Negro* makes it clear that she believed communism was the best hope for coloured people.

Rickword was closely connected to the small left-wing publisher Wishart and Co., working for them as well as writing essays and criticisms for left-wing journals (in 1921 he had reviewed Nancy's *Outlaws* for the *New Statesman*, for which he wrote regularly), and he managed to persuade Ernest Wishart to publish *Negro* at Nancy's expense. As Rickword said later, 'We ... felt to some degree that literature must be understood and practised as a part of a culture wider and deeper than any single art form, because culture was the essence of the way in which people lived and thought and felt.'

Now began a frenetic time of work as Nancy, helped by Rickword, worked on the book, planning its layout, selecting illustrations, writing captions and so forth. At the same time, she was involved in raising funds for the defence of the Scottsboro Boys as the case, with its endless postponements and retrials, rumbled on. She was also pursuing libel actions against various newspapers for their reporting of her time in the US. These were eventually settled out of court, with Nancy gaining an apology and an award of £1,500. 'A settlement was announced by Lord Hewart in the libel actions brought by Miss Nancy Cunard against Allied Newspapers, Ltd,' ran one report in July 1933. 'Mr Roland Oliver K.C. (for Miss Cunard) said that Miss Cunard has for some time past been keenly interested in the the colour question. She has been engaged for some time collecting material on that subject. In the spring of last year she was in America and became the subject of a number of libellous articles and suggestions about her work.' Most of the money she was awarded went towards the publication of *Negro*, which was costing far more than she had expected.

At the same time, she was still in correspondence with Henry, to whom she had been sending occasional small sums of money to help with the pitiable turn his life had taken. In one of these letters, she suggested that he come back to Europe. But even at this low ebb Henry knew that he could not face returning to the same conditions as before – a life of dependency on Nancy, interspersed with the quarrels, jealousies, cruelties and uncertainties that such a life would involve. He must, he said, have a job to do that would bring him in an independent income.

More letters passed between them, in which Nancy proposed that he took charge in London of a black-centred institution that would be part welfare centre, part information bureau, contain a bookshop and a reading room, and have a register of hotels and boarding houses where coloured people might stay. It was to be run in conjunction with the Negro Welfare Association* of London, Nancy told him, but he would definitely be in charge.

For Henry this sounded like a godsend. Nancy sent him his fare and he first went straight to Paris, going after two days to London – and to a Nancy he had not seen for twenty months. Rather unkindly, he wrote that she seemed older (she was now thirty-six) and more tired. Nevertheless, she rushed him straight off to a party; this time, it was not with her usual crowd of London friends, with whom he got on well, but a group of black Africans – although he noted that most of the women there were white – whom he found he could not like. Afterwards, she and Henry went back to the large studio she had rented, where she told him, to his surprise, that she was leaving for France the following morning. The reason was Raymond Michelet.

The completion of *Negro* had heralded the gradual ending of the love affair between Nancy and Michelet. He was as deeply interested in the subject as ever, but by now he was a young man rather than a boy and, though he loved Nancy, felt he could not go on being 'run' by her and needed to strike out on his own. He was grown up and had become financially independent – his father had died and left him some property, which he had sold.

---

* One of the most prominent black organisations in Britain in the 1930s.

He had also met a girl much nearer his own age. Nancy, sensing that he wished to end their long affair, was dashing over to see what she could do about it. Before she left, she showed Henry a small bundle of clothes and told him that, if anyone called and asked for them, to hand them over and say that she was away.

When she returned, it was clear the relationship with Michelet was over. He had become a snob, she told Henry, perhaps to justify the rupture. What came as no surprise to Henry, however, was to discover that Nancy already had another lover. This was Edgell Rickword, the man through whom *Negro* was eventually published.

He had arrived at the studio flat the day Nancy left, asked for her and was told by Henry – who found his appearance 'rather pleasant' – that she was away. When Henry asked if the clothes were his he agreed that they were but would not take them, saying he would wait until her return.

As Henry soon learnt, Rickword had been living at the studio until his own arrival. 'This amused me very much,' said the now disillusioned Henry. 'I could not help thinking "just another one of the boys". I certainly had nothing against the lad but his naivete amused me because I knew he had not yet learned all there was to know about Nancy.'

At first all seemed hopeful, but two things soon became clear: that Nancy's interest in the projected black-centred institution was fast diminishing and that Henry found he disliked her new friends, whom he considered nondescript and uneducated. Nancy, he gathered, was trying to organise them into some sort of committee to be affiliated with the Communist Party – another focus of his disapproval. For Henry was at heart conservative and in favour of a settled way of life rather than radical campaigning. It was not long before he realsed that the job for which he had returned to England was never going to materialise. 'So there I was again,' he recorded. 'Right back in the same position I had sworn I would never find myself in again. Stranded, in a foreign country where I could not get a working permit even if I found a job. The future looked about as bright as the eclipse. What was I to do?'

When Nancy told him she was planning to take a flat with Rickword, Henry offered no opposition but said that he would never live in the same building. Instead, he found quarters near Regents Park – later noting that Nancy only visited his flat twice during the five or six months he lived there.

For the final burst of work on *Negro* Nancy went away to the country, leaving Henry an allowance of five shillings a day [worth about £25 today]. Then, on her return, came the work of getting the flat she had taken ready for her and Rickword. It was on a top floor in Percy Street, conveniently near the Eiffel Tower, and consisted of two bedrooms, a large sitting room, a large kitchen and a bathroom. Henry did most of the work needed, painting floors, making bookshelves, having rugs stored and cleaned. Nancy had organised the arrival of all her possessions that had been stored in the rue Guénégaud – furniture, books, paintings, hangings, African art.

Nancy, whose need for sex had become almost as powerful as her craving for alcohol, now turned her amatory attention back to Henry, whom until then she had seen little of. 'She wanted me to be one of her lovers in the intimate sense of the word,' he wrote of that time, 'and I absolutely refused. Not only was I afraid but I certainly had no intention of doing anything like that as long as there were so, so many men in her life.' In addition, Henry had met a black English girl on whom he had become keen and was spending as much time as possible with her.

Nor would Henry follow her into the enthusiasm for communism which she was now showing, refusing to attend demonstrations or protest meetings that she and her new friends were engaging in: 'Although she was keeping me I felt I owed Nancy nothing as she had certainly not kept her promises.'

Rickword was an enormous help to Nancy during the last part of the year, working hard with her on *Negro*, his gentle nature and belief in what they were doing allowing him to ignore Nancy's demands, expostulations and outbursts of annoyance. Henry, who had seen it all before, watched with detached and somewhat sardonic pity: 'I knew from experience that regardless of how hard he worked that his time to be "dumped" would come eventually. Whether he realised this I had no way of know-ing but I did feel sorry for him for I felt he was being played for a dupe.'

Henry had managed to stay on the edge of Nancy's life, making excuses to avoid going out with her, largely because of his distaste for her new black friends. But when she asked him to accompany her to a special Christmas dinner given by one of them, so long in advance that he could think of no reason for refusing, he felt he had to agree to go – but planned that on the night he would stay at home. He had already gone to bed and switched out the light when Nancy turned up, walked in, switched on the light and talked him into coming with her. 'If ever there was a time I wanted to be free to do as I liked it was that night,' he said to himself. 'I could not help feeling like a "hunted man". I wanted freedom; I wanted to get away . . . but I couldn't.' They were, of course, late for the party – Nancy was always late for everything – which lasted all night. Henry took Nancy home but firmly refused her amorous advances.

But the real question for anyone reading his autobiography, with its many disparaging references to Nancy, is: why did Henry stay with her so long if he was so disenchanted – and why did he keep returning every time he had sworn never to see her again?

It was not simply money: Henry was an extremely talented musician who had kept himself by his playing and singing before and who knew many others in 'the business' through whom he could, eventually, have got work. The answer must be that his retrospective and rather grumpy view of her was unclouded by her presence, the promise of a glittering future coupled with the familiar all-pervasive enchantment that he often refers to in puz-zled manner but which brought him again and again from the other side of the Atlantic. A few weeks after they had first met, he had written to her, 'Even when the bitter realities of life would tend to cause you to lose your vision of that which is ideal, or might make you feel the uselessness of love and sentiment, I shall sense it all and know that the inherent qualities of sweetness and loveableness must prevail, and that the Nancy I love is now and never can be anything but adorable.' Something of those feelings must have remained with him, even though he could not work out why.

Although *Negro* had been ready to publish in December 1933, there was a last-minute hitch when Nancy decreed that it was to have a specially made dark-brown binding. Finally, *Negro* was published on 15 February 1934; Nancy and her friends celebrated through several well-refreshed nights. Its 250 contributions, two-thirds of which were by black authors, added up to 855 pages and the whole thing weighed eight pounds – too heavy for the normal book-postage rates. To Nancy's disappointment, it did not sell well and the expected gush of publicity was not forthcoming: the book's size, price of two guineas (more than the average weekly UK wage) and general cumbersomeness made it both difficult to categorise and to review. There were approving notices in the *Daily Worker* and the *New Statesman* – both, of course, left-wing – and a mention in the *New York Times*, but little else. She sent copies to all her contributors, asking them to encourage others to buy.

A first copy went to Michelet with the affectionate inscription, 'Dear Raymonde, comrade and collaborator-in-chief – Here is our book, your copy – it is significant that revolution broke out the moment of its release – and that here too the hunger marchers are converging on London. I go to join them right now. With all my love, 14 February 1934, Nancy.'*

Nancy's reference to the hunger marchers was one of her few open acknowledgements of the Depression (her complaints about lack of money were generally laid at her mother's door). London was still in its grip and there had been sporadic hunger marches, often to local councils and often communist-backed, with one in 1932 of 100,000 marchers that had started in Scotland and ended in a riot in London's Hyde Park. Then came the government's Unemployment Insurance Act, due to be made law

---

* Many of the remaining copies were destroyed in a warehouse fire when London was bombed in the Blitz of 1940.

in June 1934, meaning that assistance rates were set nationally rather than according to local need. This triggered a nationwide hunger march, with many of the marchers and committees from the South Wales coalfields supported, for the first time, by an MP – Aneurin Bevan, himself a former miner and the son of a miner. It was a cause bound to appeal to Nancy.

One afternoon when Henry visited Nancy's flat he saw her getting ready to join the hunger marchers. Her usual elegance had gone out of the window; instead, she was dressed in a man's overcoat, a flying helmet, countless scarves, gloves and galoshes. She intended, she told Henry, 'doing a few miles' with the hunger marchers as they advanced towards Trafalgar Square.

After three days she returned – but not alone. With her was a tough-looking young man who had obviously been on the march with her. As he had a key to the flat and seemed perfectly at ease, Henry realised at once what the situation was. 'In spite of the fact that I should have been accustomed to Nancy's lightning changes of lovers, I never ceased to marvel at them,' he wrote of that episode.

For Rickword, still living in the flat and still her lover, it was a wretched shock. He went out to have a consolatory drink with Henry, with whom he had become good friends, and confided that he was still very much in love with Nancy, and very hurt. His response, however, was stalwart: he quickly found himself a girl and installed her in his room in the flat, but two days later Nancy threw them both out – she could do this as the flat was in her name.

Although living with the Hunger Marcher, as he was always known, Nancy never ceased trying to regain Henry's affections. Determined never to be sucked into such storms of emotion again, he held aloof: 'The parade of lovers that I had witnessed had long since killed any pretence of feeling I may have had for her.'

Now that *Negro* was no longer the all-consuming centre of Nancy's life, Henry realised that soon she would make an unexpected move. Sure enough, she left for France, taking the Hunger Marcher with her – he did not last long, but what happened to him is not known. By now, Henry was supporting himself in London, ending up with a decent job in a theatre orchestra, so that when after seven or eight months a letter came from Nancy asking him to go travelling with her, he had no hesitation in refusing.

Then came another letter, in the late summer of 1934, telling him she was very ill and could he come for a few days to visit her, and sending him the fare. This was a request he felt he could not refuse and set off to join her. She was indeed weak and ill, and Henry persuaded her to seek treatment in London, where she was put into a nursing home for several weeks to rest and recover.

When Nancy hinted at settling a small sum of money on him Henry began to regard the idea of travelling with her in a different light. After her spell in the nursing home they spent a couple of weeks at Eastbourne before returning to London, putting her furniture into storage, packing up the flat and returning to France.

First they stayed in a dingy Montmartre hotel, then went to Chapelle-Réanville, to find the house looking shockingly shabby, with cobwebs and weeds everywhere, the dirty dishes and pans from her last stay there still unwashed in the sink. The prospect was so unpleasing that they went down to the South of France, expecting sunshine and warmth, only to find rain and snow, and stayed in a freezing hotel while looking for a job for Henry until he convinced her that he would only find work if they returned to Paris. Here they settled in a small two-bedroom hotel apartment, and Henry realised gloomily that he had once again given up a job which had supported him in order to satisfy Nancy's endemic restlessness exhibited, as so often, in travel. This time, with her constant reiteration of her lack of money, the quarrelling began again, Henry asking for a daily allowance rather than fighting over bills.

Nancy then decided she wanted to live in the country rather than in Paris. They returned to Chapelle-Réanville, and Henry spent several hard days' work cleaning, painting, scrubbing and weeding to put the house to rights for Nancy. With less money now at her disposal, live-in servants were dispensed with. Instead, she got a cleaner from the village and decided to do her own cooking. Every fortnight she would come up to Paris for the weekend and see Henry, which involved more quarrelling as she would demand to know why he was not working.

Then, when he got a two-day contract at Cambrai – a town in northern France near the Belgian border – came the dénouement, seemingly out of the blue.

Henry, Nancy and an agreeable young African had had dinner together, the evening had been pleasant and, as Henry remarked, 'no one was drunk'. They went back to the apartment, where Henry got himself ready to leave at 5.30 a.m. for the train to Cambrai. Packed and ready, he was sitting in his bedroom reading during the last minutes before he had to leave when Nancy came into the room and said, without any preamble, 'We don't like each other any more so we might as well call it quits,' before announcing that she was leaving there and then.

Henry was staggered. He pointed out how late it was and that soon he would be gone and she would have the place to herself. But there was, as he put it, 'a sharp and vicious exchange of words', ending with Nancy leaving.

When Henry got back from Cambrai, he found a note on the table 'telling me she was through' as well as a cheque for 200 francs. She told him he could count on the same amount for six weeks – but no more arrived.

It was a sad and anti-climactic end to the longest and most formative love affair of Nancy's life. It was because of Henry that she had evolved the idea of *Negro*, it was to Henry she dedicated the book, her life's major work and in many respects her monument, and it was the patient and forgiving Henry – her 'tree', as she called him – who had tolerated her extraordinary and disruptive character longer than anyone else.

The two only saw each other twice again – once at a dinner party and once passing in the street. Yet, years later Nancy wrote, 'Henry made me – and so be it . . . Others have loved me more (?), and I, perhaps others. No, probably not, for me has this been true. In any case, Henry made me. I thank him.'

*

Slowly, Nancy's Paris life was ending; so, too, was the Paris of the past decade. As the Depression finally overtook France, so the atmosphere of the capital was one of misery and bitterness. The poverty was such that the previous year 10,000 Parisians had taken to the streets, shouting that 'Not one sou!' of war debts should be repaid to the US. 'Thousands of young men, forced out of their jobs by the crisis, struggled on to their last penny, to the end of their tether then, in despair, abandoned the fight,' wrote the journalist Morvan Lebesque of that time, describing how groups of them would congregate on street benches and – for the warmth – at Métro entrances. At night, destitute women slept on piles of newspapers in the shadow of Notre-Dame.

As life got tougher, the focus had moved from the arts to politics; instead of violent arguments in a bar about the merits or otherwise of a painting there were violent fracas, largely between left and right, in the street. That February a demonstration culminated in a vicious riot in the Place de la Concorde, in which canes tipped with razor blades were used to slash the legs of police horses, three of the *Garde mobile* were tossed into the Seine and never seen again, and something like 20,000 rounds of ammunition were fired. The official estimate of deaths was twenty to seventy, although Janet Flanner, who had watched the whole thing, believed it to be much higher.

There was no doubt that *Les Années folles* were well and truly over. With the repeal of the Eighteenth Amendment (in December 1933) Prohibition was finally over, and freedom to drink no longer the lure it had once been. Movements once new and to some profoundly shocking had been absorbed into mainstream culture and figures that had formerly dominated the cafés of Montparnasse had either become famous, fallen by the wayside, moved on or been forgotten. Hemingway was already a star; Picasso had become so rich that he owned a Louis XV château near Gisors, to which guests were often driven in his luxurious Hispano Suiza with its mirrors and cut-glass flower vases. Harry Crosby was dead, Aragon, uncritically admiring of the communist regime, was in Russia most of the time – and how many people now remembered Djuna Barnes?

Even Harold Stearns, the man who had induced so many to come, had departed. In 1930 he had left the *Tribune* to work for the *Daily Mail* ('going over to the Limeys,' said his friends), but his alcohol-based life meant that soon his health gave way. Doctors diagnosed infected teeth and extracted them all; no jobs were left so that finally, broke and toothless, he had to return home, his passage on a freighter paid for by friends and the American Aid Society of Paris. With the departure of so many Americans, Shakespeare and Company, the bookshop run by Sylvia Beach, had hit hard times; the woman who had so bravely and generously published *Ulysses*, now in its eleventh edition, had not made a penny from it despite the agreement with Joyce – he, on the other hand, invariably travelled first-class, ate in the most expensive restaurants and even tried to get Sylvia to fight the legal battles ensuing from the pirating of his work.* Friends, including Ernest Hemingway, supported her by giving paid-for readings of their works.

For one Montparnasse monolith, success on a grand scale had come at last. With the publication of Gertrude Stein's *The Autobiography of Alice B. Toklas* both she and Alice had become literary celebrities. When they returned to the US for an extended lecture tour, everywhere they went they were treated like royalty, and Gertrude often spoke to standing-room-only crowds who listened to her with baffled reverence as she read from her work in a sonorous monotone. Her audience, noted one *New York Times* critic on 2 November 1934, 'listened intently for nearly an hour to the frequently puzzling involutions and repetitions of [Stein's] diction and went away afterward to argue'. (Of an earlier Stein lecture, organised by Harold Acton, Acton had written, 'Hers was the only possible way of reading those flat sentences. But it was difficult not to fall into a trance.')

One of the few who had changed little, except in size, was Kiki, a few years earlier crowned 'The Queen of Montparnasse'. She had grown so much larger that Ernest Hemingway, in his

---

* As *Ulysses* was banned in the US it did not have the protection of copyright.

introduction to her memoir, said that 'Kiki now looks like a monument to herself', although she still had the same wild spirit. When horrified at the number of bourgeois customers in her favourite café, she flashed her naked breasts and bottom at them, while the barman looked on with indifference,* and when her latest lover advised her to put money away for the future, she merely replied, 'All I need is an onion, a bit of bread and a bottle of red. And I will always find somebody to give me that.'

Nancy's friends Janet Flanner and Solita Solano, though still together, had both found other lovers. The cafés were catering more and more to tourists. 'And the Rotonde?' wrote the *flâneur* Basil Woon, 'There too the proprietor has succumbed to the lure of the plush seat and the clean fingernail – I am talking about the waiters now – and, to add to the complete criminality of the catastrophe, he has added a grill room and jazz band upstairs.'

Gone was the life that Nancy and her friends had led, excitedly discussing art, literature, love and ideas night after night in a favourite café as the saucers piled up or dancing in smoky *boîtes* until dawn crept along the dark streets.

Although Nancy had plenty more transient lovers, there was never another to match those five of the Paris years. In search of what to do next after *Negro* her communist sympathies drew her first to Moscow; communism, she felt, was the only way to fight the injustices of class and colour as well as the growing menace of fascism. In Germany, where once Berlin had rivalled Paris in its freedoms, Hitler's Nazi Party was tightening its grip on all aspects of the state and in 1935 Mussolini's Italy invaded Abyssinia (now Ethiopia). Nancy, like all her friends fiercely anti-fascist and anxious to do what she could, managed to obtain a job reporting to the Chicago-based Associated Negro Press on the Abyssinian War. This was followed by reporting on the Spanish Civil War

---

* Recounted by Evgeny Zamiatin, then living in Paris, in a letter to a friend 5 January 1933. See *The Englishman from Lebedian*, by J.A. Curtis.

that broke out in 1936 (Nancy, almost needless to say, was hotly on the side of the Republic).

She spent most of the Second World War years in London, sustained largely by her many close friendships – the return of Norman Douglas to England was a particular joy – and the organising and publishing of another anthology, *Poems for France*, for which she obtained seventy contributors. Although she lived within half a mile of her mother, who since 1942 had taken up residence in the Dorchester Hotel in Park Lane, the estrangement was so complete that the two never met, although they had various friends in common, such as the Sitwells and Harold Acton.

After the war, Nancy returned to France, where she found her home at Chapelle-Réanville wrecked. During the German occupation the local mayor, a fascist sympathiser, had invited German troops and the local villagers to pillage freely. Nancy's wooden sculptures and masks had been burnt by the soldiers as fuel, letters and documents destroyed, and almost all of her books, including first editions and a rare 1598 edition of the works of Chaucer, had been stolen, burnt or thrown into her well. What had happened made it impossible for her to face occupying the house again and she began thinking of living in the south-west of France. After travelling around she eventually settled in a small village called Lamothe-Fénelon; it was near Souillac, where she had been so happy with Aragon and, later, Michelet.

Nancy never saw her mother again, not even returning to England when Emerald was on her deathbed – she died in the Dorchester on 10 July 1948 – nor did she even go to her funeral. Emerald's brief, handwritten will, made out a month before her death and witnessed by her solicitor and the reception clerk at the Dorchester, left her collection of letters from George Moore to Sacheverell Sitwell, her clothes, furs, crêpe-de-chine sheets, silver and £1,500 to her faithful maid. Of the residue, £35,574 10s and 3d, one-third was left to Nancy, with another third to Diana Cooper, who must have seemed so much the daughter she would like to have had, and the remainder to her young friend Sir Robert Abdy.

*

Nancy's last days were appallingly sad, a round of wanderings, arrests and violent altercations, of being thrown out of hotels and burning pound notes, as her mind and body gradually gave way after a lifetime of alcohol, smoking and barely eating. Her drinking was now so excessive that she was often incoherent, violent or abusive, 'a heroic figure in dilapidation', said Raymond Mortimer. Arrested in London for assaulting the police who had picked her up while she was soliciting, she threw her shoes at the magistrate who sent her to jail. In prison, she was deemed mentally incompetent and transferred to an East End hospital where she tore the buttons off her clothes, tossed them into the bath and wrote to everyone she could think of. There was no one to take charge of her (her cousin Victor's health was too poor to care from someone in her condition). She refuted the idea that alcohol could have anything to do with her situation, claiming that it was political – the work of fascists.

The last journey of this constant traveller was up from Lamothe-Fénelon by train and then by taxi across Paris to the flat of Raymond Michelet, where she arrived delirious, frail, penniless and, as Georges Sadoul wrote later, 'thin as a Buchenwald corpse'. Once she had been carried in she asked for rum, then for the friends of her old days – Aragon, Becket, Sadoul and Thirion.

Sadoul was the only one whose address Michelet knew; the two of them took her to the hotel where she said she had a room and where she insisted on climbing the stairs by herself, refusing to let either of them help her. She was so weak that this took almost two hours. Michelet then went to Aragon to tell him all this and to ask him to come and help, but Elsa furiously opposed the idea. While Michelet was arguing that the two men who owed so much to Nancy should care for her at this time, Nancy, having set fire to papers in her room, had somehow got down the stairs and found a taxi. Her incoherence was such that the driver took her to the police, who brought her, unconscious, to the Hôpital Cochin where she died that same night, 17 March 1965. She weighed a mere twenty-nine kilos.

*

It is difficult to find an epitaph for this extraordinary woman. Society beauty? Tireless campaigner against injustice? Wonderful friend? Selfish, promiscuous lover? Muse? Alcoholic? Poet? So deep was Nancy's impact on the lives of many that her friends composed a Festschrift for her, published three years later, *Brave Poet, Indomitable Rebel*. Perhaps most important of all, this book of memories was, as another friend wrote, 'laced with love' – something that she had been seeking, in one way or another, all her life.

ACKNOWLEDGEMENTS

I am greatly indebted to David Ross, now the owner of Nevill Holt, for so kindly showing me over what was Nancy Cunard's birthplace and childhood home, and for pointing out so much of interest that pertained to her and her family.

Most of Nancy's collection of letters and other papers was destroyed, along with many of her possessions, when her Normandy farmhouse was occupied by German troops during the Second World War, and by local people after she had left. Almost all of the rest of her papers, including her scrapbooks, diaries and photographs, are in the Harry Ransom Center, Austin, Texas. Here my particular thanks and my greatest gratitude go to Kathryn Millan, who painstakingly, over many days, photographed Nancy's diaries for me during lockdown and sent other useful information.

I would like to thank Anne Chisholm for allowing me to use several quotes from her masterly biography of Nancy, on which I relied heavily. I would also like to thank Roger Conover for permission to quote from Mina Loy's poems, 'Nancy Cunard' and 'Gertrude Stein', and Alma Books for permission to quote from 'Seven Dada Manifestos and Lampisteries' by Tristan Tzara.

I owe the confirmation of T.S. Eliot's one-night liaison with Nancy to the kindness of Lyndall Gordon, who made a summary of Eliot's second letter to Emily Hale available to me.

I am most grateful to Lewis Wyman, the Reference Librarian in the Manuscript Division of the Library of Congress, for finding me several letters from Nancy to Janet Flanner.

Richard Aldington's papers are in the New York Public Library. The papers of Janet Flanner and Solita Solano, including

Solano's unpublished memoir, are in the Library of Congress.

There are a few letters from George Moore to Nancy in the New York Public Library.

The Claude McKay papers are in the Beinecke Rare Book and Manuscript Library, Yale University.

Henri-Pierre Roché's diary is in the Harry Ransom Humanities Research Center, University of Texas, Austin, Texas.

Finally, I would like to offer my most grateful thanks to my wonderful editor, Alan Samson, and my equally wonderful agent, Isobel Dixon. I am, as always, enormously grateful to Linden Lawson, nonpareil copy-editor, and the marvellous staff at the London Library.

LIST OF ILLUSTRATIONS

༺•❀•○•❀•༻

Page 1
Nancy as a debutante (Mary Evans/Illustrated London News Ltd)
Nancy's parents (Getty/W.G. Phillips)

Page 2
Emerald Cunard (Getty/Topical Press Agency)
Nancy Cunard by Ambrose McEvoy (© Bradford Museums &
    Galleries/Bridgeman Images)

Page 3
George Moore (Alamy/Pictoral Press Ltd)

Page 4
Michael Arlen (Alamy/Granger Historical Picture Archive)

Page 5
Ezra Pound (Getty/Bettmann)

Page 6
Aldous Huxley (Alamy/Everett Collection Inc.)

Page 7
Nancy and Henry Crowder (Getty/Keystone France)

Page 8
Louis Aragon (Getty/Keystone France)

Page 9
Top left: Nancy in Paris (Man Ray 2015 Trust/DACS, London 2022,
    ADAGP image: Telimage, Paris)

Top right: Nancy and Tristan Tzara (Man Ray 2015 Trust/DACS, London 2022, ADAGP image: Telimage, Paris)

Below left: Nancy in a feathered headdress (Victoria and Albert Museum, London)

Page 10

Top: Nancy with John Banting and Taylor Gordon (Getty/Hulton Deutsch)

Below: Group portrait of artists, writers and performers (Alamy/Everett Collection Inc.)

Page 11

A group of Bright Young Things (Mary Evans/Illustrated London News Ltd)

Page 12

Top left: Kiki de Montparnasse (Alamy/Matteo Omied)

Top right: Man Ray (Alamy/Granger Historical Picture Archive)

Below: The Dome (Getty/Apic)

Page 13

Top: The Select (Getty/Albert Harlingue)

Below: France's National Holiday, 14 July (Getty/Keystone France)

Page 14

Top left: Iris Tree by Modigliani (Alamy/Classic Paintings)

Top right: Robert McAlmon (Getty/Berenice Abbott)

Below left: Wyndham Lewis (Getty/Hulton Archive)

Below right: Sylvia Beach (Bridgeman/ARCHIVIO GBB)

Page 15

Top left: Ernest Hemingway (Bridgeman/Archive Charmet)

Top right: F. Scott Fitzgerald (Getty/Bettmann)

Below: Harry and Caresse Crosby (Alamy/ARCHIVIO GBB)

Page 16

Top left: Janet Flanner (Shutterstock/Granger)

Top right: Solita Solano (Getty/Berenice Abbott)

Below: Gertrude Stein (Getty/Fotosearch)

BIBLIOGRAPHY

Acton, Harold, *Memoirs of an Aesthete*, Methuen, 1948.

Aldington, Richard, *An Autobiography in Letters*, ed. Norman T. Gates, The Pennsylvania State University Press, 1992.

Antheil, George, *Bad Boy of Music*, Hurst & Blackett, 1947.

Arlen, Michael, *The London Venture*, Cassell, 1920.

Beach, Sylvia, *Shakespeare and Company*, Faber and Faber, 1960.

Beaton, *The Glass of Fashion*, Weidenfeld & Nicolson, 1954.

Bedford, Sybille, *Aldous Huxley, A Biography*, Chatto & Windus, 1973.

Bonham Carter, Violet, *Champion Redoubtable: Diaries and Letters 1914–45*, Weidenfeld & Nicolson, London 1998.

Bouvet, Vincent and Duruzoi, Gérard, *Paris Between the Wars: Art, Style and Glamour in the Crazy Years*, Thames & Hudson, 2010.

Carpenter, Humphrey, *Geniuses Together*, Unwin Hyman, 1987.

Charlton, Anne and Charlton, William, *Putting Poetry First: A Life of Robert Nichols*, Michael Russell, 2003.

Cooper, Duff, *The Duff Cooper Diaries*, ed. John Julius Norwich, Weidenfeld & Nicolson, 2005.

Crowder, Henry, with Hugo Speck, *As Wonderful as All That?* Wild Trees Press, 1987.

Cunard, Nancy, *These Were the Hours*, Southern Illinois University Press, 1969.

Cunard, Nancy, *GM: Memories of George Moore*, Rupert Hart-Davis, 1956.

Cunard, Nancy, *Grand Man: Memories of Norman Douglas*, Secker & Warburg, 1954.

Curzon, Grace, *Reminiscences*, Hutchinson, 1955.

Daix, Pierre, *Aragon avant Elsa*, Tallandier, 2009.

Evans, Sian, *Queen Bees*, Two Roads, 2016.

Fielding, Daphne, *The Rainbow Picnic: A Portrait of Iris Tree*, Eyre Methuen, 1974.

Fitch, Noel Riley, *Sylvia Beach and the Lost Generation*, W.W. Norton, 1983.

Flanner, Janet, *Paris was Yesterday, 1925–1929*, Angus and Robertson, 1972.

Forest, Philippe, *Aragon*, Gallimard, 2015

Glassco, John, *Memoirs of Montparnasse*, Oxford University Press, 1970.

Hemingway, Ernest, *A Moveable Feast*, Jonathan Cape, 2010.

Horn, Pamela, *Country House Society*, Amberley, 2015.

Huddleston, Sisley, *Bohemian, Literary and Social Life in Paris*, George G. Harrap, 1928.

Huxley, Aldous, *Antic Hay*, Chatto and Windus, 1923.

Huxley, Aldous, *Point Counter Point*, Chatto and Windus, 1928.

Kapp, Yvonne, *Time Will Tell*, Verso, 2003.

Keyishian, Harry, *Michael Arlen*, Twayne Publishers, 1975.

Kluver, Billy and Martin, Julie, *Kiki's Paris, Artists and Lovers, 1900–1930*, Harry N. Abrams, 1994.

Lancaster, Marie-Jaqueline, *Brian Howard: Portrait of a Failure*, Anthony Blond, 1968.

Luke, Michael, *David Tennant and the Gargoyle Years*, Weidenfeld & Nicolson, 1991.

McAlmon, Robert, *Being Geniuses Together*, Secker and Warburg, 1938.

McAuliffe, Mary, *When Paris Sizzled*, Rowman & Littlefield, 2016.

Moore, George, *Letters to Lady Cunard, 1895–1933*, ed. Rupert Hart-Davis, Rupert Hart-Davis, 1957.

Moore, Lucy, *Anything Goes*, Atlantic Books, 2008.

Murray, Nicholas, *Aldous Huxley*, Little, Brown, 2002.

O'Keeffe, Paul, *Some Sort of Genius: A Life of Wyndham Lewis* Jonathan Cape, 2000.

Patmore, Brigit, *My Friends when Young*, Heinemann, 1968.

Paul, Elliot, *The Last Time I Saw Paris*, Random House, 1942.

Thomas, Hugh, *John Strachey*, Eyre Methuen, 1973.

Vaill, Amanda, *Everybody was so Young*, Little, Brown & Co, 1998.

Weber, Ronald, *News of Paris*, Ivan R. Dee, 2006.

Wilhelm, J.J., *Ezra Pound in London and Paris*, The Pennsylvania State University Press, 1990.

Williams, William Carlos, *Autobiography*, Random House, 1951.

Wineapple, Brenda, *Genet, A Biography of Janet Flanner,* Ticknor and Fields, 1989.

Wiser, William, *The Crazy Years, Paris in the Twenties,* Thames and Hudson, 1983.

Wiser, William, *The Twilight Years, Paris in the 1930s*, Robson Books, 2001.

Ziegler, Philip, *Diana Cooper*, Hamish Hamilton, 1981.

INDEX

❯─┤◆❯─○─❮◆├─◄

Nancy Cunard is denoted by NC.

Abdy, Sir Robert 312
Acton, Harold
  on Douglas 252
  Maud and 9
  on Moore 120
  on NC 64, 232, 243, 250
  Negro anthology piece 296
  poetry by 251
  on Pound 71
  stays with NC 199
  Stein and 113, 310
  writes to NC 266, 284
Adderley, Peter Broughton 36–7, 38
African-American troops 154–5
Aga Khan, Prince Aly 40
l'Age d'Or (1930 film) 254–5, 256, 260
Albert Hall Ball 25, 52, 54
Aldington, Richard 73–4, 218–21, 245–8, 261–2
  marries H.D. 75
  work by 250, 251
  Death of a Hero 218, 245
  The Eaten Heart 226–7, 246
  Last Straws 252, 261
Americans, in Paris 57–9, 138–43, 240, 270–1
Antheil, George 104, 109, 115, 177
Aragon, Louis 168–81, 199–200, 203–6, 210–15
  Aldington on 246
  Barney's and 115
  Dadaist 76
  and Elsa 224–6, 231
  NC and 167, 192–4, 216, 229, 253
  in Russia 309
  style 132

Surrealist 150
Thirion and 236
'Chant de la Puerta del Sol' 195–6
Le Con d'Iréne (*Irene's Cunt*) 194–5, 203
La Défense de l'infini 185, 195, 196, 224
Le Roman inachevé 173
Les Voyageurs de l'impériale 186
Poème à *crier dans les ruines* 222–4
Snark translation 221
Traité du style 192, 203
Arlen, Michael 'the Baron' 60–70
  Aragon and 186
  on the Gargoyle 154
  stays with NC 79, 99
  The Green Hat 60–1, 69–70, 133, 154, 164
  The London Venture 62–3
  Piracy 69, 89–90
Art Deco 157–8, 190, 201
Asquith, Cynthia 36, 44
Asquith, H.H. 7, 16, 20, 36, 48
Asquith, Margot (*later* Lady Oxford) 7, 16, 20, 36, 257, 281
Asquith, Raymond 20
Asquith, Violet 30
Associated Negro Press 311
Astaire, Adele 154
Athenaeum magazine 94

Bagnold, Enid 27
Baker, Josephine 165, 175, 270
Balfour, A.J. 13
Ballets Russes 148, 204
Banting, John 89, 174, 199, 243, 261, 285–8, 291, 296
Barnes, Djuna 115, 137, 310
Barney, Natalie 104, 114–15, 135–6

322